AF541258

ESSAYS ON SCHOOL CURRICULUM

By

Dr. Marlow Ediger

Emeritus Professor of Education

Truman State University

201 West 22nd Street

North Newton KS 67117

United States of America

&

Dr. Digumarti Bhaskara Rao

M.Sc., M.A., M.A., M.Ed., Ph.D.

Principal & Research Director

R.V.R. College of Education

D-43 (277) S.V.N. Colony

Guntur — 522 006

&

Member, Board of Studies in Education

Acharya Nagarjuna University

digumartibhaskararao@rediffmail.com

DISCOVERY PUBLISHING HOUSE PVT. LTD.

NEW DELHI-110 002

Published by:
Tilak Wasan

DISCOVERY PUBLISHING HOUSE PVT. LTD.
4383/4B, Ansari Road, Darya Ganj
New Delhi-110 002 (India)
Phone : +91-11-23279245, 43596064-65
Fax : +91-11-23253475
E-mail : parul.wasan@gmail.com
discoverypublishinghouse@gmail.com
web : www.discoverypublishinggroup.com

***First Edition:* 2012**

ISBN: 978-93-5056-082-2

Essays on School Curriculum

Printed at:
Shree Balaji Art Press
Delhi

Dedicated
to
Beloved friend
and
Able administrator

Prof. G.V. Chalam

M.Com., M.B.A., LL.M., Ph.D.

Department of Commerce and Business Administration
Acharya Nagarjuna University
Nagarjuna Nagar-522510
&
Coordinator
PG & Professional Courses
Acharya Nagarjuna University
Nagarjuna Nagar-522510
Guntur, Andhra Pradesh, India

Preface

The school curriculum has many different conceptions. It may include any educational experience. It may also be conceived as a conversation, relationships, and it is this phenomenon of plurality that is inherent in the new paradigm view of curriculum. It must be understood as encompassing not only those experiences that take place within schools, but the entire scope of formative experience both within and outside of schools. Further, it includes experiences that are not planned or directed, as well as experiences that are intentionally directed (in or out of school) for the purposeful formation of right citizenry of society.

The school curriculum includes subjects such as languages, mathematics, social studies, science, etc. Many aspects of the curricular subjects are discussed in this book. This book will be of great use to curriculum designers and teachers and administrators at school level.

Digumarti Bhaskara Rao

Contents

1

CHAPTER

Philosophy and Curriculum Organization

There are several philosophies involved in organizing the curriculum. How the curriculum is organized may mean much to pupils in the school setting. Teachers, school administrators, and curriculum directors need to study, analyze, and implement that which assists learners to achieve as optimally as possible. In an era when public schools are asked to aid pupil progress in passing mandated tests as well as avoid dropouts from school, it behooves planners of the school curriculum to provide necessary inputs to assist all to be successful learners (Ediger 2010).

Plans of Curricular Organization

One of the oldest methods in organizing the curriculum was to use the separate subjects approach which is still popular presently. The philosophy here stressed the saliency of keeping each academic discipline separate with its objectives of instruction, learning opportunities for pupils to achieve these objectives, and evaluation procedures which measure pupil progress. A watered down curriculum results when each discipline loses its clarity and uniqueness. There are essential bodies of knowledge from these disciplines which each pupil needs to master, according to advocates. William Chandler Bagley (1874-1946) emphasized the separate subjects curriculum and essentialism. He believed strongly that each academic discipline should maintain its integrity and not be integrated with others since this simplified knowledge and selected academic areas would then be minimized. The No Child Left Behind (NCLB) law of 2002 in USA mandated testing of reading and mathematics in grades three through eight for pupils to meet standards for promotion purposes. Science was added in 2009; this left social studies out as a member of the big four curriculum areas. Dr. Bagley was opposed to the social studies as a curriculum area due to its emphasis upon integrating content in relating subject-matter areas. Rather, he wanted history to be taught as a separate subject. Dr. Bagley believed that only exacting content be taught such as in mathematics, history with its names, dates, places, and salient events, as well as the different branches of science. Thus, social studies stressed vague content in its implementation. (In NCLB, history/social studies was not included in mandated testing). Dr. Bagley was opposed to:

- lax discipline in the classroom.
- the correlated and fused curriculum, to be discussed later.
- the interests of students being heavily emphasized. Bagley wanted stability.
- an activity centred curriculum which John Dewey stressed.
- student input in planning objectives, learning activities, and evaluation procedures (Wahlquist, 1942).

But, essentialism lives on under different names such as in mandated academicareas. Thus, a body of knowledge and skills has been identified which all school pupils should master and be tested upon. The measurability of mandated testing comes from the measurement movement advocated by E. L. Thorndike (1874-1946) and B.F. Skinner (1902-1986). The essentials or basics in mandated objectives stress the importance of

- precise objectives to be used by teachers in emphasizing targets to aim for when teaching.
- aligning instruction with these highly specific objectives.
- testing to see how well students have achieved.
- the test results are stated numerically in terms of percentiles, as well as grade/ age equivalent scores, when compared with the norm group listed in the Manual.
- grade and district as well as state averages may be compared (in the media) with other schools by grade levels, school districts, and states, in the Nation's Report Card.
- teacher achievement, compared with other classrooms, may be evaluated based on his/her classroom test scores (Ediger, 2008).

The separate subjects curriculum may be emphasized with/ without measurement philosophy of education and the following summary statements may be made:

- students may become highly familiar with an academic discipline.
- students may develop a deeper understanding of that academic discipline being studied.
- students may achieve sequence in one academic discipline without interference from other subject matter areas.
- students may understand the scope of a single academic discipline better by limiting content to one subject matter area.

- students may focus upon using the methods of acquiring subject matter as advocated by academicians, such as historians, scientists, mathematicians, among others (Ediger and Rao, 2003).

A second plan in organizing the curriculum emphasizes relating two academic disciplines in teaching (Ragan and Shepherd, 1982). A block of time may stress fusion or students perceiving the relatedness of two academic areas. A ninety minute block may then be devoted to teaching history and literature. This doubles the amount of time in this block as compared with the usual 45 minute period traditionally. The history and literature teacher, for example, might then cooperatively plan the objectives and subject matter to be taught. The Great Depression and the literature written during that time may be fused, and not taught separately. This might well be a good way to have proper perspective in relating literature to the time it was written. How much relationship of knowledge should pupils perceive? No doubt, it is a role of educational philosophy to determine the degree of integration of subject matter. Why should there be fusion and other interrelated subject matter be taught?

- pupils perceive the whole of knowledge, not separate categories
- pupils find it easier to remember content if they can relate it to other academic disciplines
- pupils become increasingly creative when engaging in combining academic disciplines
- pupils find knowledge more useful when fusion/integration of subject matter occurs in learning by discovery.

The following summary statements indicate the advantages of using a block of time in teaching:

- teachers would teach fewer subjects and teach them in greater depth.

- teachers would be responsible for fewer students, such as eighty as compared to 175 in the separate subjects curriculum. Diplomas would be awarded upon mastery of subject matter.
- teachers need to know each student well and realize there are individual differences.
- teachers must realize students possess different learning styles.
- teachers need to provide situations with many questions for students to ponder upon (Watkins,1990).

A third philosophical plan of curricular organization emphasizes the unified curriculum whereby teachers, school administrators, and students, believe in subject matter increasingly losing its boundaries and borders. Knowledge is perceived holistically by learners, not fragmented. Thus, history, geography, science, literature, and mathematics become unified. A team of teachers might then plan the objectives, learning activities, and evaluation procedures for any given unit of study. For example, if students are studying a unit on The Age of Discovery (history), place location in geography may be brought in, in terms of where these discoveries took place. Science discoveries, such as Galileo's experiments in the 1600s on gravity from the leaning tower of Pisa, bring on much student interest and a myriad of experiments may be brought in to the ongoing unit of study. With science experiments, mathematics is the language of expression in terms of measurement of phenomenon. Developmentally appropriate literature may be brought in such as *The Prince* by Machiavelli. The degree of unification of subject matter emphasizes a philosophy of education. How do students learn best in curriculum organization? Is it with the separate subjects, the fused or unified curriculum? (See Ediger,2006).

There is one additional plan which needs discussion pertaining to curriculum organization and that is problem solving. Problem solving stress the identification and solving of lifelike problems. John Dewey (1859-1953) was a leading proponent of problem solving with experimentalism as a philosophy of education. Dr. Dewey had a laboratory school at the University of Chicago in the late 1890s which stressed experimentalism. This philosophical school of thought emphasized the following:

- change is paramount in school and in society
- school and society are integrated, not separate entities
- schools need to stress the practical since individuals live in the societal arena
- pupils in school are actively involved in learning, not passive recipients of knowledge
- life consists of solving personal and social problems
- ultimate reality cannot be known but experiences are knowable (Dewey, 1916).

In the school setting, students identify problems, develop related hypotheses, and these are tried out, not through test taking, but in lifelike situations. The following school situations involve problem solving:

- developing standards of conduct for students interacting with each other
- planning and doing a project directly related to an ongoing unit of study
- organizing and implementing a formal or informal dramatization
- constructing a model pertaining to a concept or generalization being studied
- working cooperatively in pursuing an ongoing activity.

Problems arise within an ongoing experience which require clarification, an hypothesis, and an approach in its evaluation. Experimentalists are also strong in looking at the consequences of an act or action.

Conclusion

Teachers and supervisors need to study and plan effective methods of organizing the curriculum. Criteria which need emphasizing in organizing the curriculum include the following:

- does it minimize one or more academic areas?
- will it assist pupils to establish meaning in an ongoing activity?
- will learners become more motivated and perceive purpose in learning?

The plan chosen may be used for one academic area for a single unit or part of a unit of study. Other approaches may be added as needed. Flexibility in organization of the curriculum makes it possible to adapt each to assist optimal learner achievement and progress.

REFERENCES

Dewey, John (1916), *Democracy and Education*. New York: The Macmillan Company.

Ediger, Marlow (2006), Teaching Mathematics in the High School Setting," *College Student Journal*, 39 (4), 711-715.

Ediger, Marlow (2008), "Psychology of Parental Involvement in Reading," *Journal of Instructional Psychology, Reading Improvement*, 45 (1), 46-52.

Ediger, Marlow (2010), "Issues in Social Studies," *International Journal of Educational Research, Development and Extension*, 1 (1), 43-49.

Ediger, Marlow, and D. Bhaskara Rao (2003), *Philosophy and Curriculum*. New Delhi, India: Discovery Publishing House Pvt. Ltd.

Ragan, William, and Gene Shepherd (1982) *Modern Elementary Curriculum*. New York: Holt Rinehart and Winston.

Wahlquist, John T. (1942), *The Philosophy of American Education*. New York: Ronald Publishing Company.

Watkins, Bevertey T. (1990), "An Education Professor Tries to Put on His Fantasy School into Effect," *The Chronicles of Higher Eduction*, November 7, p. A3.

2

CHAPTER

Psychology and Curriculum Development

Teachers, Supervisors, and School Administrators desire to Assist Pupils to Attain Optimally

The psychology of learning certainly may help in this area and is designed to do so. There are selected principles of learning which when used might guide pupils to achieve objectives of instruction. Pupils differ from each other in a variety of ways such as interests possessed, purposes perceived, attitudes acquired, as well as values developed. Thus, individual differences among learners must be provided for in the classroom. Using the same methods of instruction, the same materials of instruction, and having the same expectations for each is not realistic. Rather, the teacher must adapt methods used which are suitable to assisting learner achievement and progress. Materials of instruction need to engage pupils in the learning process, while achievement expectations for each pupil's achievement must be high but reasonable. Teachers need to be well prepared for each day of teaching and incorporate salient tenets of educational psychology. Securing the interests of pupils is of utmost importance. Disconnected from studying and attending will not maximize learner progress. The teacher needs to secure and maintain intense pupil interest in ongoing lessons and units of study. He/she must observe pupils rather continuously to notice if adequate pupil concentration is there. Each educational psychologist to be discussed focused upon a selected psychology which, if applied, should aid pupil progress (Ediger, 2007).

Relevant Psychologies of Education

There are educational psychologists who have contributed much to curriculum development and teaching/learning situations. The influence of their thinking and research is quite evident in what is being emphasized presently. Behaviorism as a psychology of learning stresses the saliency of measuring pupil learning in precise numerical terms, such as percentile, age/grade equivalent, and stanine results. B. F. Skinner (1902-1986) was very prominent in advocating measuring pupil achievement and not leaving subjective judgements of learner achievement up to the teacher. Dr. Skinner advocated Stimulus/Response theory in his written programmed materials. In using programmed learning, pupils rarely made mistakes in a tightly knitted sequence. Here, pupils, for example, read a sentence or two and then responded to a multiple choice test item. If the response was correct, reinforcement was in evidence; rewarding correct answers is known as operant conditioning. Thus, Skinner placed the stress upon the correctness of a response, rather than the stimulus. Earlier, Pavlov, Russian physiologist in his experiments with dogs, emphasized the stimulus. Changing the stimulus brought on a different response. Thus, a dog was conditioned to salivate with the sound of a bell only whereas the unconditioned stimulus (UCS) such as meat caused the dog to salivate. The site of meat and the sounding of a bell (conditioned stimulus) together, ultimately lead to the dog salivating solely through the sounding of the bell. With operant conditioning, Dr. Skinner brought to the attention of educators the importance of properly ordered materials of instruction as well as building the self concept due to learner success in achievement. Testing then becomes very important; generally standardized tests are favoured with those containing high validity and reliability. This can be noticed with mandated testing which provide standards for pupils being promoted to the next grade level, if a passing score is received (See Donahue, 2000).

Mandated testing advocates also use behaviorism as a model for prescribed learning. Standardized tests used are aligned with the measurably stated objectives and are written, generally, by specialists in each academic area. The classroom teacher selects learning activities which assist pupils to achieve the stated objectives of instruction. Operant conditioning within behaviorist psychology in programmed learning emphasizes a high success rate in each pupil's learning whereas mandated testing stresses sorting pupils in terms of those passing/failing the test, as well as making comparisons among different classrooms, schools, school systems, and states (See Gore, 1993). The following are major summary statements pertaining to behaviorism as a psychology of learning including mandated testing and operant conditioning:

- precision is emphasized with measurably stated objectives
- tests are aligned with the objectives of instruction
- test results from pupils generally are quantifiable
- tests usually consist of multiple chpice items
- machine scoring is used with mandated testing in which many students take the tests on the state or national levels
- pupil, classroom, school system, and state achievement levels of learners may be compared to notice successful and failing schools.

Jean Piaget, Swiss educator who studied children for over 50 years, came up with a maturation theory of learning. What children can learn depends upon their stage of maturity, dependent upon age levels. He came up with the following approximate levels of maturity in learning:

- psychomotor stage, ages birth to age 18 months. Here, infants learned from objects which move such as clatter balls fastened to a crib. The young child might then move the spheres attached to soft rod. While doing this, the eyes of the infant watches the movement and hears the sounds involved. Many toys that can be held by/for the child are then used to shaking with the attending different noises. The gradual movement, soft noise, and the feeling of the toys make for learning.
- preoperational stage, eighteen months to seven years. Here, the child sees one variable when making comparisons among objects. Thus, a glass of water as compared to pouring that same water into a taller thinner container makes the youngster believe that the taller, thinner container has more water as compared to the original glassful, even though the water was poured from one container to the next directly in front of the observer. Perceiving one variable only is quite typical of these children, ages 18 months to seven years, as they continue to learn.
- stage of concrete operations, ages seven to eleven. Here, the learner needs real objects to learn from as the abstract leanings are being emphasized. Thus, a small model horse is necessary when reading the related abstract word. The school may not possess all the needed models, but it is good for the learner to associate the concrete with the abstract. Reasoning skills are starting to enter into the teaching and learning situation with further and indepth skills added in sequential achievement.
- stage of abstract thought, beginning at age, eleven and twelve in which children increasingly possess the

ability to problem solve notice variables, as well as engage in critical and creative thinking without referring directly to concrete materials of instruction.

Jean Piaget, then, emphasized the saliency of maturation in teaching and learning situations. Abraham Maslow developed a humanistic theory of learning whereby the child and his/her environment need careful consideration in the curriculum. Maslow, first of all, believed the physiological needs of children need attention. Thus, adequate nutrition, good shelter/homes, and clothing need to be taken care of. These are prerequisites to developing the desire to learn in school. Second, pupils need to have safety needs taken care of. Abusive situations and harassment should not be experienced by children. Achievement comes about if pupils feel secure from all alarm. Third, all like to feel they belong in a class or school. Being an isolate and not being accepted makes for uncomfortable situations. Teachers need to assist pupils in becoming a part of the group setting. Fourth, esteem needs must be met; pupils like to feel successful and be recognized for achievement. Pupils, no doubt, do not like school due to the lack of recognition for deeds and acts. Eventually, dropping out of school may occur. When all these preceding needs have been met, pupils are ready to achieve more optimally.

Jerome Bruner viewed subject-matter as being main ingredients in learning. He emphasized that pupils achieve structural content in different academic disciplines. The structural ideas may be identified by subject matter specialists such as a professors of history identifying key ideas in history; these main ideas are then available to teachers who assist pupils in achievement. Thus, teachers must meticulously identify major generalizations of learner attainment. So often trivia is emphasized such as irrelevant names, dates, and places, and this may be avoided or minimized with helping pupils acquire structural content. The structure provides the framework of an academic discipline upon which related subject matter may be built. Learning opportunities need to emphasize pupil's attaining inductive these structural ideas. The teacher must possess a good knowledge of subject-matter to help pupils learn content, using discovery methods of teaching. He/she encourages and assists whenever necessary. The structure of knowledge approach used in teaching has the following advantages:

- assistance is available to teachers in selecting what is salient for pupils to learn
- teachers may focus upon teaching what is relevant, not the mundane and insignificant
- pupils are excited in learning subject-matter by discovery rather than lecture or telling methods
- pupils may work as academicians do using the same tools and approaches
- learns might well meet up with the same/similar structural ideas as different units of study are taught
- evaluation may consist of pupils achieving and attaching meaning to identified key, structural ideas.

Daniel Goleman (1995) focuses upon emotional intelligence (EQ). He emphasizes the importance of psychological factors which might well create problems at school and the work place. A worker, for example, may have the know how to succeed at these places, but have difficulties in getting along with others. Negative feelings and attitudes get in the way of being proficient. Goleman states the EQ may be more salient than IOs possessed. Teachers in the classroom notice the following situations:

- pupils who are isolates and seemingly fail to be able to connect with others
- pupils who pout when they do not their way and might frequently feel sorry for themselves
- pupils who disturb others and keep them from studying

- pupils, individually, who roam around the classroom and cannot settle down to learn
- pupils who like to entertain and want to be class clowns which disrupt discussions
- pupils who are quick to pick fights on the playground
- pupils who harass others in diverse ways (Ediger, 2010).

There are pupils who become angry soon at the least provocation. This is shown as consistent behaviour. Anger management is important since an angry individual may do many things which are regrettable later on. This has ruined a person's life. Teachers need to view and diagnose those who have problems with anger, among other forms of unapproved behaviors, and assist all pupils to be accepted by others as well as be well adjusted. They need to emphasize committee work whereby each does his/her fair share of work as well as working harmoniously with others. Good human relations and social development of each pupil is significant. Individuals must know and manage their emotions, as well as know the feelings of others. Social skills need developing and using when relating to others. Non-verbal skills need honing such as having appropriate facial expressions, tone of voice, and postures/ gestures.

Howard Gardner (1993) emphasized multiple intelligences theory in providing for individual differences in a classroom. Thus, more than one intelligence (IQ) is possessed by learners in a school setting. Teachers need to provide for pupils of different intelligences. Thus, the following, among others, are important to consider in teaching and learning situations:

- verbal intelligence such as learner experiences in reading and writing activities in diverse curriculum areas. In gathering information, these pupils achieve much in terms of reading subject matter content.

- logical intelligence in which learners do well in using logic as is true in mathematics as well as in other academic disciplines.
- musical/rhythmical as in writing lyrics and putting these to music to reveal what has been learned. This activity may be correlated with any facet of unit teaching by putting that which has been learned to music. Rhythmical experiences, also, are salient as in folk dances related to social studies units of instruction.
- intrapersonal experiences whereby the student prefers to work by the self and does well in achieving objectives of instruction.
- interpersonal intelligence whereby the pupil prefers to work collectively in committees to attain and accomplish in ongoing lessons/units of study.
- bodily/kinesthetic intelligence stresses the importance of manual dexterity as well as eye hand coordination. There are pupils who do well, for example, in constructing models, science equipment, and engaging in the project method. Athletic endeavors also stress bodily/ kinesthetic intelligence.
- Scientific intelligence whereby the pupils shows high capabilities in objective thinking. Objective thinking is stressed in all curriculum areas, and especially in science.
- artistic intelligence in which the child shows proficiency in creative thinking in using space to reveal what has been produced in art work. When viewing art products in national museums, the viewer is fascinated with the following: media used and blended to produce a product, unique interpretations used by the artist, perseverance which went into completing a work of art, as well as beauty expressed by the artist.

Conclusion

Teachers, supervisors, and principals might gain much from *a* study of leading educational psychologists and their beliefs and ideas with the intent of applying selected major generalizations in improving the curriculum. Thus, the following are salient:

- Skinner with his emphasis upon learner success when activities are sequenced appropriately.
- Piaget with stress placed upon stages of pupils maturing properly before learning opportunities are implemented.
- Maslow with his emphasis on meeting pupil needs holistically.
- Bruner with relevancy placed upon teaching significant subject matter.
- Goleman with importance placed upon developing well socially and emotionally.
- Gardner with placing saliency upon abilities possessed by individuals and providing for important differences.

REFERENCES

Donahue, P. (2000),"Evaluating Teaching," *ADE Bulletin*, 126 (1), 46-47.

Ediger, Marlow (2007), "Learning Activities in the Curriculum," *College Student Journal*, 41 (4), 967-969

Ediger, Marlow (2010), "Constructivism and the Social Studies," *Edutracks*, 9 (7), 13-15.

Gardner, Howard (1983), *Frames of Mind: The Theory of Multiple Intelligences*. New York: Basic Books.

Goleman, Daniel (1995), *Emotional Intelligence; Why it Can Matter More Than IQ*. New York: Bantam Books.

Gore, G. R. (1993), "What is Good Teaching?" *Physics Teacher*, 31(8), 482.

Collaboration Versus Individual Endeavours in the Curriculum

Which is the better approach in pupil learning—working together in collaborative situations or working by the self in ongoing learning activities? Howard Gardner (1993), Harvard University psychologist, emphasized that these are two different intelligences. Collaboration is preferred by selected pupils in learning. These learners do best when working in a small group to complete ongoing activities and experiences. Individuals working by the self may have this intelligence as a preference. Individually, pupil achievement is at a higher level as compared to working cooperatively with others.

Collaboration Versus Individual Endeavors

In working collectively within a lesson/unit of study, pupils experience a social situation. Quality interaction among participants is needed to agree upon objectives in an activity as well as making plans to achieve these objectives. Further interaction is necessary to carry out the plans to fruition as well as evaluation procedures must be developed to evaluate the final product as well as processes used along the way.

Cooperatively developed standards are necessary in collaboration which include:

- all members need to contribute as much as possible
- contributions need to circulate among members and not between two pupils only
- politeness and acceptance of each other must prevail
- an attitude of assisting each other to succeed is crucial
- processes used in committee work need to be appraised regularly.

Progress reports should be made periodically to notice formative achievement as well as to aid in sequential attainment. Collaborative endeavours will succeed if appropriate standards are followed in ongoing activities. The role of the teacher is to observe pupils carefully in terms of desired goals as well as provide assistance as needed to help learners to persevere in an orderly manner. The processes involved are as salient as the products produced from collaborative work. Pupils, too, are responsible for endorsing criteria for effective committee work. Both product and processes emphasize learning and stress goal attainment within an ongoing unit of study. Quality experiences assist achievement and progress. Thus, the topic or project must be interesting to pupils and involve active engagement. Pupils are not passive recipients but are engaged in the ongoing activity. Information being processed must relate to the pupil's own sphere of purpose in order that relevancy is in evidence. The purpose is related to the learner's interests and thus propels effort in achievement. The learner is not passive in receiving knowledge and skills, but rather is an active being who seeks and finds that which is relevant and purposeful. Then too, meaning theory becomes salient in that the learner attempts to find what makes sense. Attaining meaning as well as understanding what is taught is vital to the learner. If pupils engage in collaborative lessons/units of study or if individual efforts are put forth, the pupils must seek purpose and meaning within an interesting experience. Collaboration and individual endeavors should assist pupils to attain objectives in the curriculum and provide background experiences tor ensuing learning activities.

With collaboration, the pupil is in an advantage of developing feelings of belonging. In Maslow's hierarchy (1954), the following needs are listed for human beings:

- physiological (nutrition, shelter, sleep and rest, thirst alleviation, and proper clothing)
- safety (freedom from danger and abuse)
- belonging (wanting to be an accepted member of a group)
- esteem (desire for recognition and reward for goal accomplishment)
- wishing to be the kind of person desired.

The desired need fulfilment may be in any order of the above asterisked items, but generally follow the order given and they are interrelated. Cooperative endeavours does emphasize the importance of achieving feelings of *belonging*. Thus, persons do not wish to be isolates but be an accepted member of a group. By working together on selected tasks, pupils develop increased proficiency in working with others, providing the learning environment is suitable. Thus, appropriate standards must be followed. The writer in supervising university student teachers observed where pupils in a committee were on task rather continuously. They were exited and enticed with the task being pursued. When recess time came, these participants wanted to keep working on the ongoing activity. Interest made for motivation as well as acceptable peers made for quality human relations. The writer also noticed whereby small group work did *not* materialize to achieve goals. The following were reasons for the failure in the collaborative endeavour:

- seemingly the student teacher and the cooperating teacher did not introduce the project appropriately to secure interests of learners.
- pupils did not understand their respective roles in small group work.
- there were pupils in the small group who did not respect each other; definite cases of rudeness were noticed readily. Membership in a collaborative endeavour need to learn to work together if goals are to be accomplished. It may be necessary to put pupils in a committee who function well together; later, pupils, as they progress, may be more accepting of others.
- those who are isolates, initially, might be placed with others who are highly accepting of others. The teacher and pupils in the committee must evaluate if all are participating adequately. If this does not occur, diagnosis must be emphasized to ascertain causes with remediation following.

There are a plethora of activities involving collaborative experiences. One committee made a model farm scene in a social studies unit. Learners expressed purpose in doing the model being inherent in the objectives of the project. They carefully planned the project before initiating the activity. Accepting the purpose or reasons for doing the model, pupils do progress in the experience. Evaluation was continuous as the work commenced with pupils raising questions about what did not possess clarity. Pupils do need to establish meaningful learning in sequential steps when engaged in the project method. In science, four pupils were working collaboratively in developing a model volcano, folds, and faults, in an ongoing unit of study titled, "Changes on the Earth's Surface." Much research went into developing the project such as securing information through and from internet use, textbooks/ library books, journal articles, video tapes, and DVDs, among others. The completed projects were open to viewing by pupils in other classrooms. In a mathematics class, live pupils collaboratively developed models of a cone, pyramid, and a cylinder. By using a hands on approach in learning, pupils seemingly learned more about each space figure as compared to looking at and discussing textbook drawings and then finding the volume of each. Collaboration, too, stresses art work, human relations, eye hand coordination, as well as personal responsibility. Vygotsky (1933-1978) advocated collaborative work for pupils; in this way, ideas circulate and "bounce off the minds of participants." Learning, then, occurs within a social setting with pupils learning from each other as well as from the self. John Dewey (1916), also, advocated pupils learning in group settings. In his laboratory school at the University of Chicago, as early as 1896, pupils engaged in problem solving activities.

In comparing collaborative learning with individual endeavors, the latter also has responsibilities of careful listening and interacting to secure the most out of teacher explanations, task identification, understanding the objectives, assignment to achieve objectives, and appraisal procedures to optimize learning. The learner must ask for clarification of what is not understood in order to develop sequence in achieving. As a style of learning, the pupil has opportunities to pace his/her progress as individual differences provide. The kinds of activities can be the same such as engaging in the project method, problem solving, use of computers and technology, among others. The pupil does not need to wait on others to finish their segment of work as is true of collaborative endeavors. Also, these individuals do not need to:

- keep pace with others when it is difficult to do so
- feel inferior as compared to others who shine in the committee setting
- worry about criticism from peers.

When viewing the individual in society, it is quite obvious that a person interacts with others at the work place and with others in different clubs and organizations. Thus, it is very salient to be able to interact harmoniously with others in collaborative endeavors. Then too, each person needs to be able to find what to do individually. Thus hobbies, talents.as well as personal interests, may find oneself in finding what to do individually. Individuals work together with others as well as by the self. The classroom teacher then must assist pupils to do both well—work and interact well collaboratively as well as use spare and leisure time well. Then too, later at the work place the individual may need to work by the self (Ediger and Rao, 2007).

In Closing

The teacher must provide a classroom which assists pupils well in social and individual endeavors. Classroom management then becomes important in doing the following:

- structuring the classroom with a variety of interesting learning activity which meet objectives. These materials provide learning activities for collaborative and individual work.
- discuss with clarity roles for each person to perform, be it individual or collaborative, leaving much room for creative and critical thinking as well as problem solving
- model behaviours which may not be understood by learners
- evaluate pupil pursuits when monitoring learner behavior in achievement
- assist pupils as needed in order that quality sequence in learning is in evidence.

REFERENCES

Dewey, John (1916), *Democracy and Education*. New York: The Macmillan Company.

Ediger, Marlow, and D. Bhaskara Rao (2007), *Teaching Social Studies*. New Delhi, India: Discovery Publishing House.

Gardner, Howard (1993), *Multiple Intelligences: Theory into Practice*. New York: Basic Books.

Maslow, A. H. (1954), *Motivation and Personality*. New York: Harper and Row.

Vygotsky, Len (1933-1978), *Mind in Society; The Development of Higher Psychological Processes*. Cambridge, Massachusetts: Harvard University Press.

Ethics and Morality in the Curriculum

There are salient standards for living which must be stressed in the curriculum. They serve as criteria in terms of what is the good life for all. When looking back to classical writers as well as modern times, the standards for ethics and morality has remained somewhat consistent and need to be studied by all learners. Universal criteria assists the self to become less egocentric in relating to others in society. All humans have worth and need to be treated with respect and caring. Too frequently, people think of the self in terms of what is moral and good. Militarism and war endeavours favour this line of thinking. The "others" in society be it individuals or nations must be brought to defeat so as to preserve one's personal freedoms regardless of death, destruction, and ruin that follows to the victims (Ediger and Rao, 2004).

The writer will survey what has be stated pertaining to ethics and morality over time as well as what has survived.

Ethics and Morality in the Societal Realm

Socrates (470-399 BC) used a questioning procedure to assist individuals to ascertain moral truths, in ancient Athens. Thus, an inductive approach was used by Socrates and this came to be called the Socratic Method. Through questions raised by Socrates, individuals realized the lack of clarity and consistency of adhered to ethical beliefs. The Socratic method is used in the curriculum presently. Discovery methods are then used in place of lecture to help pupils learn. In Socrates time, there were skeptics who frowned at any attempt at truth. Socrates sought stability in morality and ethical behavior in a time of growing skepticism. Socrates' thinking may be compared with a contemporary, named Gorgias who taught that:

- nothing whatsoever exists
- if something exists, it cannot be known
- if it could be understood, it could not be communicated.

The Sophists were leaders at that time with beliefs stressing that each individual has his/her own truths, with nothing emphasizing universal truth. Everything is relative and "man is the measure of all things."

Aristotle (384-322 BC) advocated pure contemplation as the highest good for individuals to engage in. Contemplation involves thinking about ethics and morality. Pure contemplation emphasizes that one moves away from concrete situations of human made things and the natural environment to concentrate on the abstract and what makes for a good society. The goal stressed by Aristotle prior to and of lesser value than pure contemplation was the Golden Mean. This goal emphasized the here and the now with avoiding extremes in life such as taking foolish chances, being foolhardy, versus refraining from acting and doing in performing relevant deeds in society. There is a Golden Mean between the opposite ends of this continuum. Thus Aristotle would stress the Golden Mean in society and the highest good - pure contemplation - when individuals contemplate ethics and morality. Generally, the elite and upper class would have the most time and knowledge for contemplation to take place (See Brameld, 1955).

Stoicism, founded by Zeno (334-262 BC), advocated the good life as consisting of controlling personal feelings. Feelings could be controlled but happenings to the self had to be accepted. Thus, stoicism stressed not showing feelings toward anything that happened regardless of positive or negative occurrences. Individuals need to accept who and what they are and not complain, nor give blame for happenings one does not like. Life is like a drama in that it is short and one arrives on the stage with the good (wealth, for example) and the bad (an ugly face). Even for those occurrences which are liked, the individual should show no feelings. Stoicism then was an answer to social and personal dilemmas.

John Locke (1632-1704) emphasized four standards for the education of the elite or upper class. The highest standard was the virtuous person who has the qualities of being a good individual. This person is known for honesty, thrift, and quality behavior. These individuals have a good reputation and are looked upon in a favorable manner. Next in saliency came wisdom. The person with wisdom has foresight in making wise judgments. These individuals do not come into poverty nor do they do shameful deeds. Third is good breeding. John Locke was critical of those who exhibited sheepish bashfulness in that they were shy and did not express themselves well in social situations. They were timid and reserved when communicating with others. The outgoing person with much confidence is wanted. Fourth, Locke stressed knowledge. He admitted to being "bookish," but felt there were three other traits being more important such as virtue, wisdom, and breeding. In his curriculum then, John Locke stressed four characteristics of a well educated gentleman (See Sahakian, 1968).

Jeremy Bentham (1748-1832) advocated "the greatest good for the greatest number" in the realm of society. This meant that governments should strive to make laws which benefit the largest number of people in society. Also, in judicial reform, Bentham worked to make punishments fit the crime rather than arbitrary rules and laws being promulgated. Uniformity in laws was then advocated by Bentham. For his day, "the greatest good for the greatest number was noble indeed. This is different than advocating human rights for the elite only or largely. In a democracy, minority rights, too, should and must be upheld, something that Bentham minimized (See Wayper, 1954).

David Hume (1711-1776) was a skeptic and questioned many actions and assumptions. He stressed, for example, that one cannot know cause and effect. Thus; if a person sees/hears two things as connected, the certainty of this cannot be determined. Striking a piano key, for example, is followed by the same sound continuously, according to an observer. But, this is customarily assumed to be true in that A causes B. But, the perceiver cannot see cause and effect.

As an extreme skeptic, does this mean that anarchy should prevail in an area or nation? Hume said that even if laws, rules, regulations are arbitrary in different states, the citizen must abide by these courses of action to make for civility. However, what are conceived to be absolutes cannot be proven and are subjective. There have been a plethora of philosophers who have looked for absolutes which are always true. A leader in this area, was Rene Descartes (1596-1650) who sought that which was always true, and he finally came up with the well known, "I think, therefore I am." This belief was established by Descartes after doubting everything possible, even his own existence. Descartes still had to come up with the God concept who, he felt, could not and would not deceive. God made it possible to accept that he (Descartes) was real since being one who thinks and a thinking human is real. No deception was involved here. The quest for universal certainty has alluded many individuals (See Ulich, 1950).

Immanuel Kant (1724-1804) believed in the Categorical Imperative which stated that whatever is wanted by the self should become a universal desire. Thus, if I want *A*, then *A* should be the goal for all people. If *B* is not wanted, then *B* should not be heaped upon others. Rudeness is not wanted for the self; then rudeness must not be passed onto others. Politeness is desired and then it should be a universal in behavior. The Categorical Imperative is not an elective, but an imperative in human behavior. It is an "ought" and not cause/effect in terms of human actions. The Categorical Imperative seemingly became an absolute in the thinking of many (See Bowyer, 1970).

Francis Bacon (1561-1626) was an early philosopher who emphasized accuracy in communication. He stressed four idols which hindered in arriving at truth:

- idols of the cave. The cave pertained to subjectivity and limits of the mind to arrive at accurate conclusions. Ideas conveyed need critical evaluation to come up with truths. Personal experiences must be assessed in terms of the larger society and world. Being gullible in listening to the thinking of others may be minimized in training the mind to stress critical and creative thinking.
- idols of the tribe. Within one's own acquaintances, statements are made and passed on which lack credibility. Culture then emphasizes half truths or fiction. A goal of culture must be to correct deficiencies in expressed content.
- idols of the market place. When people interact with others in the business world, careless and limitations in use of language might well be in the offing. Due to slovenly communication as well as simplicity in wording, individuals arrive at inaccuracies and distorted ideas. Careful use of meaningful language assists individuals to understand others better. Misunderstandings accrue when a lack of accuracy is in the offing.

- idols of the theater. Here, language is used in novel and in interesting ways whereby the listener might use these ideas in vague ways in communicating with others. Presentations from theaters, if followed, bring on careless communication (Stumpf, 1973).

Basing his thinking on the mathematics model, Bertrand Russell, early twentieth century philosopher, emphasized that misunderstandings might well be minimized if precision in language was emphasized. At one point in his life, Russell stated that each word used orally should refer to something concrete. Thus, an abstract word should correlate with an object or item. These were called atomic facts. When two or more atomic facts are put together, the result is a molecular proposition. Too frequently, vague expressions, although used even in standard English, are meaningless. The presenter needs to be certain that preciseness in communication is in the offing. There is a relationship here between the thinking of Francis Bacon and Bertrand Russell. Both viewed the possibilities of using accuracy in language to communicate.

John Dewey (1859-1952) stressed the importance of experimentalism as a philosophy. Dewey believed that the quest for certainty of ideas was useless. One cannot know absolutes, but modified thinking occurs when solving problems. To solve a problem, the involved person or persons develops a tentative hypothesis and obtains information from a variety of sources to secure answers. The obtained information is used to test the hypothesis. As a result, the hypothesis may need revision or is accepted as is. New problems might arise in the ongoing problematic situation requiring an hypothesis, followed by its testing. Problem solving may definitely be used in attempting to solve ethical and moral dilemmas. Dewey used problem solving in his laboratory school at the University of Chicago and believed this procedure to be practical for pupils in the school and community setting (Dewey, 1916).

In closing, there are a myriad of questions to discuss pertinent to each of the philosophers mentioned in this writing:

- How do you like Socratic questioning as compared to lecture in a classroom?
- What have you come up with in using Contemplation as a means of getting at ethics and morality? Is this possible to do so?
- Might one's feelings be omitted/minimized when unfortunate/fortunate things happen, according to Stoicism? Is it possible to do so?
- Can virtue (John Locke) be learned by any person? What about in situations where violence in a community rules?
- Do you favor the "greatest good for the greatest number philosophy of Jeremy Bentham? Why or why not?
- Is it possible to be as great a skeptic as was David Hume?
- How is Immanuel Kant's Categorical Imperative like the Golden Rule?
- What are selected "idols" that you have heard in society?
- How helpful is John Dewey's problem solving in arriving at good ethical and moral behavior? Why do you think that way?

Students should do much reading on each philosophy. A peer approach may be used whereby committee members assist each other in word recognition and meaning making. The subject matter needs to make sense and be usable to reflect upon being ethical and moral in behavior. Concrete examples need to be given such as the teacher modeling Socratic procedures of instruction as compared to lecturing. Philosophy should be challenging as well as interesting.

REFERENCES

Bowyer, Carleton (1970), *Philosophical Perspectives for Education*. Glenview, Illinois: Scott, Foresman and Company.

Brameld, Theodore, (1955), *Philosophies of Education in Cultural Perspective*. New York: Holt, Rinehart and Winston.

Dewey, John (1916), *Democracy and Education*. New York: The Macmillan Company.

Ediger, Marlow, and D. Bhaskara Rao (2004), *Philosophy and Curriculum*. New Delhi, India: Discovery Publishing House.

Sahakian, William S. (1968), *History of Philosophy*. New York: Barnes and Noble Books.

Stumpf, Samuel Eli (1973), *Philosophy, History and Problems*. New York: McGraw-Hill Book Company.

Ulich, Robert (1950), *History of Educational Thought*. New York: American Book Company.

Wayper, C. L. (1954), *Political Thought*. New York: Philosophical Library, Inc.

Mathematics for All Pupils

Mathematics has always been considered as a basic in the curriculum. The familiar concept of the three r's reading, writing, and (arithmetic indicates its historical salience. With No Child Left Behind law passed in 2002, it is as essential as ever. This law emphasized testing of pupils in grades three through eight for promotional purposes, in mathematics, reading, and science. Then too, in society, individuals use mathematics in every day transactions. It is practical, useful, and relevant for all pupils to be successful achievers in this academic area. A mathematics curriculum needs development which encourages, motivates, and challenges learners to achieve, grow, and accomplish as much as individual abilities and interests provide (Ediger, 2010).

The Psychology of Learning and Mathematics Mathematics teachers must observe pupils carefully to notice pupil problems which arise in learning. Too frequently, teachers attempt to cover much content in a short period of time without paying attention to learners having mastered what is taught. Psychologist David Ausubel (1978) stated that that the most import factor in teaching is to start where pupils are presently in achievement. Thus, if pupils are studying a unit on addition of fractions, the teacher must be certain that learners understand why one-fourth plus one-fourth equals one half. This can be shown meaningfully with one-fourth of a circle being placed adjacent to another congruent one- fourth. Concrete and semi-concrete materials must be inherent to make learnings understandable in teaching. The abstract numerals need to be written next to the two congruent fourths which equal one half. Ensuing subject matter may then be taught in relating the new with that learned previously. The sequence must be as seamless as possible. If the sequence lacks proper order, pupils may be lost in achieving the new objective. The mathematics teacher must pay careful attention to ordering experiences properly for pupils. When learners understand the meaning of addition of proper fractions, a question may arise by a pupil on names to be applied to fractions such as numerator and denominator. Sequence then resides within involved pupils. These terms should be printed neatly on the word wall for pupil reference and also for their discussion interests when congregating here. Many pupils review and elaborate on meanings when seeing and discussing vocabulary terms on the word wall. Learners also sequence subject matter when, for example, they ask questions about other names for the above two fourths such as three sixths, four eights, among others, each being shown in meaning with three sixths of a circle being placed on one half (Ediger and Rao, 2002). Visual cues are salient in teaching fractions such as circles, squares, software projections on a white board, and slides projections.

Verbal cues should promote effectives of visuals. They should be clear with proper voice inflections to secure learner attention. Stressing selected words more so than others helps pupils to focus upon these salient vocabulary terms, such as proper and improper fractions. The teacher's voice with appropriate prosody can be a very effective means of obtaining pupil attention. Gesture clues should be used to further pupil attentiveness. Here, a logical sequence may be initiated when teacher judgement is used in pointing to the word wall to reinforce a concept and its definition, such as equivalent fractions. Included facial expressions such as a nod of approval or a smile when learners respond correctly is included in non-verbal communication (See Kindervater, 2010).

Levels of Thinking in Mathematics

Pupils need to use different levels of thinking or cognition in ongoing units of study. *Recalling of information* is salient since this provides building blocks for higher cognitive levels. After meaning has been attached, pupils may need to recall how to reduce a fraction to lowest terms. Clearly stating how this operation is performed is necessary to reveal mastery.

The next level of cognition indicates *understanding* of what was recalled. Thus, for instance, pupils need to demonstrate how a fraction is reduced to lowest terms. What are the understandings needed in reducing fractions? Sequentially, the pupil reveals understanding in the order of performing this operation.

Elaborating indicates a more complex level of cognition. Pupils may be challenged to change a mixed number to an improper fraction and describe its meaning. Scaffolding may occur here whereby the teacher may assist by using manipulative materials. This involves the teacher logically helping learners to change a mixed number to an improper fraction. With elaboration, pupils attain content in greater depth with increased understanding. Elaboration should not be hurried since "covering ground" is not the goal in teaching mathematics, but assisting learners to become ready for sequential achievement is salient. Going from the known to the unknown is sacrosanct. Teachers must assist pupils to go from what is known to the ensuing unknown in teaching and learning situations. Elaboration should assist in achieving this objective with learners raising questions to work toward clarification. Too frequently, pupils have memorized subject matter for a test, but meaning has been lacking; indepth learning should help pupils to attach understanding to loose ends of the mathematics curriculum (See Nolan, 2003).

Metacognition guides pupils to reflect upon previous learnings. Learners need assistance in thinking about what they know and what they do not understand. This could be modeled verbally by the teacher in providing a clear model for pupils. With careful attention to each step of learning, pupils individually may use this model in and for metacognition. Metacognition can help pupils to retain knowledge and skills. It does involve rehearsing previously acquired subject matter as well as having a diagnostic purpose. The diagnosis stresses viewing problematic situations in pupil learning with remedies in the offing. It is best to have a developmental mathematics curriculum whereby seamlessly pupil accomplish, develop and grow, but at times and with reflection, diagnosis reveals what needs additional attention in teaching. For example, in the division of fractions, pupils and the teacher might discover that the former does not understand the reasons for inverting the divisor and multiply. The author remembers in grade school when he was taught to divide fractions by simply "turning the divisor upside down" and then doing the familiar which is multiplying. He does not recall any reasons given for doing this. It does make rote learning a concept easier, but it does not provide for meaning in terms of building blocks for sequential achievement. Each learning acquired assists in attaining the more complex, ordered mathematical ideas (Ediger, 2007).

Critical thinking should also be a major objective in mathematics. Here, the pupil learns to separate the relevant from the irrelevant. For example, in doing a word problem, there might be information that is not needed (extraneous content) in solving the problem. Also, the learner might not be following the sequence necessary in solving the problem.

One item on a test observed by the author when supervising student teachers dealing with fractions pertained to pupils arranging four fractions from the largest to smallest in value: 2/3 3/4 5/7 6/7. Here, the test item deals with critical thinking in being able to discern the number of parts an object is divided into (the denominator) as compared to the parts being considered (the numerator) as in two of three parts being considered in the fraction 2/3. Critical thinking, here, involves analyzing and making comparisons in arriving which order to show the arranged fractions from largest to smallest (See Scafidi and Bui, 2010).

Creative thinking is also salient as a mental process. The pupil here reveals novel, unique ideas. Originality is a key concept. A pupil might be encouraged in creative endeavors in the following:

- arriving at a different solution in solving a word problem.
- making a collage from different colors of construction paper, using cut out geometrical figures consisting of circles, squares, triangles, among others. Pupils need to identify each geometrical shape in doing the art project.
- writing word problems for other pupils to solve.
- dictating a story by young children for the teacher or aid to record. Older learners may do their own writing in long hand or with word processor use.
- brainstorming how any one fraction being studied may be useful in everyday life.

The mathematics teacher must plan carefully to provide for individual differences. In most classrooms, there are English Language Learners (ELL), handicapped learners, and diverse minority groups which definitely should also have the best in mathematics teaching and learning situations. They need attainable, challenging objectives, varied learning opportunities which provide for different intelligences, as well as activities that make adequate provision for different styles of learning. A cookie cutter approach where one size fits all is not approbate in a modern mathematics curriculum. Evaluation of achievement needs to be valid and reliable. Optimal achievement is desired from each category of pupils. Diverse appraisal need to be used to assess learner progress including portfolios, teacher written and standardized tests, teacher observation, pupil and teach self evaluation, rating scales, discussions, rubrics, and checklists, among others. Feedback from pupil evaluation results should inform instruction, including the need for higher levels of cognition (See, National Council Teachers of Mathematics, 1989).

In ongoing mathematical units of study, the teacher may find it difficult to ascertain where *clarification* is needed to assist learners in attaching meaning to a concept or generalization. Pupils need encouragement to raise questions pertaining to what lacks meaning and understanding. Pupils may feel uncomfortable in asking for assistance. To minimize/ alleviate these feelings, the mathematics teacher may do the following:

- develop a classroom environment which is relaxing and conducive to learning.
- ask questions in an atmosphere of trust which pinpoint problems in pupil's understanding a specific process or particular knowledge.
- encourage self-evaluation on the part of pupils including diagnosis and remediation.
- have a support system whereby pupils assist each other to achieve.
- sequence learnings which bridge the gap for pupils between the known and the unknown.
- attain pupil efficacy whereby pupils feel confident in ensuing learning opportunities (See Palvanivassan, 2006).

Additional Factors in Teaching

With adequate inservice education and recognition given for quality teaching, the mathematics teacher might well gain self confidence in ongoing units of study. A quality self concept is needed for teachers to become increasingly effective in teaching all categories of learners. Efficacious teachers know how to provide for individual differences in assisting each pupil to achieve more optimally.

To select what pupils are to achieve, the mathematics teacher must be well versed in mathematical content and methods of teaching. Key, structural ideas need to be acquired by pupils; trivia must be avoided. Inservice education should involve not only teachers and school administrators but also professors from nearby universities who specialize in mathematics education. Major generalizations might then be identified for pupil acquisition.

Inservice education should also focus upon procedures and processes to be used by pupils in learning such as using inquiry methods, project methods, problem solving, rational thinking, a learning by doing approach, as well as constructivism as a psychology of learning. Rote learning is to be discouraged unless meanjng is stressed therein. For quality sequence to occur, the pupil needs to build on previous learnings and this emphasizes learners understanding what is taught and learned.

REFERENCES

Ausubel David (1978), *Educational Psychology: A Cognitive View*. New York: Holt, Rinehart and Winston.

Ediger, Marlow (2010), "Collaboration in Improving the Mathematics Curriculum," *Montana Mathematics*, March, pp. 13-14, Published by the Montana Council Teachers of Mathematics.

Ediger, Marlow, and D. Bhaskara Rao (2002), *Teaching Mathematics Successfully*. New Delhi, India: Discovery Publishing House.

Ediger, Marlow (2007) "Learning Activities in the Curriculum," *College Student Journal*, 41 (4), 967-969.

Kindervater, Terry (2010), "Family Literacy," *The Reading Teacher*, 63 (7), 610-613.

National Council Teachers of Mathematics (1989), *Curriculum and Evaluation Standards for School Mathematics.* Reston, Virginia: NCTM.

Nolan, Jennifer L. (2003), "Multiple Intelligences in the Classroom," *Education*, 124 (1), 115-119.

Palvanivassan, M. (2006), Analysis of Errors Committed by Higher Secondary Students in Calculus. Ph D thesis evaluated by the writer for the University of Madras, Chennai, India.

Scafidi, Tony, and Khanh Bui (2010), "Gender Similarities in Math Performance from Middle School Through High School," *Journal of Instructional Psychology*, 37 (3), 252-255.

Mathematics and the Psychology of Learning

Teachers of mathematics need to have a strong background of course in work and pedagogy, as well as inservice educational opportunities in teaching mathematics. In addition, they must keep abreast of recommended methods of instruction through reading of journal information pertaining to instructional practices.

Pupils deserve quality instruction in order to achieve as optimally as possible. Knowledge and skills secured need to be useful in school and in the community. Trivia and useless information need to be culled to make room for the relevant and functional subject matter. The psychology of learning can do much to assist mathematics teachers in helping pupils to attain objectives of instruction.

Psychology of Teaching Mathematics

Mathematics teachers need to be highly knowledgeable about the psychology of learning and how its use might well facilitate pupil learning. First of all, it behooves teachers to facilitate learners in ongoing activities to be actively involved in achieving. Passive, uninvolved pupils will hardly achieve worthwhile objectives. Thus, the teacher must develop learner interest in the ensuing mathematical experiences. Materials of instruction need to be as concrete as possible on the pupil's developmental level. Thus, for example, on the early primary grade levels, pupils might use wooden blocks in counting in one to one correspondence. As the child points to each block in counting and orally says the cardinal number, meaning is attached to an ongoing activity. For older pupils, such as on the senior high school level, the teacher assists pupils in using what has been learned in a concrete life-like situation. There is a purpose then in learning which is functional in school and in society.

Learnings which are relevant and useful aid pupils in becoming involved in achievement. What is understood and has meaning increases opportunities for pupils to actively participate in ensuing lesson and unit experiences. Next, pupils need to have ample experiences in practising what has been acquired. This may be enhanced through meta cognition strategies. Here, the mathematics teacher assists pupils to reflect and think about previous learnings. When reflecting in answer to vital questions, the pupil makes use of salient facts, concepts, and generalizations. He/she also reveals what is not meaningful; gaps in learning need to be filled with sequential information. What is lacking in sequence may make for difficulties later on when increasingly more complex subject matter is being learned. Previous learnings provide building blocks for ensuing subject matter. Retention of knowledge and skills is important for establishing meaning and understanding as well as making it possible to use these learnings in achieving higher levels of cognition. Meta-cognition skills in reflective thinking then are useful presently as well as in future endeavors such as at a work place.

Scaffolding needs equate stress in the mathematics curriculum. Here, the pupil is at a certain level, for example, in multiplying fractions with unlike denominators and with scaffolding might attain at a more complex level in multiplying mixed numbers. The knowledgeable teacher then is competent to assist learners in achieving the new objective, but this is possible with appropriate assistance by utilizing a variety of materials of instruction. Mandated testing emphasizes demonstrated pupil achievement on tests; scaffolding might very well be a psychological principle to be used in upping learner progress in measuring progress, providing that meaning is attached to acquired mathematical subject matter.

Adhering to styles of learning has assisted many pupils to do well in the curriculum. Thus, there are pupils who achieve more optimally in collaborative endeavors with each pupil in the committee contributing to their success. Pupils then cooperate as well as challenge each other to achieve, grow, and develop in mathematics. The sharing of ideas provides a framework for each to use his/her talents for the good of the group in mathematical problem solving experiences and at the same time emphasize social attainment within the committee. In comparison to collective endeavors, selected pupils attain more optimally in working by the self. These learners achieve best when personally engaged in the ongoing objective and task. There, no doubt, needs to be opportunities for both collective and individual endeavors in mathematics. Why? In the community, individuals do math both ways since the citizen solves personal mathematics problems, and also works collectively at the work place. A rational balance between the two must exist in the curriculum since individual and collective needs are in evidence in school and in society.

Another salient factor in the psychology of learning is that evaluation should provide feedback from pupils to the teacher for ensuing learning opportunities. Appraisal may well be continuous with the use of teacher observation. Here, the teacher may assist a pupil as soon as possible when an error has been made such as in carrying in addition or multiplication. The teacher may then inductively/deductively help a pupil to engage in more complex learnings sequentially. The teacher must be highly capable of diagnosis and remediation in ongoing lessons and units of study. It is best to have a developmental program of instruction for all pupils, but this is not possible when pupils, individually or collectively, reveal that which needs more emphasis in teaching. Formative evaluation is done along the way when a mathematical unit is being taught; here, the teacher assesses pupil achievement at regular intervals through valid and reliable tests. The test results give information to the teacher on success in teaching as well as what learners need more help in such as reducing fractions to lowest terms or determining the least common multiple. The items missed by pupils then provide guidance to the mathematics teacher for ensuing teaching and learning situations. Clarification of remedial objectives assist the teacher to provide meaningful experiences for teachers. Pupils need to perceive the purpose of each sequential activity for remediation. This may be stated clearly by the teacher when aiding pupils to see errors made on the formative test; this should motivate pupils to achieve ordered progress.

In addition to formative evaluation, summation assessment should also be in the offing. Thus at the end of a unit of study, the teacher notices what needs to be changed in terms of objectives, learning opportunities, as well as appraisal procedures for the next time the mathematics unit is taught. Summative evaluation then stresses end of the unit appraisal to ascertain what should possibly be modified to make for greater success in ensuing teaching and learning situations.

In conclusion

Mathematics teachers need to stay abreast of the latest psychological recommendations in order to provide more adequately for each pupil in the classroom. Providing learning opportunities which are meaningful, purposeful, and engage learner interests is vital. Metacognition skills are salient in that the learner reviews previous leanings to ascertain what was not understood and then what to do to close these gaps. Scaffolding aids pupils to reach new heights in learning with sequential content to realize the more complex ideas in mathematics. Relevant subject-matter increases the chances of pupils using previously encountered mathematical facts, concepts, and generalizations. Styles of learning, too, need ample teacher attention whether it be in collaborate or individual endeavors. Formative and summative evaluation in unit teaching assist the teacher to plan more effectively for ongoing as well as end of unit endeavours.

7

CHAPTER

Improving Achievement in Mathematics

How might pupil achievement in mathematics be improved? This manuscript will pertain to upping progress by incorporating major psychological principles. Pupils may be turned off in math lessons due to routine procedures , resulting in feelings of boredom. Instead, there is much the teacher may do to motivate learning.

Maximizing Achievement

The mathematics teacher might well reduce feelings of boredom by using a variety of activities. Thus, the teacher may utilize the concrete phase with objects and items; the semi-concrete with illustrations, transparencies, life-like problems coming from learners, the hand held calculator, the computer and internet; and the abstract such as word problems, functional worksheets, and and the basal textbook. Varying the types of activities for pupils on their individual development level might make for stimulating experiences, especially if designed to obtain personal interests. Active involvement of learners is a must in ongoing lessons and units of study (Ediger, 2007).

Second, pupils may be assisted in achieving challenging goals through bridging; thus the teacher helps pupils overcome the gap between present and a higher desired level of attainment. The mathematics teacher may then sequence questions so that the pupil might attain the ensuing objective. The ordered responses of the learner aid in attaining the new objective of instruction. Bridging is a very valuable concept for teachers to emphasize in teaching and learning situations. Pupils need to feel challenge and yet experience success in teaching and learning situations. The teacher with mathematical knowledge and skills is, especially, trained and educated to assist each category of learner be it the gifted/talented, the average achievers, English Language Learners (ELL), the special needs child, and/or pupils from lower income level homes to attain as optimally as possible (See the National Council Teachers of Mathematics, 1989).

Third, pupils need to believe in themselves to become efficacious learners. Here, pupils have confidence and a good self concept to develop achieve, and grow in knowledge, skills, and attitudes. The quality mathematics teacher, too, needs to possess efficacy in that he/she is confident in teaching any category of learner to attain optimally. Efficacy comes from developing mathematical competency in subject matter, methods of instruction, and the emotional (attitudinal dimension) domain. There are educators who advocate Emotional Intelligence (EQ) to be highly salient in that good attitudes toward mathematics instruction aids in becoming competent in the subject matter of mathematics as well as its related teaching skills (See Nolan, 2003).

Fourth, metacognition skills assists the learner to reflect upon what has been learned and what is left to learn. Through reflection, the pupil not only rehearses previous content acquired, but also assesses where gaps and misunderstandings have occurred. Diagnosis and remediation then become salient since that which is not meaningful may become so. The teacher needs to model the correct response or reasoning used to solve a word problem. Metacognition not only aids pupils to rehearse and retain mathematical learnings but also use reason to correct errors.

Fifth, it is important to identify learning styles of pupils to ascertain which procedure is most beneficial for learners. Selected pupils do best in large group instruction where a multiplicity of activities capture pupil's attention. Others prefer small group endeavors whereby collaboration is involved among participants. Each may challenge others in the small group so all achieve well. Still others, prefer individual endeavors whereby the learner prefers to work by the self. Adequate provisions must be made for every pupil and no one should fall through the cracks. Time on task is valuable with much being expected from learners within the allotted time (Ediger, 2010).

Sixth, the math curriculum needs continual updating with the latest in technology to facilitate the learning process. Technology involving computer use might well guide learners to achieve more optimally. Technology assists pupils to attain relevant content and skills needed in the 21st century and to compete favorably with other nations in the world, such as Finland and Singapore. Computer programs must emphasize problem solving, reasoning, diagnosis and remediation, as well as simulations, among others, which motivate pupil learning to attain objectives. School supervisors must provide inservice education to guide teachers in making the fullest use of technology in curriculum improvement. Mathematics teachers need to develop confidence in using technology to provide for each category of learner in securing knowledge, skills, and quality attitudes.

Seventh, mathematics teachers need continual encouragement to upgrade professional instruction. The following approaches are highly recommended:

- working toward an advanced degree at an approved college/university.
- doing an independent study on an area of weakness in teaching mathematics to fill the void in strengthening teaching and learning.
- taking online course work in mathematics subject matter and procedures of instruction
- managing the classroom effectively to maximum mathematics achievement as well as improve the attitudinal dimension.
- study innovative programs such as cognitive mapping strategies with plans, if the study so warrants, to implement salient concepts (see, Vadivu, 2010).

REFERENCES

Ediger, Marlow (2007), "Learning Activities in the Curriculum," *College Student Journal*, 41 (4), 967-969.

Ediger, Marlow (2010), "Collaboration in Improving the Mathematics Curriculum," *Montana Mathematics*," March, pp 13-14.

The National Council Teachers of Mathematics (1989), *Curriculum and Evaluation Standards for School Mathematics*. Reston, Virginia: NCTM.

Nolan, Jennifer (2003), "Multiple Intelligences in the Classroom." *Education*, 124(1), 115-119.

Vadivu, P. Pandia (2010), *Effect of Metacognitive Strategies on Concept Mapping in Learning in Biology Education*. Kodaikanal, India: Mother Teresa Women's University. Ph D thesis evaluated by the writer.

CHAPTER

Diagnosis and Remediation in the Mathematics Curriculum

The teacher must have a quality background of subject matter content in mathematics, not only for teaching but also for viewing pupil errors which need correction. In each mathematical unit of study, the teacher must choose important content for instruction, not trivia. Each pupil needs to perceive interest, purpose, and meaning in mathematics. It would indeed be excellent if the teacher, inductively/deductively, would continually sequences learnings appropriately. Even then, there are pupils who do not connect with the ongoing lesson. Thus, the teacher must be a good diagnostician and remediator of gaps in learning which learners possess (Ediger, 1997).

Assisting Pupils in Learning

Which are selected common errors pupils reveal in ongoing mathematical units of study? These need to be studied by each teacher in the classroom. Collectively, teachers should also meet to discuss the concepts of diagnosis and remediation of pupil mistakes. Improving the curriculum involves teachers working together with effective human relations involved. The relations need to involve respecting each other's ideas in an atmosphere of trust. Building on subject matter discussed, teachers might well develop a repertoire of knowledge and skills in teaching mathematics (See National Council Teachers of Mathematics, 1989). Pupils, too, need to experience an atmosphere of acceptance and belonging. It becomes more profitable then for teachers and pupils to analyze difficulties in mathematics and stress synthesis. One major problem faced by pupils is the lack of computational skills. With addition and subtraction of whole numbers, fractions, and decimals, there are numerous specifics to view. Pupils too often have memorized addition facts, for example, without understanding and attaching meaning. These are foundational learnings and pupils will later in sequence deal with increased complexity of mathematical operations. Meaningful subject matter must always be in the offing. Computational errors must be diagnosed as soon as possible and with teacher observation used to evaluate progress so that learners do not practice what is incorrect (See Kennedy and Tipps, 1991).

Second, pupils need to use reason properly when pursuing ongoing learnings. For instance, a pupil might believe that 3/8 is larger in value than 3/4 until a circle is divided into eight parts and three of these are considered whereas the second fraction, the circle is divided into four parts and three of these are being considered. Here, the pupil can see which is larger of the two fractions and use reason in ordered learnings. Being able to think through a problematic situation, most pupils are able to come up with answers to questions (Ediger and Rao, 2000).

Third, pupils need to develop a systematic approach in problem solving. Too frequently, pupils may jump around hastily from one procedure to another without additional means of solving a problem. When solving word problems, pupils fail to ask questions such as:

- what is wanted in a final answer?

- which essential information is needed sequentially to problem solve?
- is there information presented which is not needed in arriving at a solution?
- what questions do I need to ask the teacher to clarify what is not understood?
- do I know the appropriate operation on involved numbers to solve the problem (Ediger, 2007).

When giving assistance to pupils, the mathematics teacher may use inquiry methods whereby the teacher provides clues such as verbal, gestural, pictorial, audio, and concrete materials to guide pupil progress.

Fourth, pupils pupils make computational errors which need diagnosis. This might well mean that basic addition, subtraction, multiplication, and division facts have not been mastered, or haste and sloppy performance are inherent. It does save time and effort if essential leanings have been mastered when pursuing new learnings. Diagnosis would involve if the same errors are made again and again by a pupil, and yet these are not beyond the developmental level of the learner. By calling specific kinds of errors to a pupils attention, he/she should perceive purpose with remediation in ongoing lessons and units of study (Scafadi and Bui, 2001).

Fifth, lacking fluency in reading causes difficulties in doing word problems. Mathematics instruction should not become a reading course. However, it is difficult to separate reading skills from the academic discipline of mathematics. Thus, it becomes imperative for the teacher to identify the kinds of errors made by a pupil when reading math word problems. Calling pupils attention to the importance of using context clues may help many pupils. A difficulty in using phonics such as the initial consonant of a word needs remediation and provides the learner with an approach in attacking unknown words. Other phonic elements may be stressed in teaching as needed to help pupils in developing word attack skills. The mathematics teacher needs to be a teacher of reading in order lo assist learners to identify words fluently while reading to solve mathematical problems. Comprehension of subject matter is the ultimate goal (Ediger, 2010).

Sixth, vocabulary development is salient since selected learners do not understand concepts inherent in ongoing lessons and units of study. These words may come from reading word problems and also those utilized in discussions. Addends, minuend, subtrahend, factoring, inverting, among others, need elaboration and then placed on a classroom word wall. The math teacher may refer pupils to these words as needed. The writer when supervising university student teachers noticed how studious learners were when viewing these words and discussing them at break time. Pupils do have an inward desire to learn.

Seventh, selected pupils lack an adequate attention span to benefit from the ensuing learning opportunities in mathematics. If the activities are too complex, the mathematics teacher may remedy the situation by adjusting teaching and learning situations to the present achievement level of the learner. Then too, the explanations given may be simplified by using terminology which pupils understand. Materials of instruction used might be more concrete in nature. Thus, objects may be used together with the abstract words and concepts in providing for meaningful instruction. The pace of experiences provided should harmonize with what pupils can master in time. The point being that math teachers need to observe pupils at work and diagnose what needs improvement. Remediation then is based upon observations made on a daily basis. Test results, too, may provide excellent feedback on where pupils fail in attaching meaning in the mathematics curriculum. These situations might well make for turning off and loosing interest in achieving. Computers and technology have advanced to provide for selected excellent programs to secure and maintain pupils interest in the curriculum (Martinez, 2010). Eighth, pupils fail to understand and use structural ideas in mathematics. Attaching meaning to and utilizing a structure of knowledge assists the pupil in developing proficiency in doing math. Thus, for example, the commutative and associative properties of addition and multiplication provide learners a method of viewing computation and their possibilities in performing operations on number. Also, patterns involved in working with number might well fascinate and interest pupils in mathematics.

In conclusion

By diagnosing and remedying pupil progress in mathematics, learners might find interest and purpose in ongoing lessons and units of study. The curriculum then is adjusted to their present achievement levels. Being frustrated and having a feeling of being lost in an activity, pupils may experience change with motivation and interest in learning and achieving objectives of instruction.

REFERENCES

Ediger, Marlow (1997), *Teaching Mathematics in the Elementary School.* Kirksville, Missouri: Simpson Publishing Company.

Ediger, Marlow (2007), Learning Activities in the Curriculum, *College Student Journal,* 41 (4), 967-969.

Ediger, Marlow, and D. Bhaskara Rao (2000), *Teaching Mathematics Successfully.* New Delhi, India: Discovery Publishing House.

Ediger, Marlow (2010), Enjoyment in the Mathematics Curriculum, *Montana Mathematics,* 43 (3), 12-15.

Kennedy, Leonard, and Steve Tipps (1991), *Guiding Children's Learning of Mathematics.* Belmont, California: Wadsworth Publishing company.

National Council Teachers of Mathematics (1989), *Curriculum and Evaluation Standards for School Mathematics*. Reston, Virginia: NCTM.

Scafadi, Tony and Khanh Bui (2010), Gender Similarities in Math Performance from Middle School Through High School, *Journal of Instructional Psychology*, 37 (3), 262-255.

Martinez, Monica (2010), "Teacher Education Can't Ignore Technology," *Phi Delta Kappan*, 92 (2), 74-75.

9

CHAPTER

The Substitute Teacher and the Mathematics Curriculum

Too frequently, the complaint has been that substitute teachers merely baby sit and do not actually teach students. Thus, the feeling may persist that substitute teachers do not need to be prepared for their presence in the classroom. The author believes that substitute teachers need to be well prepared for each day of teaching and quality sequence in student learning is being emphasized. Student achievement needs to move forward as sequentially as possible. Well prepared and motivated substitute teachers must be in the offing. This paper will pertain to helping these teachers to grow, develop, and achieve.

Inservice education and the Substitute Teacher School districts need to provide quality inservice education for substitute teachers at the beginning of a new school year. This should make it possible for assisting learners to benefit fully from each day of teaching. The mathematics curriculum needs to stress meaningful learnings for students. Thus, the substitute teacher needs to assist young children to count, add, and subtract with the use of markers. Thus, children learn to count as they point sequentially to each marker. This makes it possible for young learners to show a set of three, for example, when using these markers. They may combine markers to show addition, e.g. two markers and one marker. The concrete representation may be shown in the abstract: 2+1=3. When ready, these students may attach meaning to subtraction-three markers minus one marker equals two markers. The inverse operation of subtraction is then shown meaningfully. These foundational concepts assist students to build upon previously understood subject matter. Inductive and deductive learning may be stressed (Ediger and Rao, 2003).

Demonstration teaching should help the substitute teacher in teaching students in the classroom. It provide models to emulate in a classroom. The substitute teacher needs to show in an interesting way place value learnings to students. A neatly developed place value chart may be constructed with the names of place holders such as ones, tens, hundreds, etc. listed at the top with pockets underneath to hold congruent paper strips (manipulative materials). Thus, for example, to show the numeral 312 in the place value chart, two slips of paper may be put into the ones pocket, one in the tens, and three in the hundreds pocket. To add 134 to 312, four congruent slips may be put into the ones pocket, and three to the tens pocket with one to the tens column. The student may then be guided to perceive meaningfully that 312 + 134= 446. The inverse operation may be indicated in subtracting 312 from 446 by manipulating slips of paper from the ones, tens, and hundreds columns. All four operations-addition, subtraction, multiplication and division-may be shown on the place value chart, using the congruent slips of paper and the related abstract numerals. When the place value chart is no longer needed, students may work with the abstract numerals only. With proper sequence in the mathematics curriculum, students should be able to achieve subject matter content in moving from the concrete (markers) to the semi-concrete (place value chart), to the abstract. Students must be actively involved in using the manipulative materials to show operations on number. An indepth understanding of base ten numeration is important for all learners. Interest in learning is a powerful factor in achievement. A variety of activities and methods of instruction need to be used including computer based instruction (Ediger, 2006).

Objectives for student attainment should include number words and mathematical symbols applicable to operation on numbers. Readiness needs to be in evidence so that students may benefit from ensuing lessons. Hurrying through different lessons is not a goal, but attaching meaning to each sequential step of learning is salient. Thus in geometry lessons and units of study, students must understand subsequent learnings pertaining to points, lines, rays, and line segments in space figures, and thus experience ordered success. Among others, learnings in congruent and similar geometric figures should become a definite part of the student's mathematical vocabulary (See Noddings, 2008).

With inservice education, the substitute teacher needs to perceive models to use in quality teaching and learning situations. Practical situations should also be used in mathematics instruction. Thus a student may have, for example, $60.35 and needs $83.59 to buy a baseball glove, how much more needs to be earned. The place value chart may be used here. Or, if the student is ready, the abstract phase of learning might well be used in determining how much more money is necessary to buy the baseball glove. Sometimes, the practical phase of learning is highly motivating to students. During the 1955-57 school year, the writer taught in a two teacher rural school near Lehigh, Kansas. There were six Holdeman Mennonite children in the classroom. Eighth grade is terminal education. The students did much better in mathematics than social studies or other subject matter areas, due to their perceiving the utilitarian value of arithmetic. Mathematics textbooks were then more rural orientated with word problems on how many bushels would go into a metal grain bin with the dimensions of the bin given. Students learned about how many pounds in a bushel of wheat, oats, and corn. This is common knowledge to the writer who grew up on a farm, but to his professional colleagues at a university, this knowledge was basically unknown. Culture, time, and place assist in determining what is relevant (See Savithiri, 2006).

Problems may always be crafted to meet practical needs of students in mathematics in diverse cultures. This merely says to adapt course work to fall within the experiences of learners. The creative substitute teacher needs to think of a variety of rich experiences for children. The NCTM Standards that pertain to early mathematics experiences for Kindergarten through grade four emphasize the following:

Standard 6: Number Sense and Numeration, the mathematics curriculum should include whole number concepts and skills so that students can:

- construct number meanings through real world experiences and the use of physical materials
- develop number sense
- interpret the multiple uses of numbers encountered in the real world (National Council Teachers of Mathematics, 1989).

Inservice Education for Substitute Teachers

A well-prepared substitute teacher experiences quality opportunities for growth and professionalism. What is presented in inservice education needs to be functional and based upon the best in research practices. These programs must present learning activities involving master teachers showing how to make mathematical learnings meaningful, interesting, and purposeful. A hands on approach needs to be used. Substitute teachers need ample opportunities to try out concepts and generalizations in a contextual classroom setting. These learnings may include the following in inservice education:

- regrouping in addition, subtraction, multiplication, and division.
- problem-solving and project methods of instruction.
- diverse algorithms and computational methods.
- the four operations on fractions and making sense of mixed numbers, as well as renaming and reducing fractions to their lowest terms.
- extending understanding of fractions to the use of decimals and per cents.
- evaluation of learner progress and reporting student progress to parents (Ediger, 2007).

Substitute teachers need to be well educated to assist students to do well in the mathematics curriculum. They must be able to guide each learner to make continuous progress in knowledge, skills, and attitudes.

In Closing

Students need to be able to monitor their very own progress. The substitute teacher then must assist each student to reflect upon his/her progress. By reflecting, the learner thinks about what was understood and what needs more work be it in mathematical facts, concepts, and/or generalizations. Also by reflecting, the student may think of new ways to use mathematics in every day life.

REFERENCES

Ediger, Marlow, and D. Bhaskara Rao (2000), *Teaching Mathematics Successfully*. New Delhi, India: Discovery Publishing House.

Ediger, Marlow (2006), "Writing in the Mathematics Curriculum," *Journal of Instructional Psychology*, 33 (1), 120-123.

Ediger, Marlow (2007), "Teacher Observation to Assess Student Achievement," *Journal of Instructional Psychology*, 34 (3), 137-139.

National Council Teachers of Mathematics (1989), *Curriculum and Evaluation Standards for School Mathematics*. Reston, Va: NCTM, 38.

Noddings, Nel (2008), "All Our Students Thinking," *Educational Leadership* 65, (5), 8-13.

Savithiri, V. (2006), Impact of Metacognitive Strategies in Enhancing Perceptual Skills Among High School Students on Learning Geometry. Ph. D. theses evaluated by the writer for Alagappa University, Karaikudi, India.

10

CHAPTER

The Innovative Science Curriculum

With state mandated testing focusing upon reading and mathematics as the two curriculum areas for annual testing in grades three through eight, as determined by the Elementary and Secondary Education Act (ESEA) beginning with the 2005-2006 school year, it behooves school officials to emphasize science, also, as a basic. Science is all around us in the natural environment. Science provides knowledge for technological advances and can provide the good things in life. There are also issues in how technology should be used. Thus, drilling for petroleum in wild life areas, such as in Alaska, has truly become an issue. Science then provides knowledge and skills for advancement in society, but also can be used in a detrimental way. The school curriculum then needs to provide pupils with a quality science curriculum which provides the needed subject matter, skills, and attitudes necessary in a democracy (Ediger, 2000, 10-12).

Recommendations for a Quality Science Curriculum

The science curriculum needs to meet selected standards in order to stress *excellence*. Inquiry approaches are highly recommended. Thus, pupil are curious learners and identify problems. Problem identification come about from observing natural phenomenon in the environment. There are questions which then arise in the mind of the learner. The senses of using sight, taste, smell, hearing, and touch are used in learning about natural phenomenon. Observations, too, are extended such as through the use of a microscope.

A science rich classroom setting helps pupils to use the senses and identify problem areas. The author while supervising university student teachers in the public schools noticed classrooms which had one or more of the following:

- an aquarium in which goldfish were observed carefully by pupils. A question which arose pertained to the goldfish living and swimming in water was, "How can *fish* live in water while I can't" This question, among others, can be very appropriate to begin inquiry learning.
- a glass jar containing frog eggs and then developing into tadpoles. The tadpoles then further developed into young adults and placed into a suitable area. Amphibians live part of their life in water and par time on land.
- a terrarium whereby a small garter snake, in a carefully developed setting, was still or moving around cautiously. Pupils noticed how the reptile generally lived on land, not in water. Pupils while observing the garter snake, asked, "Why does the garter snake hurriedly stick its tongue in and out?"
- a parent brought a caged canary to the classroom. Here, learners noticed and listed distinguishing characteristics of *birds*. Comparisons were made with fish, amphibians, and reptiles.
- another parent brought to the classroom, for a brief period of time, a mother cat with three small nursing

kittens. The concept of *mammals* was then discussed indepth as to what makes for this category of vertebrates (Ediger and Rao, 1996, Chapter Four).

Once pupils have identified problem areas or questions, about an one animal or category, they are readily to secure information to obtain answers or hypotheses. The hypotheses are tentative and subject to further inquiry for testing purposes. The hypothesis is then revised or *accepted* as is.

There are a plethora of related learning activities for pupils in studying more about each category of vertebrates. Pupils might brainstorm lists of names for each category of vertebrates. Higher order thinking skills are vital for pupils to develop, such as divergent thought, when branching out to other animals in a vertebrate category. For example, names of birds to branch out a category might include, blue jays, blue birds, sparrows, cardinals, among others. Pictures may be collected or drawn for each species of bird, placed in chart form, and labeled for all to see/review. Classification skills are salient for pupils to develop in science such as classifying fish, amphibians, reptiles, birds, and mammals.

Second, pupils with teacher guidance may make models of each category of vertebrates. Paper mache' models make for attractive visuals. Rules need to be established to make models using paper mache', otherwise it can be a messy activity. A hands on approach in learning is used here.

Third, pupils individually or collectively may do research on a particular vertebrate and present the findings to the total class. For example, a committee of three may research, using a variety of reference sources, the habitat of a member of the reptile family, such as turtles. Turtles with their protective shell do fascinate many pupils. These fascinations may then be explored further with a depth study. Visuals such as collected pictures and drawings may accompany the report given to the class. Communication skills are highly important to develop within pupils in ongoing lessons and units of study.

Fourth, committees may be developed to read selected library books on a certain facet of vertebrate life such as amphibians. Thus a committee may read and share information on the life cycle on fish. The committee needs to use proper rules for sharing such as all participating and no one dominating the discussion, as well as staying on the topic being pursued.

Fifth, pupils may make a biological chart showing the different Eras of time. These periods of time included:

- Paleozoic with fish coming into being through evolutionary means.
- Mesozoic with turtles arriving on the scene. Pupils may wish to do some branching put here to include the age of dinosaurs. Birds also came into being in the Mesozoic era with the archaeopteryx.
- Cenozoic with the development of mammals, including human beings.

The biological chart with the above named Eras may include background scenery to show plant life in relationship to animal life. The dates need to be given for each Era such as the Paleozoic (ancient life), 570 million years to 200 million years ago, approximately. Interesting plants carpeted the earth such as green mosses, ferns, horsetails, club mosses, and seed plants. These plants provided the basis for the coal forests of the Paleozoic era which provided, in time, for conversion from wood to coal formations. Much planning and work go into the development of a biological chart showing the different Eras of plant and animal life. The chart may be a part of an exhibit whereby other classrooms are invited to view the displays. This is an excellent way for all pupils to learn more about science and the interesting activities therein. Much research, effort, and time go into achieving objectives in the science curriculum (See Ediger, 2001, Chapter Four).

Fifth, a quality current events programme updates ongoing science lessons and units of study. In the unit on vertebrates, for example, a current events item from Science News (Bower, April 20, 2002), reveals the following:

The evolutionary roots of primates, the group of mammals that gave rise to humans are murky. Paleontologists generally think that the first primates appeared about 65 million years ago, whereas the genetic analyses of the DMA from living primates yield an estimate of 90 million years.

The DMA-derived number comes closer to the mark, according to a research team led by biologist Simon Tavare of the University of Southern California in Los Angeles, California. Using a new statistical model of primate evolution the scientists conclude that the older common ancestor of today's primates lived approximately 81.5 million years ago.

The common ancestor of primates, the model suggests, rose before dinosaurs disappeared. The ancestor resembled a modern dwarf lemur, weighing 1 to 2 pounds, and led a nocturnal life in tropical forest, the scientists theorize. Early primates therefore would have expanded northward from tropical areas, rather than originating in northern regions, as many researchers now assume.

A variety of sources need to be used in a science current events program. These include qualified resource persons who communicate well with pupils, internet, world wide web, science magazines written for age and developmentally appropriate pupils, CD ROMS, videos, audio recordings, newspaper articles, among others. Problems and questions may arise from the readings. These need to be clearly stated and information gathered to secure necessary information. Information needs to be evaluated with additional obtained content. The comparisons made make for critical thinking. A resolution among the different information sources involves a synthesis. Creativity in thinking may generally be inherent in working out a synthesis among the data gathered or information acquired. Thus, higher levels of thinking involving critical and creative thinking, as well as problem solving, should be in the offing.

Sixth, reading is an important skill to be used in information gathering. It is not science, in and of itself, but rather a procedure used to secure vital information. Thus, the pupil needs to become proficient in word recognition skills. These include phonics, syllabication, and use of context clues. Word recognition skills are tools, not ends, to use in comprehension of subject matter read. Vital facts, concepts, and generalizations read need to be acquired in comprehension strategies.

The basal science text, library books, among other sources, may well provide content for problem solving. Reading is one way of finding out!

Seventh, experimentation is the heart of the science curriculum. Experiments should involve children in their use. The experiment needs to be performed whereby each participant can observe readily what is going on. Thus, if learners are studying what plants need in order to grow, diverse variables may be evaluated. Two plants from the same/similar stock, properly potted, may be used in the experiment. All variables except one, need to be held constant. For example, one variable such as the amount of water used for plant growth may be tested for. One potted plant receives a proper amount of water, whereas the adjacent plant does not receive any. One variable then has been tested as to what plants need to survive and grow. Of course, the experiment may be made increasingly complex by having several of the same/similar stock. Each plant is given a different amount of water. In time, children may observe which plant grows best. A line or bar graph may be drawn to show plant growth in comparison with the amount of water received. Other variables to be tested include sunlight versus no sunlight, sandy soil versus loam, as well as different environmental temperature readings for two or more plants. The amount of sunlight may also be tested in terms of degrees as variables (See Ediger, 1994, 24- 25).

Eighth, community service may be integrated into the science curriculum. Clarkin (April 21, 2002) wrote the following pertaining to elementary age pupils in the Hutchinson, Kansas School District planting trees to beautify a section of the Jim P. Marinez nature trail:

The ingredients for creating a living, rose colored ribbon along the bank of the Arkansas River came together Thursday:

- 50 redbud seedlings.
- about 60 eager school children.
- an assortment of shovels and buckets of water.
- and grownups to help channel good intentions into finished deeds.

Avenue A elementary School adopted a two mile portion of Hutchinson's Jim P. Martinez Sunflower Trail, which swings through the school's enrollment territory, for cleanup. It's a task tackled a few times during the school year. The Hutchinson Tree Board provided money for purchasing the red bud trees, plus a "song bird bundle" containing trees and shrubs. A forestry technician shows students the proper way to dig a hole and leave enough room to spread the tree's roots out. There are a plethora of possibilities in learning scientific principles in planting trees as well as engaging pupils in a community based beautification project.

Ninth, a multicultural emphasis needs to be stressed in science whereby equality of opportunity is in evidence in the classroom for all pupils. Opportunities to learn stressing equity extends to handicapped pupils. Each pupil needs to experience success in teaching and learning situations as well as achieve optimally. A science curriculum design needs to emphasize a developmental curriculum in which acceptance and belonging are in evidence. Good attitudes are paramount in developing the science curriculum along with cognitive and psychomotor objectives for pupil attainment.

Tenth, learning by discovery is salient which involves careful, meticulous observation together with making predictions, doing exact measurements of scientific phenomenon, and generalizing on the information gleaned (Ediger, 1995, 14-15).

There are a plethora of educators who believe that the present emphasis upon state mandated testing might well minimize the importance of science in the curriculum.

State Mandated Testing and the Measurement Movement

State mandated testing addresses concerns which selected educators and lay people have on demonstrated pupil accomplishment and teacher accountability. Thus, state mandated tests are given to indicate what pupils have learned. Generally, a percentile is provided to show where a pupil is in achievement, such as the fiftieth percentile. Weaknesses of state mandated testing, as given by science educators are the following:

- multiple choice test items cannot measure science processes such as careful observation, problem solving skills, critical and creative thinking, as well as inquiry learning, in contextual situations.
- multiple choice test items cannot measure quality attitudes toward science.
- multiple choice test items have emphasized drill in preparing for the state mandated test. Drill is opposite of an inquiry orientated science curriculum.
- multiple choice test items on reading and mathematics in state mandated tests de-emphasize pupils achieving

science objectives and the role of science in the school setting.

Further weaknesses of state mandated tests include the following:

- these tests lack validity in that pupils in many cases have not been taught that which is covered in the test.
- the tests may not have been pilot tested before general use was made of them.
- science may receive short shrift, in practice, if teacher salaries are tied to pupil test results in reading and mathematics. Monetary resources for teaching may then be designated for teaching reading and mathematics (See Jorgenson and Vanosdall, 2002).

Testing and measurement beliefs are based on realism as a philosophy of education. Realists believe one can know in whole'or part the teal world as it truly exists and is. For example when looking at chemical formulas, preciseness is in evidence such as in the following: $C_6 H_{12} O_6$, the formula for sugar. Thus, 6 atoms of carbon, 12 atoms of hydrogen, and 6 atoms of oxygen make for sugar. The formula is consistent and never varies. Chemistry is precise and accurate. It is true that new elements may be found in the universe, but the number given now is 107 elements and has remained so for sometime. This preciseness and accurateness is then applied to testing pupils to determine what has been learned in the school setting. It is doubtful if the human mind operates in this manner. A pupil's test results may indicate, for example, that he/she is on the fortieth percentile, meaning that out of every 100 pupils, forty are below and sixty above the fortieth percentile. Other precise numerals used to show pupil achievement are standard deviations, and stanines. Sometimes grade equivalents are given, but these are less objective as compared to standard units of measurement such as standard deviations and stanines.

Who writes test items for state mandated tests? Generally it is under the supervision of the state department of education. Human beings do the writing. Usually, they include measurement specialists from a university. Subjectivity is involved here in that other test items could appear on a state mandated test than those chosen by test writers. Readers of literature need to look at a Manual of a standardized test to see how the test items are chosen and how a norm group is selected. The norm group's test results are then used to make comparisons with one's own pupils in the classroom. For example, if a pupil received a score of 45 on a mathematics test, then that score is compared to the norm group in the Manual and may correspond to the fortieth percentile and/or be one standard deviation below the mean. Thus, it is only after the test items have been written, in which subjectivity has been in evidence, that numerals are used to arrive at objectivity as to the precise place where a pupil is in academic achievement. Pupils test results also may indicate "exemplary," "satisfactory," or "needs improvement." These indicators are quite subjective as to where the cut off points are for each of the three levels.

State mandated tests need to be studied, analyzed, and revised to improve the assessment process (See Ediger, 1999, 112-117).

Harmonizing Testing with Portfolios

Perhaps, a solution may be found in using state mandated test results along with a portfolio approach. Portfolios are quite different in their construction as compared to testing. Portfolios are developed by the pupil himself/herself with teacher guidance, not by external sources as is true of developing state mandated tests. Portfolios emphasize showing the every day classroom work of the student rather than a single numeral indicating achievement on a yearly basis. Thus, a portfolio may include the following representative work of a pupil:

- essays, biographies, poetry, autobiographies, outlines, summaries, conclusions, among other written work.
- objects, models, dioramas, construction work, and murals completed by the learner. If the items are too large for a portfolio, snapshots may then be taken for inclusion.
- illustrations drawn, pencil sketching, water color paintings, among others.
- audio recordings of reading aloud, talks given, oral book reports, and group discussions, among other oral communication activities.
- video tapes of creative and formal dramatizations, as well as of pantomiming.
- self evaluations made in terms of quality criteria.

Portfolios should not become too voluminous, especially since two raters, as a minimum, will assess each on a five point scale. They will reveal actual progress of pupils in listening, speaking, reading, and writing across the curriculum. Inter-scorer reliability will be a problem when the two raters assess each portfolio. Quality rubrics and their use should help in achieving appropriate reliability.

Test results and portfolio data provide much information on a pupil's progress. Test results provide a numeral for one school year of achievement whereas portfolio endeavors reveal pupil progress from everyday classroom work (See Ediger, 1999, 112-117).

REFERENCES

Bower, B. (April 20, 2002), "Older Ancestors, Primate Origin Age in New Analysis," *Science News*,161 (16), 243-244.

Clarkin, Mary (April 21, 2002), "A Ribbon of Redbud," *The Hutchinson News*, Hutchinson, Kansas, 67504.

Ediger, Marlow (2000), "Project Methods on Science," *Becoming*, 11 (2), 10-12.

Ediger, Marlow and D. Bhaskara Rao (1996), *Science Curriculum*. New Delhi, India: Discovery Publishing House, Chapter Four.

Ediger, Marlow, and D. Bhaskara Rao, (2001), *Teaching Science Successfully*. New Delhi, India: Discovery Publishing House, Chapter Four.

Ediger, Marlow (1994), "The Unexpected in Science," *Investigating*, 10 (3), 24- 25.

Ediger, Marlow (1995), "Designing Science Units of Study," *School Science*, 33 (1), 14- 15.

Ediger, Marlow (1999), "Problems in Teaching Science," *Experiments in Education*, 27 (7), 112- 117.

Jorgenson, Olaf, and Rick Vanosdall (2002), "High Stakes Testing, The Death of Science?" *Phi Delta Kappan* 83 (8), 601-605.

Pointers in Teaching Science

There are selected criteria which need to be followed in teaching ongoing lessons and units of study in science. By following each criterion, pupils optimize achievement in the science curriculum. Achieving objectives in science teaching, pupils may progress sequentially in a carefully designed programme. Which criteria should science teachers follow in teaching/learning situations?

Guidelines in the Teaching of Science

Teachers need to have high expectations from instruction and pupil learning. Too frequently, teachers expect minimal achievement from selected learners. Instead, the science teacher must expect optimal progress from each pupil. With carefully chosen learning opportunities, pupils feel challenged to grow and accomplish. These activities need to engage pupils, are interesting and possess perceived purpose. All seem to be actively involved if the activities attract attention. This is the way it should be in teaching science. When supervising university student teachers with cooperating teacher guidance, the writer observed in one class where pupils were inattentive in a science unit on "The Changing Surface of the Earth".

Much lecture was used in teaching and pupils appeared lethargic, and yet the content might have been very engaging for pupils. Pupils, for example, tend to be fascinated with volcanic eruptions, glaciers, soil/wind erosion, floods, hurricanes/tornados, among other destructive forces. Models, power point, illustrations, videos, print sources, science experiments and demonstrations, as well as excursions (erosion of soil might well be observed on the school grounds), provide relevant materials of instruction for learners to attain carefully chosen objectives. There are excellent reading materials, for instance, pertaining to natural disasters in current events newspapers, internet sources, as well as the basal science textbook. High expectations, within reason, as well as interesting materials and discussions can certainly engage pupil in ongoing lessons and units of study. Scaffolding may be utilized by the science teacher to assist pupils in achieving more complex learnings (Ediger and Rao, 2010).

Purpose in learning is very significant in aiding learner progress. If pupils do not see relevance in subject matter being studied, they will tend to possess low energy levels for achievement. There are numerous approaches then which may be used to guide pupils to notice how subject matter content might be utilized. Selected pupils have read how a tornado completely wiped out a small town or did heavy damage in larger cities. For example, Greensburg, Kansas, a small city and now almost completely rebuilt, was totally destroyed by a tornado in 2007, except for a very few structures. A well built, brick grade school was entirely demolished to show tornado strength in an aftermath. The President of the United States made several visits to this small city. There are other tornados such as hurricane Katrina in New Orleans which pupils have heard/read about which were equally powerful. Pupils need to be actively engaged in ongoing learning opportunities in current events involving science news (Ediger, 2010).

Meaningful experiences need to be in the offing for pupils in science. These must be personalized which assist to ensure learner success. Thus, for example to lecture/explain to pupils that air has weight and takes up space, learners may be engaged in putting a tissue paper in an inverted tumbler and press it straight down into the water filled aquarium. Prior to doing this experiment, learners need to hypothesize as to what will happen to the tissue. These may be printed on the board for all to see clearly. Pupils need to understand that hypotheses are subject to testing. The experiment needs to be performed where all can clearly notice a dry tissue inside the tumbler. Meaning is attached to an important science concept. Additional experiments may be performed to confirm the correct hypothesis. Understanding of subject matter is salient; memorization, alone, is inadequate. Ensuing meaningful subject matter will be based upon what is dearly understood in the present learning opportunities. Success in meaningful achievement is significant for all in the school/classroom setting (See National Research Council, 1996).

Metacognitive strategies should be used so that pupils recognize what has/has not be acquired. Thus, the pupil is assisted to reflect upon what was learned in order to reinforce and retain relevant concepts and generalizations. Then too, the pupil will realize gaps in learning. These gaps need to be alleviated through additional sequential learning opportunities. They may also be filled through scaffolding. Here, the teacher may deductively present brief meaningful explanations which the pupil can utilize in understanding ensuing knowledge and skills. Scaffolding may also fill gaps through inductive experiences whereby the science teacher raises ordered questions which assist the learner to arrive successfully in understanding the new content (See Bybee, 1 997).

Problem solving and inquiry learning are at the heart of teaching and learning situations in science. Pupils, individually or collectively, with teacher guidance raise purposeful questions which require effort and perseverance in their solving. The questions are meaningful since the pupil has an inward desire to achieve necessary answers. Quite frequently, experimentation provides needed information. Depending upon the maturation level of learners, a question, for example, may arise pertaining to what plants need in order to grow. Thus, two potted bean plants containing equivalent stock and soil with the same appropriate moisture, may be set on a window ledge. Pupils then may hypothesize what happens when a paper sack is placed over one plant. Careful observation is necessary with not jumping to hasty conclusions pertaining to the results. Testing for one variable may also involve differences in moisture provided, differences in the type of soil, and differences in temperature readings for one potted plant as compared to the other. Methods of science may be stressed here with testing one variable, as well as developing/ revising an hypothesis, if necessary. New problems are identified along the way as an experiment progresses (See Martinez, 2010).

Problem solving is a useful skill in that individuals rather continuously identify major/minor problems which need solutions. Then too, problem solving is useful in society as well as in school.

Pupils need to feel confident in problem solving and inquiry methods as approaches in securing information. Self efficacy must then being an ongoing objective in science. The efficacious science teacher possesses the following:

- feels challenge in teaching arid learning situations.
- believes he/she is capable of teaching any set of learners regardless of socio-economic levels or ethnicity.
- enjoys teaching science due to being able to motivate learning in science.
- reads science subject matter from a variety of reliable reference sources including the internet. Ideas gleaned are used to improve the science curriculum.

- does science experiments and demonstrations on his/her own as well as providing background knowledge and skills for teaching.
- is able to utilize technology effectively in teaching and learning situations (See Jones, 2010).

The teacher is highly capable in using feedback from evaluation to assist each pupil to do well in ongoing lessons and units of study. Mandated tests, teacher observation, valid and reliable teacher written tests, supervisory visits, pupil and teacher self evaluation results, rating scales, checklists, among others should provide information/data on necessary steps to help learners individually to achieve well. Motivated pupils, actively interested in achieving, need to ascertain meaning and purpose in optimizing learner progress.

REFERENCES

Bybee, R. W. (1997), *Achieving Scientific Literacy*. Portsmouth, New Hampshire: Heinemann.

Ediger, Marlow, and D. Bhaskara Rao (2010) *School Science Curriculum*. New Delhi, India: Discovery Publishing House.

Ediger, Martow (2010), "Children's Literature in the Science Curriculum," *Journal of Instructional Psychology*, 37 (2), 117-119.

Jones, Alex D. (2010), "Science Via Photography," *Science and Children*, 47 (5), 26- 30.

Martinez, Monica (2010), Teacher Education Can't Ignore Technology," *Phi delta Kappan*, 92 (2), 74-75.

National Research Council (1996), *National Science Education Standards*. Washington DC: National Academy Press.

12

CHAPTER

The Science Curriculum and Levels of Pupil Thinking

It is salient to develop pupils ability to think since this pervades all curriculum areas as well as in the societal domain. Too frequently, pupils achieve in the lowest level such as recall of information. The recall level is important and provides building blocks for higher levels of cognition. However, in school and in society, increasingly complex thinking patterns must be stressed. What might the science teacher do to implement these kinds of activities in the science curriculum?

Sequencing Diverse Levels of Thought

A variety of rich learning experiences must be provided pupils to achieve vital objectives in science. These should be concrete, semi-concrete, and abstract in nature as well as provide for pupil optimal progress. Individually, each needs to attain as optimally as possible. Thus, for example within an ongoing unit of study, pupils need to carefully observe igneous, sedimentary, and metamorphic rocks, as concrete learning materials. They must feel and handle these specimens, using a magnifying glass. Here, pupils are learning facts at the *recall* level. Pupils, individually, may then recall and identify each type of rock. Additional experiences include seeing each of these rock classifications using a computerized projection on the white board, as well as on power point slides. With related discussions, pupils might infer characteristics of selected rocks (Ediger and Rao, 2010).

The level of *understanding* follows with pupils attaching meaning to how each of the three rock categories were formed. Here, the spoken voice may use verbal cues in teaching in that voice inflection is in evidence. Thus, appropriate enunciation, stress, and pitch of selected words assists learners in attending to ongoing presentations. The attention of pupils then is drawn toward how rocks are formed. A quality video tape together with the accompanying spoken voice, for example, may indicate clearly how sedimentary rock are formed in bodies of water by cementing small fragments of limestone, over time. Illustrations in the video tape provide visual cues in focusing learner attention on relevant content. Environmental cues further assist pupil understanding such as words on a word wall which pupils may refer/relate to for previous as well as ongoing concepts in an ensuing unit of study. Reinforcement of learnings is in evidence with revisits to concepts and vocabulary previously studied. The science teacher may incorporate non-verbal clues within those clues previously mentioned by using hand motions as well as using facial expressions (nods of the head, smiles, and using eye contact) which encourage learning, the teacher maximizes pupil achievement (Ediger and Rao, 2002).

In an appropriate sequence, the level of *critical thinking* might well be stressed. The learner increasingly analyzes relevant for that which is not relevant to the topic or subject matter being discussed. Too frequently, pupils focus upon the trivial rather that what is essential to attach meaning. In discussing volcanic eruptions, for example, pupils might study lava and metamorphic rock, with clarification on their differences and how these were formed when uncovered from volcanic eruption. Elaboration goes further into topics of formation and involved differences. An indepth sequence is emphasized here. The science teacher always must be aware of sequence when elaborating to create elucidation of ideas. Otherwise, pupils may become lost in the shuffle (Frey and Fisher, 2010).

Synthesizing Information obtained stresses, among other things, for learners to attain conclusions and summaries. Pupils being able to synthesize accurately and holistically is salient in every day studies in school as well as in the societal arenas. A summary/conclusion must contain vital gleaned information, with no room for fragmented content. It may be compared to the central idea which, in one sentence, states saliency of subject matter in a lead topic sentence within a paragraph/summary. The teacher in sequence may have pupils read silently a selection from the basal science textbook on the utilization of rocks and minerals after which the teacher models aloud how to arrive at a summary. Learners must notice carefully the order of content used here. This may be followed with modeling of the central idea. Pupils might then read aloud, in turn, subject matter on soil erosion. Reading fluently and with prosody acquires pupil attention and develops proficiency in comprehension, as well as in thinking about a conclusion. The conclusion, as well as the previously mentioned summary, must hold water in that each has supporting details (Tiedt, 1982).

Creative thought stresses the importance of developing unique, novel ideas. Creative ideas helps a society to move forward from where it is presently to something new which improves, beautifies, and enhances. Poetry is one avenue of creative expression and these poems may be written in different forms. Thus, acquired science subject matter may be written with rhyme such as:

- a couplet with two lines rhyming
- triplets with three lines rhyming
- quatrains with four lines of rhymed verse
- limericks with lines one, two, and five rhyming, as well as lines three and four with rhyme
- haiku with five, seven, five syllables respectively per line
- tanka with five, seven, five, seven, seven syllables sequentially per line
- free verse with no set number of lines or syllables, nor of length.

Acrostic poems are fascinating for numerous pupils to write. Thus, the pupil may take any vocabulary term from the science unit being studied and write it vertically, with continuance in writing a phrase or sentence such as in the following:

Erosion
Engraven in soil and rocks
Biding in force with wind or water
Often appearing in time on the earth's surface
Softens as well as hardens by forces of nature
Inbedded in the weathering process
On the surface of the earth
Nature's way of telling a story (Ediger, 2010).

Creative stories, art products, among others, are good to emphasize in teaching science. Ingredients may be added such as alliteration which contains two or more successive words beginning with the same sound.

Information based library books might well interest pupils in a specific topic in science. In a unit on Desert Life, for instance, there are a plethora of library books written on different reading levels for children. The learner may select sequential books to read which capture his/her attention and these might well be used to supplement discussions in an ongoing science unit of study. In several classes observed by the author, when supervising university student teachers, pupil discussion on desert life was based entirely from library book content. Each contributed in an atmosphere of respect. This might well be a method of varying the kinds of learning opportunities for pupils, along with science experiments, demonstrations, AV aids, oral reports, portfolios, writing experiences, and the use of computers and technology (See National Science Education Standards, 1996).

REFERENCES

Ediger, Marlow, and D. Bhaskara Rao (2002), *Philosophy and Curriculum*. New Delhi, India: Discovery Publishing.

Ediger, Marlow (2010), "Children's Literature in the Science Curriculum." *Reading Improvement*, 37 (2), 117-119.

Ediger, Marlow, and D. Bhaskara Rao (2010), *School Science Education*. New Delhi, India: Discovery Publishing House.

Frey, Nancy, and Douglas Fisher, (2010), "Identifying Instructional Moves During Guided Learning," *The Reading Teacher*, 64 (2), 84-95.

National Science Education Standards (1996). National Research Council.

Tiedt, Iris M. (1982), *Language Arts Handbook*. Englewood Cliffs, New Jersey: Prentice-Hall, Inc.

13

CHAPTER

Reading Critically in the Science Curriculum

With the tremendous emphasis placed upon reading in the educational literature and in the news, it behooves science teachers to place heavy stress upon achievement in this curriculum area. Mandated testing has been strong on evaluating reading progress. High stakes testing, therein, puts reading on a pedestal for learner achievement. Teachers have been pressured to teach more reading due to its importance in testing situations. Reading then needs to be included in each curriculum area, science included. To be sure, there is much reading in science and it can make its numerous contributions to learner success. However, individual differences do need to b provided for with the diverse interests, purposes, and abilities involved (Ediger, 2007). What might the science teacher do to encourage pupil achievement in critical reading?

Helping Pupils to Succeed in Reading

The science teacher needs to be a teacher of reading well as of academic content in earth, physical, and life sciences which provide content for the science. If basal textbooks are used in teaching, the teacher must be certain that new learnings are based upon what pupils have achieved previously. This is an important factor in teaching which might well make for pupil success in achievement. The new and the old just previously learned should be seamless in sequence. Failure occurs in learning if the new subject matter is too complex to master or if the content is too easy which might well make for boredom in learning. Challenging facts, concepts, and generalizations may be acquired through scaffolding. Thus, the teacher assists each pupils to attain what otherwise might be too difficult (Ediger 2006). This might well be illustrated with the new vocabulary to be introduced to learners prior to their reading from the basal science textbook. These should be neatly printed on the experience chart which all can see clearly. The words need to be meaningfully defined and/or used within sentences to fit the contextual use in the textbook. The science teacher assists pupils to bridge the gap between previous and the ensuing subject matter. What pupils know about vocabulary might then be extended to what they will be reading from the textbook. Contextual illustrations from the text need to be utilized to help learners attach meaning to the new vocabulary. Illustrations from the teacher's file as well as in a video tape may further illuminate understanding. Accuracy in meaning separates what is correct from the vague and the hazy (Ediger 2010).

Assessing the topical headings in the reading selection should aid pupils in providing readiness for comprehension. They need to be turned into questions; necessary information might then be gleaned to secure answers. It is wise to provide readiness experiences, prior to pupils reading the textbook selection. Reading critically may then be in evidence.

During this time, pupils should be encouraged to raise questions which provide an additional framework for seeking answers during the ensuing science reading experience (See DeRoche and Kostelny).

Followup activities should consist of in-depth discussions. Here, pupils need to read critically to separate accurate from inaccurate information, as well as facts from opinions. Then too, reading between the lines is salient since not all content might not or cannot be written with precise language. Metaphors and similes are a case at point. When these are used, a discussion should clarify intent.

When supervising university student teachers in the public schools, the writer observed several lessons taught with pupil contributions coming from library books largely. The unit emphasized prehistoric life and the age of dinosaurs. The topic is generally very interesting to pupils and the ensuing discussion was vibrant indeed. Pupils obtained library book content on the plesiosaur/mosasur, the tyrannosaurus rex, the diplodocus, the stegosarus, duck billed dinosaurs, among others. Illustrations were shown of each which was followed, in sequence, by a video tape to further clarify ideas and extend meanings. A myriad of questions were raised and committees formed to answer questions and solve problems such as the following:

- were most dinosaurs warm or cold blooded? What major differences would this make?
- why weren't a few dinosaurs saved from the catastrophic event of their annihilation?
- why did the archaeptorex possess claws on its wings?

Committees gathered data which was then presented to the class.

Enthusiasm tends to be high when learners themselves identify and solve dilemmas experienced. Art work was brought in to the unit with committees making models contained in the ongoing unit if study. Thus, from lightly soaked paper towels, a committee made a sea turtle from the Mesozoic era. The turtle was molded from the paper toweling and let to dry. Tempera paint used to show specific features of the model turtle made helped make for motivating displays of art work (See Parker, 2001).

Children's literature can make for valuable contributions in pupil learning. They may be displayed at an interest center from which pupils might browse and select to read. If pupils find the contents of interest, they tend to choose other interesting books for personal reading. These may be of the same/similar author or genre. Pupils must practice much reading in order to improve skills as well as increase knowledge. Achievement is cumulative and it contributes to further growth and progress. Knowledge and skills presently acquired provide building blocks for ensuing achievement.

A free reading time might also be in the offing whereby learners select sequential library books to read. If a pupil is unable to settle down to reading a book, the teacher needs to assist and offer guidance in sustained silent reading. He/she may pronounce unidentified words, as needed, to pupils during this time. Ideas gleaned may be brought into ongoing discussions in the unit being studied.

Peer reading can be beneficial in that pupils in the small group read from the same book and assist each other to develop higher levels of cognition as well as with word recognition. Reciprocal reading might also be stressed here with peers taking turns reading the content aloud. Then too, oral reading may be emphasized when a peer member lacks necessary reading skills. The latter should follow along, viewing the printed words in the book, as the reading aloud activity continues. Children must be encouraged to checkout library books to read at home. There are myriad ways of assisting pupils to read and analyze books with critical reading.

One more idea pertaining to encouraging reading, the writer observed a co-operating/student teacher read aloud during story hour which related to the ongoing unit of study. These teachers in a conference mentioned that pupils would later read the same titles in spare school time. Reading skills and critical thinking improved in the curriculum over time (See Stiggins, 1997).

Writing in the Science Unit of Study

There are a plethora of ways to utilize abstract content read in a unit of study. One way is to emphasize a hands on approach in learning through constructing a model our doing an experiment. This requires careful planning, implementation of the plans, and evaluation of the completed product. Hands on procedures in learning opportunities assists in providing for individual differences in interests, talents, and abilities among pupils.

Abstract activities also may be implemented to help pupils use what has been acquired through reading from the basal textbook and library books, among other media. The teacher needs to model developmentally appropriate tasks so that learners understand what is being emphasized. The latter should always be guided to perceive purpose in the writing experience. It should not be that writing is stressed for the sake of doing so, but there are practical reasons for becoming a good writer, useful in school and in society. Which kinds of written works are salient? The following are recommended:

- *Summaries:* Pupils need assistance to summarize what has been read. The summary must pay attention to major ideas as well as subordinate content, otherwise there is a lack of organization in the written product. Topic sentences to begin with in written instruction should orientate the reader of the summary to ensuing subject matter. Pupils may be lead through what are major as well as subordinate ideas. The balance of the summary supports the topic sentence or main idea. Pupils, too, need help in sequencing the subordinate ideas. Pupils should be lead through the order here and change/modify what must be altered in subsequent content. Critical thinking is inherent (See Shareeja, 2010).

- *outlines:* Through outlining content, pupils are aided in noting the orderly progression in writing. The teacher may begin here by discussing sequence within an outline containing blank spaces. Thus, the topic sentence is given and pupils need to fill in one or two subordinate ideas with one already provided. If details are to be added, the science teacher may omit one detail with pupils determining the other subsequent ideas in sequence. All of the preceding parts of an outline might come from a section in the basal science textbook. Pupils with teacher guidance may then check for accuracy of the outline with the comparison made.
- *diary entries.* Each learner needs to keep dated diary entries of subject matter acquired as well as skills attained. This helps pupils to note major ideas attained as well as those of lesser significance. Practice in writing is then stressed, along with the other forms of written work stated above.
- *log entries.* These are to be emphasized so that pupils learn to combine diary entries into an organized whole. The entries are good to use for review purposes (Ediger, 2007).

The above writing activities assist pupils to read, proof read, and engage in critical thinking. The important ideas, always, must be separated from the less salient.

REFERENCES

DeRoche, and Susan J. Kostelny (2006), "An Adventure in Problem Based Reading," *Phi Delta Kappan*, 87 (9),708-709.

Ediger, Marlow (2006), "Scaffolding in the Reading Curriculum," *Iowa Educational Leadership*, 8 (4), 24-26.

Ediger, Marlow (2007), "Meaning in Reading Instruction," *Reading Improvement*, 44 (4), 217-220.

Ediger, Marlow (2010), "Issues in the Social Studies," *International Journal of Research, Development, and Extension*, 1 (1), 43-49.

Ediger, Marlow (2007), *Teaching Science in Elementary Schools*. New Delhi, India: Discovery Publishing Hoscienceuse.

Parker, Walter C. (2001) *Social Studies in Elementary Education*. Upper Saddle River, New Jersey: Prentice-Hall, Inc.

Shareeja, AN M. C. (2010), "Macognition: Concept and Development," *Edutracks*, 9(9), 10-13.

Stiggins, Richard J. (1997), *Student Centered Classroom Assessment*. Upper Saddle River, New Jersey: Merrill.

The Psychology of Learning and Teaching the Social Studies

The social studies teacher must use the psychology go learning in planning and implementing the curriculum. This assists pupils to achieve more optimally. Motivating disinterested pupils, who have little purpose in achieving stated objectives, with stimulating learning opportunities, aids learners to develop, attain, and grow. Quality attitudes should be an end result of achievement. They facilitate learners in developing an inward desire to learn. Too frequently, there is a low energy level for learning on the part of some pupils. Achievement then tends to move in a negative direction. The social studies teacher must possess a repertoire of knowledge and skills in helping pupils to attain objectives (Ediger, 2010).

Intrinsic Versus Extrinsic Motivation

Intrinsic motivation emphasizes that pupils have an inward desire to learn. Pupils are interested in learning more about each social studies lesson and unit being pursued. On their own as well as with teacher guidance, pupils gather information in subject matter content. The sky may well be the limit in learning in these situations. It would be good if all pupils have this inward motivation. There are teaching suggestions in facilitating inward motivation with the following:

- change the learning activity before pupils become disinterested
- modulate the teacher's speaking voice so that appropriate pitch, stress, and enunciation secures learner attention
- have adequate pupil input into the lesson/unit of study by raising stimulating questions
- develop active pupil involvement in the social studies
- use committee endeavors as well as individual work
- provide pupil choice, at intervals, in terms of which tasks learners would desire to accomplish (See Ritchhart and Perkins, 2008).

Extrinsic motivation, also, has its advocates. The social studies teacher then uses external factors in motivating pupils. For example, the teacher might motivate extrinsically by giving praise judiciously to work well done*. This should spur pupils on to desiring praise with continuous achievement. The following additional examples are provided:

- providing time for free choice of activity following one or more tasks well done.
- having a popcorn party, Friday afternoon when pupils meet definite, high criteria in learning. The criteria are established prior to pupils working on achieving them.
- giving an inexpensive prize for attaining a specific goal in a social studies lesson.

The token economy or direct giving of a prize is utilized for work well done where the standards were stated prior to the announcement of the award. The social studies teacher must decide, here, under what conditions a prize is to be given (Ediger, 2009).

Sequence in Learning

Who largely should determine sequence in learning? Toward one end of the continuum, the teacher might choose in which order learning opportunities are to be provided for pupils. Here, the social studies teacher studies pupils, individually, to ascertain sequence. He/she must choose that which assists pupils to achieve optimally. The lear/iing opportunities must not be too complex to preordain failure or so easy that learners feel bored. Scaffolding might be used, where feasible, in ongoing lessons and units of study. A variety of kinds of activities may well be used to provide for individual differences in growth, attainment, and progress. The teacher attempts to secure the interests and purposes of pupils in teaching and learning situations. Success in learning is always salient (See, National Council for the Social Studies, 1997).

Toward the other end of the continuum, the teacher may serve as a guide and facilitator of learning. A learning stations procedure might be utilized. The teacher or teacher/pupil planning may be used in developing four stations, for example, with five tasks for pupils to select from at each station. There are more tasks than pupils can complete so that those most appealing might be chosen sequentially. The teacher introduces each station to pupils in a stimulating learning environment, which may consist of a bulletin board, a word wall, a mural, a video presentation, among others. Pupils, individually, might then select sequential tasks to work on, be they individual or committee endeavors. The learner ascertains sequence within the learning activity when making these choices. For example, the pupil might choose to make a model and with the available necessary materials order his/her own experiences with teacher help as needed. The model may pertain to developing a medieval manor. Otherwise, the pupil is free to pursue in the planning and executing of the task.The teacher scaffolds when needed to aid pupil achievement. Encouragement is used to enhance achievement. The final product is evaluated in terms of desired standards (See, Parker, 2001).

Perhaps, both teacher determined as well as a pupil centered procedure should be used in the social studies. This aids in providing for the needs, interests, and purposes of learners, individually as well as collectively.

A Subject Centred Versus an Activity Centred Curriculum

The psychology of learning involved here pertains to essential content, as determined by academicians, to be learned within a unit of study as compared to pupil purpose/ input in ongoing units of study. With essential subject-matter, pupils acquire major concepts and generalizations as identified by social scientists in history, geography, economics, political science, as well as anthropology/sociology. The subject matter to be acquired by pupils is deemed necessary to become a good citizen as well as to be an informed person in school and in society. The social studies teacher explains to pupils what is not understood or is rather vague in the minds of learners. There are selected video tapes which can truly make learnings meaningful to pupils, such as one on the Renaissance period of time viewed by the writer. Here, pupils may view clothing worn, means of transportation, building of churches, university buildings, and the manor. Visual and related audio aids help pupils to attach meaning to historical and and social science concepts and generalizations (See, Fosnot, 1996).

Acquiring Basic Subject Matter can be Vitalized and Meaningful to Pupils

Toward the other end of the continuum, social studies teachers feel that pupils learn facts, vocabulary, and main ideas through a learning by doing approach. A hands on procedure is then being emphasized. Salient subject-matter is then learned at the time that a construction or art product is being created. Careful planning is necessary to develop'and complete the ensuing product. Evaluation in terms of desirable criteria is used to assess its worth and neatness. To construct a model Parthenon, of ancient Athens, pupils need to see models, have the needed materials, and do meticulous work. The making part becomes meaningless unless it is accompanied by indepth related knowledge. The teacher is a facilitator, but not a "sage on the stage." The writer viewed a model Parthenon at a social studies fair. The pupil was well versed in knowledge about the Parthenon and its history. He was able to tell clearly how it was made and the obstacles faced during its sequential development from cardboard. It is indeed fascinating for pupils to construct, design, and model (See Bain, 2004).

Most social studies teachers will use both a subject centered and learning by doing. It is important that pupils garner relevant abstract learnings in the social studies and for some it may mean making models, murals, relief maps, puppets, among others to portray concepts and generalizations from the different disciplines making up content in the social studies. Learning styles of pupils vary due to individual differences in interests, talents, and abilities.

Determining objectives prior to instruction has been quite common, especially with state and district wide stated goals. Generally, these are stated in measurable terms so that pupils can be certain if they have/have not achieved these ends of instruction. Tests are aligned with the objectives to measure pupil achievement. With mandated objectives and aligned test, pupil achievement may be measured through the use of multiple choice test results. Percentiles usually are given to show learner progress. High stakes tests and their results indicate if a pupil is to be promoted to the next grade level. How effective this procedure in teaching is depends upon the quality of the standards (objectives), the implemented learning opportunities to achieve the stated objectives, as well as the validity/reliability of the multiple choice test items. There are selected weaknesses in using this procedure of instruction:

- there is little opportunity for pupil involvement in the curriculum such as questions they may wish to have answered within a lesson.
- with the accountability movement, teaching to the test may become sacred. What is tested might be what is taught. Teachers are held accountable for pupil achievement based on standardized test results.
- stating all objectives prior to instruction is risky business, due to impairment of selected pupils in attaining these ends, especially when they are stated well ahead of and prior to instruction as well as being too complex to achieve.

Somewhat toward the other end of the continuum is to utilize teacher/pupil planning in the social studies. Planning effectively is a highly complex skill, useful in school and in society. Adequate background information is necessary to plan well. Thus, within an ongoing unit of study, pupils with teacher guidance may plan learning opportunities to accomplish open ended objectives. The following need planning:

- which activities should be offered? This may involve developing a time line, dramatizing events from history, giving an oral book report, doing an art project related to the unit being taught, peer/group, discussions, writing summaries and conclusions, among others.
- how should each activity be evaluated so that quality is in evidence? Pupils must become proficient in doing things well and with evaluation, the final process/product might well show quality work.

Pupil responsibility is significant here. Pupils need to do the learning, and the teacher must provide encouragement and effective modeling.

In Conclusion

The psychology of learning, applied to teaching and learning situations, assists pupils to achieve more optimally. Then too, humaneness is involved when pupils experience that which meets academic, social, emotional, and physical needs. Learnings then need to provide for individual differences and be:

- engaging and interesting;
- purposeful and relevant; and
- motivating and encourage curiosity.

REFERENCES

Bain, K. (2004), *What the Best College Teachers Do. Cambridge,* Massachusetts: Harvard University Press.

Ediger, Marlow (2009), "Supervising the Student Teacher in the Public School," *Education,* 130 (2), 251-254).

Ediger, Marlow (2010), "Issues in the Social Studies," *International Journal of Educational Research, Development, and Extension,* 1 (1), 43-49.

Fosnot, C. (1996), *Constructivism: Theory, Perspectives, and Practice.* New York: Teachers College Press.

National Council for the Social (1997), *Curriculum Standards for the Social Studies.* Edison, New York: Whitehurst and Clark.

Parker Walter C. (2001), *Social Studies in Elementary Education.* Upper Saddle River, New Jersey: Merrill, Prentice Hall.

Ritchhart, Ron, and David Perkins (2008), "Making Thinking Visible," *Educational Leadership,* 65 (5), 57-63.

This is a recommenced approach for all schools of educational psychology.

15

CHAPTER

Vocabulary Development in the Social Studies

Social studies vocabulary must receive high priority in teaching and learning situations. A meaningful vocabulary assists pupils to do well in listening, speaking, reading, and writing in ongoing lessons and units of study. A variety of methods and procedures need to be used to guide more optimal attainment. Pupils differ from each other in the level of vocabulary growth and these differences need to have prime consideration in the learning process. Objectives need incorporation which stress word meanings, and concepts which are salient should become an important part of the child's repertoire. The social studies teacher needs to evaluate which terms are poignant in the curriculum and incorporate these into relevant subject-matter for pupil achievement.

Pupils tend to like to play with words which are relevant and useful in school and in society. They are increasingly able to communicate more effectively with others when variety and diversity of vocabulary terms are used more precisely. Vagueness in communication occurs when clarity in intended meanings are not in evidence. Sometimes words are not used correctly in context making for misunderstandings in human relations. Thus, social studies teachers need to identify vital words and phrases to emphasize when instructional procedures are developed and implemented (Ediger, 2010).

Vocabulary Development

Various ways will be discussed pertaining to helping pupils enrich their listening, speaking, reading, and writing vocabularies in the social studies. When reading from the basal textbook, learners should see new words in print, prior to reading its content. Learner attention must be focused on these words on the white-board. A meaningful discussion should focus upon the context within which each word will be used. Background information is then provided in word recognition as well as in vocabulary development with pupils then possessing readiness factors for reading. They also need to discuss with teacher guidance illustrations in the text which might well illuminate meanings of these new vocabulary terms. There are additional ways in which pupils reinforce attached meanings such as when actually reading from the basal as well as discussing main and subordinate ideas read. The new vocabulary terms may be printed on the word wall in the classroom. The writer when supervising university student teachers has observed how pupils congregate at a word wall to review words and raise contextual questions. Review and metacognition strategies are then in the offing(See National Council for the Social Studies, 1997).

A second procedure in aiding pupil vocabulary growth emphasizes the social studies teacher using new concepts in discussions. The are a plethora of vocabulary terms which may come from different social science disciplines which provide subject matter for the social studies. These may include the following used in context as well as added to the word wall when stressed:

- economic concepts such as consumption of goods and *services.* Pupils may look around the classroom and school setting to notice inherent meanings. Thus, pupils may notice items of clothing purchased, as well as school supplies consisting of paper, pen/ pencils, among others. Gross national product, production and distribution are additional valuable economic concepts.

- anthropological/sociological concepts including culture, language, artifacts, socio-economic levels, and other related concepts.

The above-named academic disciplines may be expanded to include the following within ongoing social studies units: ,

- historical concepts such as duration in time, World War One, the Great Depression, World War Two, recessions, oil spills, off shore drilling, global warming, etcetera.
- geographical concepts—latitude, longitude, meridians, parallels, plains, plateaus, and polar regions.
- political science concepts such as federal, state, and local governments, as well as the United Nations. Socialism, democracy, communism, and totalitarian are additional salient political science concepts (See Parker, 2001).

A quality current events programme keeps the social studies curriculum updated. A rich vocabulary is then embedded. A pupil-centred curriculum needs to be emphasized in that learners must understand what is taught and its relevancy. With relevancy, use is made of subject-matter acquired. Content then is not taught and learned for its own sake, but it has utilitarian values in school and in society. Developmentally and age appropriate learnings must be provide with the style of learning preferred by the pupil. The style of learning might well stress constructivism with sequence determined largely by the pupil with teacher guidance, or deductively presented by the teacher in meaningful ways. A challenging curriculum may be in the offing through scaffolding or the vocabulary terms may need to be made concrete through understandable meanings.

Acceptable criteria for selecting vocabulary terms must be followed by the social studies teacher and might well involve the following:

- high expectations exist and yet the vocabulary encountered is achievable in meaning.
- success in vocabulary learning for each pupil is paramount within the framework of being understandable.
- indepth learnings involving quality sequence needs to be in the offing.
- positive interactions in the classroom eliminates rudeness and inconsiderate behavior in achieving positive attitudes.
- good citizenship behaviors integrate with purposeful vocabulary development activities (Ediger, 2010).

There are significant achievement levels in vocabulary development with, first of all, the pupil being able to recognize and pronounce the word correctly. This also has prerequisites such as using necessary phonetic principles as well as context clues when reading sentences and paragraphs. The pupil might then be able to define the vocabulary term and/or use it in a sentence. The recall level of cognition may be involved here. Next, the pupil is able to utilize the word in oral communication and written experiences. There needs to be planned experiences whereby the level of application is possible. This aids the learner to expand the use of these words and multiple meanings are attached. In the writer's experiences of supervising university student teachers, he has noticed pupils enjoying playing with words in providing a plethora of uses for each and possessing clarity within a contextual situation. Breadth of attached meanings for each vocabulary term indicates growth in learning as well as precision in usage. Flexibility in higher levels of thought makes it possible to be productive in usage of myriad vocabulary words in a variety of situations.

There are creative uses of newly acquired words which provide interesting learning opportunities. The writer noticed the development of acrostic poetry in a classroom which included new terms such as following in an ongoing unit of study:

producing food items for a supermarket
restocking the shelves for shoppers
ordering what is needed on the shoppers list
diligent workers keep shelves stocked
under careful supervision of the manager
canned goods are displayed attractively
the meat counter makes one hungry for steaks
in the midst of different kinds of bread
on the minds of consumers who do the shopping
no one complains about the distribution (See Tiedt, 1982).

A vocabulary concept, such as the above titled Production, may then be chosen for writing a creative poem. Acrostic poetry is relatively easy to write since it requires no rhyme, nor be of a specific length. It becomes difficult to determine words which rhyme as well as have a certain length. Pupils do need to see the acrostic in print which the social studies teacher needs to model. To initiate the individual writing of an acrostic, a group poem might be written with pupils brainstorming the title as well as sequential lines, with the teacher recording the ideas for all to see clearly. The content clearly reflects pupil knowledge of *production*. A pupil's poem may become a part of his/her portfolio.

Evaluation of Achievement

A portfolio is a random selection of learner products. The latter does the selecting of entries with teacher guidance. Sequential progress might then be noticed in vocabulary growth as well as other facets of social studies achievement. Although test scores may be included in the portfolio, the entries therein provide direct evidence of pupil achievement in vocabulary development as well as progress made in ongoing units of study. Thus, the following, among others, may be included:

- written summaries, outlines, diary/log entries, and poems
- recordings of oral book reports, committee endeavors, and dramatizations related to ongoing lessons in social studies
- drawings, diagrams, charts, graphs, and other forms of statistical information
- digital photos of products and processes studied within a unit of study (Ediger, 2007).

The portfolio provides excellent content for parentAeacher conferences whereby parents can discuss present levels of pupil achievement and what needs further emphasis. Test results may be included such as standardized tests. However, the following limitations need to be kept in mind when viewing test scores:

- multiple choice test items generally prevail which limits pupils to select from among four options with no opportunities to vary words used in personal, contextual written experiences
- pupils, individually, are compared with each other in vocabulary progress and not in growth from past achievement
- the finer nuances are not noted in test results such as the ability to use contextually acquired vocabulary in new situations
- personal definitions are not listed, generally, in choosing a correct response from the multiple choice form
- pupils may not have had opportunities to learn meanings related to the correct response in a multiple choice test item

- validity is always a problem in that selected test items have not been aligned with the local curriculum (See Guilfoyle, 2006).

In closing

Vocabulary achievement is a highly salient factor in understanding subject matter in different academic disciplines; it is poignant for the pupil presently in the social studies and for future achievement in academia. Some will continue with technical education and all will eventually need to be knowledgeable in social studies content as a member in society. An informed citizenry is highly important.

REFERENCES

Ediger, Marlow (2007), "Balance in the Curriculum," *The Elementary Principal*, 20 (4), 7-8.

Ediger, Marlow (2010), "Constructivism and the Social Studies," *Edutracks*, 9 (7),13-14.

Ediger, Marlow (2010), *Effective School Curriculum*. New Delhi, India: Discovery Publishing House.

Guifoyle, Christy (2006), "NCLB: Is There Life Beyond Testing?" *Educational Leadership*, 64 (3), 8-13.

National Council for the Social Studies (1997), *Curriculum Standards for the Social Studies*. Edison, New York: Whitehurst and Clark.

Parker, Walter C. (2001), *Social Studies in Elementary Education*. Upper Saddle River, New Jersey: Prentice-Hall, Inc.

Tiedt, Iris M. (1982), The Language Arts Handbook. Englewood Cliffs, New Jersey: Prentice-Hall, Inc.

16

CHAPTER

Oral Communication in the Social Studies

Oral communication skills are salient in all curriculum areas as well as in the societal realm. Social studies, as one academic discipline, can make definite contributions in assisting learners to effectively communicate with others. Of all language arts skills, orally communicating with others is the most frequently used in society There need to be definite objectives in each unit of study as well as emphasis therein in daily lesson plans. How might oral communication be stressed in the social studies?

Learning Opportunities in the Social Studies

To provide for individual differences among pupils, variety is a key word here. Also, pupils are on different achievement levels, and this is a prime consideration in choosing objectives of instruction. Scaffolding must be included as a definitive possibility in oral communication when thinking of stressing high expectations in teaching and learning situations.

Discussions in ongoing units and lessons are important to include frequently. Within discussions, pupils are able to clarify ideas presented and attach related meanings. Higher levels of cognition such as critical and creative thinking need inclusion. At the same time quality in effective oral communication might well be emphasized. Proper stress, pitch, rate, and enunciation must be practiced by learners. The social studies teacher presents a role model here in each lesson taught where ideas circulate among members of the class and of the teacher to effectively present subject matter (Ediger, 2010).

Listening is an inherent part of quality communication. The listener needs to perceive purpose and pay careful attention to what is said. Periodic assessment of careful listening should become an integral part of the curriculum. Distractions must be eliminated and factors which facilitate communicator/listener should be enhanced. Respect for each pupil and his/ her contributions need reinforcement. Rudeness and impolite behavior must be eliminated with rational rules and regulations which are enforced. These standards of conduct may be planned with class members and under teacher supervision. Evaluation of pupil achievement in meeting these standards provides additional opportunities for purposeful oral communication (National Council for the Social Studies, 1997).

Small group collaboration is a method of teaching which provides individuals opportunities to participate more frequently. Here, pupils may practice staying on the social studies topic at hand. Active participation by all is needed to have the group move forward. Leadership may emerge as individuals ask for clarification of ideas and offer suggestions. Learners may scaffold content as challenges in thinking occur. Subject matter achievement accrues with high expectations from pupils, as well as the teacher, might well come about as a result of active pupil involvement. The topic my relate to the ongoing social studies unit and chosen by learners with teacher guidance. Practising courtesy within a small group might well make for feelings of cohesion as well as respect for each other (See Guilfoyle, 2006).

A project method stresses the importance of developing construction and human relations skills. The project needs to be relevant to the involved learners. Careful planning of the construction experience is a must. The teacher needs to demonstrate orally how a project is chosen and planned. The carrying out of the plans emphasizes responsible behavior by those working on the project. Tools, materials, and equipment must be used and returned to their proper places before, during, and after the activity is completed. Cleaning up after each work period necessitates leaving the environment clean. Individual as well as committee endeavors may be planned with teacher guidance. Developing of standards and assessment in terms of these criteria helps pupils stay on track and persevere. Quality oral communication is inherent in the project method of instruction.

Problem-solving experiences aid pupils in perceiving the need to communicate effectively with others. A relevant problem in an ongoing lesson/ unit of study may be identified. The problem is salient and must be clear in meaning for participants. Seeking information from a variety of reference sources including knowledgeable resource personnel, the internet and the world wide web, might well bring much content to bear for discussion in attempting to solve the problem. An hypothesis needs to be developed which needs testing in a lifelike experience. The hypothesis might then be accepted as is, modified, or refuted (See Parker, 2001).

Project methods as well as problem solving activities emphasize heavy pupil involvement in sequencing leanings from beginning of each to the end. The teacher serves as a resource person and assists learners to stay on task toward completion of the project as well as the problem solving experience. Oral communication skills are greatly needed in any group endeavour, be it small or large group settings. It is a basic in the curriculum and applicable to all curriculum areas. In social studies, in particular, each inherent academic discipline requires clarity in speaking and quality listening behaviors. Among committee members, the flow of the discussion should circulate within the group. All need be to participate actively with no one dominating the discussion. Thus, in the following examples, pertaining to oral communication, it is salient to communicate clearly in each academic discipline:

- history in planning a time line to show sequence of events
- geography when developing a relief map of the geographical region being studied
- economics involving the making of a chart showing goods and services in dollar amounts, produced, within selected nations in the ongoing lesson/unit of study
- political science in planning cooperatively showing lines of organization in government. This could relate to the federal level (legislative, executive, and judicial), the state level, as well as the city government level
- sociology/anthropology with culture being integrated into the social studies. Society and how it affects people in every day affairs is the focal point of discussion. The Old Order Amish, for example, provide subject matter for a study of culture. They dress in unique ways which differentiate from members in the larger society. Women and girls wear prayer caps and long dresses which extend to the ankles and the wrists. The dresses, with high neck lines, are always of a plain color such as blue, purple, black, never striped or checked. The men and boys wear blue denim trousers and single colored shirts for weekday work duties. Straw hats are worn in summer. Worship services are conducted in German, bi-weekly in homes as well as in barns in spring and summer (See Medina and Costa, 2010).

A sample of learning activities for each of the above named academic disciplines involving subject matter for the social studies is given. These need expanding so that pupils may understand and attach meaning to what is being studied. People must be studied from diverse academic disciplines. They possess an historical background within a geographical region, buying goods and services, and are governed by federal, state, and local levels. Culture influences behavior within society. Society then has its values, customs, and beliefs which it inculcates in the societal arenas. The influence of culture may be seen most strongly in primary groups such as The Old Order Amish, as well as the Hutterite Mennonites, a communal society, in South Dakota, North Dakota, Montana, Washington state, and in Canada.

Social Action in the Curriculum

There are improvements which need to be made in society. Advocating actively that these need to be made stresses social action. Recommendations must be made based on evidence, not shallow thinking. Pupils may choose a learning station in the classroom titled Social Action. There are possible tasks for pupils to work on which they perceive as being poignant. The ideal is that these come from learners with teacher guidance. There are problems such as the following which exist in school/society:

- stop signs needed at selected intersections due to heavy traffic. Stop lights might well be necessary in some of these places
- a polluted stream or creek Ipcated near to the local school
- litter on the school grounds which learners may take pride in eliminating so that an attractive school ground may come about
- odors in the school bathrooms
- unattractive classrooms. Perhaps some easy to do items can improve the situation such as bulletin boards,

neatly displayed library books, and putting all waste paper in the trash container.

Increasingly, more salient items may be tackled with a social action approach in the curriculum. The major goal and objective in the social studies is to develop good citizens. Certainly quality social action programs may make their contributions to societal improvement (Ediger, 2007).

REFERENCES

Ediger, Marlow (2007), "Learning Activities in the Curriculum," *College Student Journal,* 41 (4), 967-969.

Ediger, Marlow (2010), "Constructivism and the Social Studies," *Edutracks,* 9(7),13-14.

Guilfoyle, Christy (2006), "Is There Life Beyond NCLB?" *Educational Leadership,* 64 (3),8-13.

Medina, Carmen L., and Maria del Rocio Costa (2010), "Collaborative Voices Exploring Culturally and Socially Responsive Literacies," *Language Arts,* 87 (4), 263-276.

National Council for the Social Studies (1997), *Curriculum Standards for the Social Studies.* Edison, New York: Whitehurst and Clark.

Parker, Walter C. (2001), *Social Studies in Elementary Education.* Upper Saddle River, New Jersey: Merrill, Prentice-Hall.

17

CHAPTER

Pointers in Teaching the Social Studies

A Quality Social Stuqies Curriculum is Needed to Assist Pupils to Do Well in Relating Well to Others in School and in Society. Multi-culturalism needs to be emphasized in ongoing lessons and units of study due to a society which has numerous ethnic groups and nationalities. Thus, there are a plethora of cultural groups which need to be studied so that learners experience positive interactions, feelings, and acceptance. Pupils in the school setting need to be grouped so that maximum collaboration is possible.

Encouraging Multi-cultural Experiences

Increasingly, public schools have pupils who speak another language than English. When entering first grade in 1934, the writer spoke low German largely. In his Mennonite church affiliation, the language of the Church was high German. As early as 1950, English largely became a predominate language of the Church. The appearance of men and women then and now were/are exactly like other people in society including hair styles, suits and dresses. Change, in many factors.was somewhat rampant, although selected cultural factors, in degrees, remained such as the following:

- being in alternative rather than military service in times of conscription. Although, there were individuals who entered military service.
- being a farming population; however, this is changed dramatically due to a lack of farm land and farming opportunities. Rural culture, however, remains salient.
- living in a homogeneous community. Presently, many different vocations, occupations, and professions are being followed whereby people tend to move to areas where work opportunities are such as in urban and suburban areas.

A more stable society, with less change, are the Old Order Amish. They use horse and carriage for transportation rather than modern vehicles. Those who farm, less than twenty five per cent do, use draft horses instead of tractors. Grain drills pulled by horses are used for crop seeding as wells harrows and disks for soil tilling. There are a few Amish communities which operate tractors for pulling farm implements. These may be used, too, for going into town for buying needed goods. Grain binders and threshing machines are used for harvesting crops rather than self-propelled combines with air-conditioned cabs. Married women are housewives and take care of the home and family, generally with five or six children. There are a few exceptions such as a rural grocery store being operated by an Amish family. Amish men have entered into a variety kinds of occupations such as construction work, the making of furniture, and repair work on small engines.

The same pattern of dress is inherent for Amish Women with high necklines, long sleeves which go down to the wrist, and length of dress extending to the ankles. Amish men wear beards, have suspenders for holding up trousers, wear black suits for Sunday services with no ties. All clothing for men and women as well as for children possess a plain color, not stripes nor checks in design.

Amish children go to school for eight years which is terminal. Usually, these are parochial schools operated by the Old Order Amish with teachers of their own faith doing the teaching. Generally, these are Amish women who teach. Textbooks used may be from leading publishing companies; however, basals from the Rod and Staff Publishing Company may be utilized containing sequential phonic lessons and biblical stories such as biographies of Abraham, Lot, Isaac, and Jacob, among others. Mathematics is a secular subject and the Macmillan, Harcourt Brace and World, or other publishing companies provide subject-matter content in these textbooks. Social Studies content comes from subject matter contained from a secular publishing company. Grammar is emphasized heavily in written work, that tends to stress factual, not creative content.

Recess time may consists of playing softball, volley ball, and croquet when the weather is favourable. In cold weather, if there is an ice pond or creek near the school building, ice skating is popular. Running games such as tag, handi-over, and 23 eskadoo are also popular in winter. Otherwise, Amish children stay indoors on cold days and play quiz games or checkers/dominos. The internet contains much information on the Amish as well as other Mennonite groups. Reference sources for children's and adult library books are given pertaining to these cultural societies.

Multi-cultural Activities in the Social Studies As the name indicates, multicultural education emphasizes diverse ethnic as well as minority groups for studying. There are a plethora of Latinos in society. These may speak Spanish, largely or only. They possess salient customs, religious beliefs, as well as philosophies of life. These need to be pinpointed as vital objectives of instruction in an integrated social studies curriculum. Learning opportunities need to be selected in order that learners might achieve the chosen objectives. Video tapes, musical recordings, digital and actual Latino art work, architecture such as large Catholic cathedrals, need to be studied and appreciated, native foods eaten (there are, of course numerous Mexican restaurants in society serving authentic foods), native folk dances may be taught, as well as important facets of the Spanish language such as greetings used. Learning opportunities then must be accurate, authentic, as well as valid and reliable. Pupils need to have ample opportunities to interact with diverse minority groups in favorable situations whereby positive feelings are developed among Latinos, as well as African Americans.

In studying an integrated with other primary and secondary cultures, African American culture needs to stress harmonious relationships with others. Good will and positive human relationships need achieving. Respect and caring are salient features to become a part of each social studies unit of study. Knowledge, skills, and attitudinal ends need careful attention so that representative cultural factors pertaining to African Americans are forth coming. African American content must emphasize leaders in American society such as The Rev. Al Sharpton, Rev. Jesse Jackson, the late Supreme Court Justice Thurgood Marshall, the late Rosa Parks, writer Angelou Mayou, and President Barak Obama. There are many athletes such as Mohammed Ali.and Kobe Bryant, as well as actors/ entertainers who have been/are famous such as the late Michael Jackson.

The literary works, art products, music, architecture, foods, and the many other accomplishments of African Americans need to be studied and become a salient part of the pupil's repertoire.

A multi-cultural social curriculum is needed in order that pupils understand the many contributions made by Latinos, African Americans, native Americans, as well as Jewish Americans. My own experiences lead me to the Middle East in the early 1950s in alternative to military service. On the

West Bank of the Jordan, then a part of the nation of Jordan, I assisted in clothing distributions in Palestinian refugee camps. The clothing distributions, in general, were orderly. These people lived in clay huts with thatched roofs and no sanitation facilities in Aqaba Camp, directly south of Jericho. Their food consisted of United Nations rations for refugees. Water was generally carried in clay pots from Ein Sultan or Elisha's fountain in Jericho, four miles away.

I also taught at Friends Boys School, a boarding school for boys, located in Ramallah. Approximately, half were Muslims whereas the other half were Greek and Armenian Orthodox Christians. Personally, I did not notice any major differences in school behavior among the different groups. Pupils should have opportunities to visit with and interact with people of Muslim Beliefs. This needs to be done in a positive atmosphere whereby acceptance is a key concept. Essential beliefs of Muslims for pupils to study are the following:

- after performing ablutions, they pray five times a day at prescribed times and with proper postures, facing Mecca, Saudi Arabia, the birth place of their prophet Mohammed.
- once in a life time, devout followers of Islam make a required trip to Mecca, during Ramadan, and thus receive the title *Hajj*. There are exceptions to this rule, such as a person having ill health.
- the Muslim creed is recited at prayer time - There is no God, but one God, and Mohammed is His prophet
- the *Quar'an* is the Holy book of Islam and devout followers generally worship in a Mosque. A nearby minaret is used by the leader, known as an Imam, to call people to prayer.
- *tithes* are given to the poor and less fortunate such as two and one half per cent of one's wealth, annually.

With an increased population of Muslims and the building of Mosques, it behooves schools to implement quality units of study on Islam. Less than thirty miles from my home is a Muslim school for children, on the northern outskirts of Wichita, Kansas. The school building represents the likeness of the Dome of the Rock, a beautiful, octagonal mosque, inside the walls of the walled city of Jerusalem. This mosque was built in AD 691, and is the third holiest site of Islam, with Mecca being the holiest, followed by Medina, 200 miles to the north and containing the tomb of Mohammed (AD 570-632).

A very rich cultural experience, for the writer, was to eat meals with nomads (bedouin). Bedouin tents were located outside of Jericho, the West Bank. The temperature is mild in winter, above freezing, but is warm from January to October with extremely hot temperature readings—April through August. Bedouin men sit in one side of the tent and the women in the other. I sat with men for eating, squatted on the ground. The hands were used for eating rice and lamb's meat, the latter reserved for special occasions, from a metal platter. It is truly a skill to eat using the hands. Furniture and utensils are kept to an extreme minimum due to the necessity of moving to where the grass is suitable for grazing by sheep, goats, camels, and donkeys. Bedouin hospitality is excellent due to the respect for visitors.

In addition to first hand experiences with diverse cultural groups, reading from internet, viewing video tapes, reading library books as well as content from basal textbooks, there are numerous rich construction experiences emphasizing eye/hand coordination which extend previous learnings obtained. These include the following:

- making a model cloth tent, paper mache desert animals, and clay figures of bedouins
- scrolls as used in the Roman Empire, as well as bound booklets of compiled children's stories written in ongoing lessons and units of study

- musical flutes as used by bedouins for entertainment when herding sheep and goats. The flute may consist of a paper tube coming from the inside of a role of paper toweling with small openings made along the tube. Air may then be blown in from a flattened sturdy card board mouth piece. The fingers are utilized to open and close these holes, making for different levels of pitch.
- a small scale Dome of the Rock, representing a Mosque inside the walled city of Jerusalem. My grandson, for example, made a model ancient Greek parthenon in an ongoing sixth grade unit of study.
- a "television set" consisting of a cardboard box with an open front. Two wooden dowel rods may be inserted into the cardboard box with a roll of butcher paper around these rods. The butcher paper needs to be flat on the floor or desk top so that illustrations and related wording might be printed thereon. The butcher paper is then placed around the dowel rods of the "television set" for a committee of pupils to tell and show the story of the segment of the social studies unit taught.
- sock puppets which pertain to multi-cultural experiences such as decorating a sock with costumes pertaining to people of the middle East. These may then be used to tell a story of an ongoing lesson or unit of study.
- making and using a loom to make cloth as bedouins do in a tent setting.
- doing a relief map made of an equal mixture of flour and salt and enough water to hold the ingredients together to show vital cities/ features such as Tel Aviv, Cairo, Jerusalem, Ammon, Damascus, Baghdad, the Judean Hills, The Sea of Galilee, Dead Sea, among

others. The relief map should be tempera painted with a legend to show elevation.

- shape clay animals such as sheep and goats as well as into pottery to hold water.
- make a mural showing the walled city of Jerusalem, the Church of the Holy Sepulcher, the Mosque El Aqsa (adjacent to the Dome of the Rock), and the Western wall, a holy place for devout followers of Judaism.

The above are examples of hands on approaches in teaching and learning situations in the social studies. Additional learning opportunities include the following, among others:

- use of reading materials involving basal text-books, library books, internet sources, newspapers and news-magazines
- video tapes, CDs and DVDs, as well as transparencies and the overhead projector
- power point presentations, slides, and illustrations
- single concept film loops and tape recordings
- quality resource personnel

It is salient to provide for the talents and abilities of each pupil. Pupils possess different styles of learning and each must achieve as optimally as possible.

18

CHAPTER

Quality in the Social Studies Curriculum

The social studies needs to be designed carefully and with much thought and deliberation so that the best curriculum possible is implemented for pupils. Within the social studies, pupils need to understand their past (history), the regions which affect them (geography), the political institutions which govern (political science), the economic institutions which provide needed goods and services (economics), the institutions which provide structure and influence in society (sociology), and culture (anthropology). These six social science disciplines provide core knowledge for the learner in ongoing units of study in the social studies. One of three categories of objectives for pupils to achieve are *knowledge* ends; here, the six social science areas provide subject matter for learner achievement. Pupils though instruction may then achieve vital facts, concepts, and generalizations (Ediger and Rao, 2002, 6-11).

Objectives of Instruction

Selected knowledge objectives which pupils may achieye in each social science discipline and emphasized in unit teaching are the following:

- *history:* The pupil will select a present day news happening and provide three events which lead up to the selected occurrence.
- *geography:* The pupil will describe the region where each of the above named events occurred, while using a map and a globe.
- *political science:* The pupil will compare and contrast the system of government being stressed within the region being studied with a different form of government in a removed area.
- *economics:* The pupij will survey the goods and services developed and exchanged within each region.
- *sociology:* The pupil will study, reflect upon, and indicate how religious institutions affect human behavior.
- *anthropology:* The pupil will state how culture (language, customs, attire, music, art, foods eaten, and types of homes, among other items) affect human behavior (Parker, 2001).

Knowledge objectives provide subject matter for pupils to achieve. Subject-matter, here, needs to be relevant and developmental for pupil attainment. Objectives need to be challenging and yet attainable. Worthwhile objectives can come from social scientists, the teacher, and learners. The latter contribute objectives when they raise questions in class for reflection and for problem solving.

A second category of objectives emphasizes *skills* ends. Skills stress the importance of pupils using and applying subject matter (knowledge) acquired in ongoing social studies units of study.' Uses and applications may include the following:

- analyzing. Here, the pupil separates facts from opinions, fantasy from reality, accurate from inaccurate statements, as well as detects band wagon approaches, and political correctness.

- *creative thinking:* This might well involve putting ideas together after taking out the unimportant and irrelevant as in analyzing. Novel and unique ideas also are salient in creative thinking.
- *problem solving:* In problem solving, a problem or dilemma situation is identified, information gathered in answer to the problem, an hypothesis developed, the hypothesis is evaluated and modified if need be.
- *analogizing:* To be able to draw analogies is important. Thus, parallels may be drawn between and among cultures/nations studied, even though differences do exist. But, the differences are not antonyms, but rather relationships may be observed. Many decisions in life are made through the use of rational thinking. Human reason based on knowledge is vital in ongoing units of study. It is important then for pupils to use knowledge in one way or another so that learning does not stress gaining inert ideas. Thus, knowledge may serve practical, recreational, creative, and theoretical purposes (See Ediger and Rao 2002).

A third category of objectives stresses the affective dimension. These kinds of ends emphasize quality attitudes, values, and feelings for pupils to develop. Good attitudes, for example, might stress the following:

- getting along well with others.
- accepting others as having extreme worth.
- using quality human relations approaches in relating well to others.
- assisting others as needed so that each may achieve optimally.
- using language appropriately to achieve objectives, rather than to develop ill will (See National Council for the Social Studies, 2001).

The social studies teacher then must have standards available for all to acquire so that proper behavior in the classroom might result. Each standard needs to be clarified to become meaningful to learners. Pupils need to know which is/is not acceptable behavior in the class-room and in society.

Organization of the Social Studies Curriculum

There are selected ways of organizing units of study in social studies. The oldest approach is the separate subjects pattern. Here, history, for example, alone provides content for ongoing lessons and units. Most social studies educators prefer that subject matter be more connected in designing the curriculum. Thus, geography might be *correlated* with history. Historical events are then taught as occurring in a geographical region. To further relate social science disciplines, the teacher may stress *fusion*. History and geography then may be taught as being related to political science. The type of government of a particular nation/state may then be studied. To further emphasize fusion, economics may be brought into ongoing lessons and units of study. Thus, the economic system of a particular nation might then be taught as related to history, geography, and political science (See Curriculum Advice, 1994). The social studies may also be organized in which all disciplines are brought in to the unit of study such as science, mathematics, art, music, and physical education. Scientific developments such as the great Italian scientist Galileo occurred in a specific period of time such as the 1600s with his experiments pertaining to falling objects from the leaning tower of Pisa. History may not be understood well, of course, unless scientific developments, past and present, are brought into the teaching of social studies.

Social studies educators stress the importance of pupils perceiving knowledge as being related, as compared to the separate subjects approach, due to the following reasons:

- pupils retain learnings longer.

- pupils perceive the relationship of knowledge whereas the social scientist may perceive separation of an academic specialty due to its depth study.
- pupils when engaging in problem solving use whichever academic discipline is needed to arrive at solutions.

Sequence in the Social Studies

The social studies teacher needs to be aware of the sequence or order of learning opportunities presented to pupils to optimalize achievement. A pupil centered sequence may be stressed. Here, the learner with teacher guidance orders his/her own experiences. For example, in reading a unit related social studies library book, the pupil sequences ideas as they are being read. Or in viewing a related AV aid, the pupil achieves order in content being presented through viewing successive open ended scenes. When teacher/pupil planning is being used within a unit of study, the learner is heavily involved in sequencing experiences. The objectives, learning opportunities, and appraisal procedures may then be cooperatively planned by pupils with the assistance of the teacher. A psychological sequence is then in evidence.

Toward the other end of the continuum, the social studies teacher may solely determine the sequence of established objectives, learning activities, and evaluation procedures with little/no pupil input. With the teacher being the decision maker, a logical sequence is being emphasized (Ediger and Rao, 2001, Chapter Two).

Methods of Teaching Social Studies

There are a plethora of methods which may be used in teaching the social studies. Methods used need to be developmentally appropriate and meet the personal needs of pupils. The following are examples of methods to be considered in teaching a specific set of pupils:

- *Explanation:* Explanations need to be given as necessary in an ongoing lesson and unit of study. Young children have a short attention span and cannot benefit from lengthy explanations as can upper elementary age pupils. The teacher must observe learners carefully to notice when to change from the use of explanations to a different method of teaching.
- *Problem-solving:* Problem solving is important in school and in society and thus needs thorough emphasis in the social studies. It takes time to stress quality problem solving procedures in the curriculum, but it has its many values.
- *Inductive method:* From specifics, pupils are guided to come up with a generalization. A questioning approach is used to help pupils arrive at a generalization. The Socratic method, named after Socrates of ancient Athens, is another name for the inductive approach in learning.
- *Deductive method:* Here, pupils are presented with a generalizations and are to achieve related, supportive specifics or details. From the general to the specific is a good clarifier of the deductive method of instruction.
- *Project methods:* Here, the pupils with teacher help plan and make items and objects directly related to the ongoing social studies lesson or unit of study. A hands on procedure in learning is involved with constructing, doing, and making. A laboratory method is another way of describing the project method (See Ediger and Rao, 2000, Chapter Two).

A variety of methods should be used to teach pupils. If pupils attention should wane in a lesson, the teacher may then change to a different method of teaching. Along with the methods of instruction, the social studies teacher may also choose suitable experiences for pupil engagement in the social studies curriculum. Among others, these experiences may include the following within a social studies unit of study:

- reading from the basal text-book, library books, and other print sources.
- dramatizing what has been read (See Emery, 1992).
- constructing models of what is being studied.
- taking excursions which clarify major concepts and generalizations in the social studies.
- writing diary entries, and doing journal writing covering learnings acquired.
- giving individual and committee oral reports on selected social studies topics.
- developing a related mural, individual drawings, and/or water color illustrations.
- making a relief map or model globe using paper' mache.
- doing a flow, organizational, vocabulary, and/or classification chart.
- developing models to indicate what has been learned.

The above-named learning activities need to be developmental together with the appropriate method(s) of instruction. For example, if reading from the textbook is chosen as the learning activity for pupils to pursue with an inductive procedure or method of instruction, then the teacher needs to guide pupils to use the specifics in content read to arrive at a suitable generalization. The generalizations must be supported by specifics or facts (See Banks, 1997).

Assessment of Achievement in the Social Studies

Diverse procedures need to be used to assess pupil achievement. A single approach is not adequate. Different assessment procedures evaluate diverse facets of a learner's achievement.

Thus, a paper/pencil test may assess cognitive learnings such as understanding facts, concepts, and generalizations. Pupil progress in quality attitudinal development cannot be measured adequately with paper/pencil tests, but rather be assessed continually through teacher observation. In addition to required state mandated tests, the following may be used to notice pupil achievement:

- true/false, multiple choice, completion, essay, and matching test items. Validity and reliability are salient in test writing.
- teacher observation of pupil attitudes, social development, and emotional growth in ongoing activities.
- rubric use to assess the quality of discussions, construction work, and art endeavors as related to social studies units of instruction.
- journal writing to assess the quality of committee work.
- diary entries written to show individual achievement in goal attainment within ongoing daily lessons.
- pupil self-appraisal in terms of desired criteria.
- use of performance assessment.
- pupil portfolio development.

Each of the above-named assessment techniques has its place to assess learner achievement and progress. Thus teacher written test items such as true/false cannot measure the affective development of pupils, but teacher observation may be used to determine achievement in learner development of positive feelings toward others.

Assessment should relate directly to the objectives of instruction. It should pinpoint which objectives have/have not been achieved by pupils. Feedback from assessment results provide the teacher with knowledge of what needs to be emphasized in teaching and learning situations. Diagnostic approaches may then be used in that the teacher may remediate what pupils have not attained. The objectives of social studies instruction need to be clearly stated so that assessment may ascertain that which has/has not been acquired. Authentic tasks need to be in evidence, as learning opportunities, to measure pupil achievement. Multiple assessment procedures should be used to notice and verify pupil achievement. Pupils should achieve high standards but the standards need to be achievable (See Wiggins, 1993).

Educational Psychology in the Teaching of Social Studies

Principles of learning taken from educational psychology have much to offer teachers in assisting pupils to achieve more optimally. These principles of learning are to be inherent with the methods of teaching being used as well as the subject matter taught. Also, the objectives, learning opportunities, and the assessment procedures are all interrelated and the principles of learning must become an integral part here, in teaching and learning situations.

To guide pupils to achieve well, the teacher, first of all, needs to guide learners to be actively engaged in ongoing learning experiences. To be engaged is to be interested in ongoing presentations. With a yariety of activities, the teacher may change to a different activity before engagement starts to wane. Interested pupils learn more as compared to those who lack interest.

Second, pupils need to perceive reasons for learning. Reasons for leaning involve perceiving purpose for active participation in the tasks being presented. With purposes inherent, pupils become increasingly more motivated.

Third, pupils need to perceive meaning in each learning experience. Meaning pertains to understanding what is being taught. It also stresses that the pupil accepts the worthwhileness of learning and achieving.

Fourth, pupils individually possess different styles of learning. Learning styles theory (Searson and punn, 2001) has much to offer the teacher in helping pupils achieve objectives of instruction. Vital ingredients here include the following:

1. acceptable noise levels, temperature readings, and informal versus formal seating arrangements.
2. emotional elements such as conformity versus non-conformity, as well as preferences for structure versus choice in terms of what to learn.
3. sociological factors such as studying alone or with others as well as preferring collegial versus a more authoritarian teacher.
4. physiological factors such as using auditory, tactual, and/or kinesthetic ways of learning. Included are moving around or sitting still as well as eating versus not eating, while concentrating on the involved task.
5. psychological factors such as analytic learners who focus on facts in a step by step fashion which leads to an understanding, as compared to global learners who desire to understand what is learned and then how it relates to themselves before focusing on facts. Analytic learners respond best to printed words whereas global learners respond better to illustrations and pictures.

REFERENCES

Banks, James A. (1997), *Educating Citizens in a Multicultural Society*. New York: Teachers College Press.

Curriculum Advice (1994), *Geography for Life; National Geography Standards*. Washington, DC: National Council for Geographic Education.

Emery, Donna W. (1992), "ChildrerTs Understanding of Story Characters," *Reading Improvement*, 29 (1), 2- 9.

Ediger, Marlow (2002), "The Teaching of Social Studies," *Edutracks*, 1(6) 6- 11.

Ediger, Marlow, and D. Bhaskara Rao (2000), *Teaching Reading Successfully*. New Delhi, India: Discovery Publishing House, Chapter Two.

Ediger, Marlow, and D. Bhaskara Rao (2001), *Teaching Social Studies Successfully*. New Delhi, India: Discovery Publishing House, Chapter One.

Ediger, Marlow, and D. Bhaskara Rao (2001), *Teaching Science Successfully*. New Delhi, India: Discovery Publishing House, Chapter Two.

National Council for the Social Studies (2001), *Curriculum Standards for Social Studies*. Washington, DC: NCSS, pp 3-6. Excerpted from the Original by Walter C. Parker, and John Jarolimek

Parker, Walter C. (2001) *Social Studies in Elementary Education*. Upper Saddle River, New Jersey: Merrill, Prentice Hall, Chapter Four.

Searson, Robert, and Rita Dunn (2001), "The Learning Styles Teaching Model," *Science and Children*, 38 (5), 22-26.

Wiggins, Grant (1993), *Assessing Student Performance: Exploring the Purpose and Limits of Testing*. San Francisco: Jossey - Bass.

19

CHAPTER

Reading Creatively in the Social Studies

Creative reading in the social studies is important since much interpretation of concepts and generalizations are required. The social studies does not have the objectivity which science and mathematics content possess. To be sure, the social studies has its precise names, dates, and places, as well as geography containing parallels, meridians, longitude, and latitude on maps and globes with precision, but with events and happenings in foreign policy, for example, creative interpretations are necessary as well as actions therein. For example in viewing a solution to the Palestinian Arab/Israeli conflict over the land of Palestine, the conflict continues to linger on over the decades. There have been a plethora of solutions offered here, but none has been implemented/ worked. There is none in sight presently. Creativity is needed to solve problems in this case and a myriad of others (Ediger, 2003).

Reading Subject Matter Creatively

One must have adequate background information to come up with creative solutions to problems. Thus in reading from a carefully chosen basal, pupils must experience readiness. New subject matter learnings need to be related to previously acquired content. This should be done as seamlessly as possible. Thus, the social studies teacher needs to introduce new concepts for pupil viewing and discussing. This provides necessary background information for reading from the textbook. Thus, for example, the following must be seen in print so that they will be recognized in the ensuing reading experience:

- *the land of Palestine:* A map should clearly show the boundaries and neighboring nations.
- *Israel:* With its present boundaries together with the occupied West Bank need to be seen by learners on a large map.
- *Palestinian Arab refugees:* These locations may be viewed on a map of Palestine together with refugee camps in Jordan, Egypt, Syria, and Lebanon.
- *the Jordan River:* This river separates the nations Jordan and Israel.
- *the walled city of Jerusalem:* This city has a surrounding wall two and one-half miles in length (Ediger, 2010).

Pupils need clarification of ideas when questions arise. Inductively the teacher assists pupils to develop knowledge and skills in these situations. If a question arises pertaining to the fundamental beliefs of Islam, the following questions might well lead to tentative answers:

- Why do devout followers make a pilgrimage once, as a minimum, during their lifetime to Mecca, Saudi, Arabia? Here, pupils may be guided to read about the birthplace of their Prophet Mohammed in AD 570, his flight from enemies (the Hegira) to Medina where he was later entombed in AD 632; in the meantime, he returned to his native Mecca. The recordings, in the *Koran* of Mohammed's messages, were received as he meditated in a cave just outside of Mecca. Additional information, from a variety of reference sources, may be added as needed to assist pupils in arriving at conclusions.

- Why do Imams call the faithful to prayer five times a day from a minaret?
- What is the importance of Mount Moriah, located inside the Dome of the Rock sacred to both Jews and Arabs?
- Why is the Church of the Holy Sepulchre sacred to devout followers of Christianity?

In each of the above, the social studies teacher needs to help, but not provide direct information to each question/problem. Creativity is involved in finding unique solutions to problems. Developmentally appropriate assistance must be provided. *Scaffolding* is an excellent concept to use here in that the teacher might well guide pupils through small progressive steps to secure an answer. The scaffold moves a pupil from where he/she is in achievement presently to some reasonable higher expectation. The learner's own creative thought propels the individual to reach out and upward to a desired level of accomplishment. Success in achievement is salient when the self concept is involved in creative thought. Pupils also need to respect each others ideas in order for novel ideas to come forth. Ridiculing and rudeness have no roles to play in the social studies curriculum. They hinder in productivity of ideas. Creativity thrives when pupils feel free to think and then come up with unique ideas for problem solving (See Shanklin and Rhodes, 1989).

Brain storming is an excellent procedure to use in stimulating creativity. The more ideas presented, the better in brainstorming. For instance, pupils may be encouraged to come up with as many responses as possible for the following:

- Why do both Palestinian Arabs and Israel want to govern, within a state/nation, the land of Palestine?

- Why is most of the land of Palestine hilly and mountainous? The triangular shaped Plains of Esdraelen in contrast, twenty by twenty by thirty miles, is quite level and free from protruding limestone rocks.

Motivating and assisting pupils when needed is important, but ideas must come from pupils when creative endeavors are being implemented. The social studies teacher must know at what point to intervene so that learners have needed knowledge to pursue ensuing thoughts (See, De Roche and Kostelay, 2006).

Written Work and Creativity

There are myriad ways in which pupils may proceed with writing activities. Poetry certainly can and does emphasize unique approaches in presenting ideas. The teacher needs to assist pupils to recognize what makes for each type of poem as the printed poem is compared with other types of verse. The following guidelines are provided for poetry writing:

- pupils inductively should attach meaning to each kind of poem.
- they need to observe carefully how the teacher models the writing of a poem being emphasized in the ongoing unit of study.
- the teacher must find motivating approaches in assisting pupils to write poetry enthusiastically.
- enjoyment of diverse forms of poetry is salient as well as pupils desiring to write different kinds of verse.
- liking novel, unique ideas is of utmost importance (Ediger, 2006).

There are selected pupils who prefer rhyme in verse such as is true in writing couplets (two lines with ending words rhyming), triplets (three lines with ending words rhyming), quatrains with all four lines having rhyme), and limericks (lines one, two, and five rhyme whereas lines three and four rhyme).

(See Tiedt, 1982). As an example, the following triplet written by a sixth grader reveals ending words rhyming:

The City of Amman
It bustles with cars in a busy nation
With over one million people in population
It strives to grow even more as individuals show elation.

In each of these poems, pupils utilize acquired subject matter in writing verse. Syllabication might also be used in poetry writing such as haiku containing five, seven, five syllables respectively for each of three lines, whereas a tanka contains five, seven, five, seven, seven syllables respectively for each of five lines of verse. The following haiku, for instance, was also written by a pupil in grade six:

Bedouin in the Dessert
Living in black tents
With camels nibbling sagebrush
Hoping for a rain.

Alliteration may be inserted as words within any poem written. Thus two or more sequential words beginning with the same initial sound make for alliteration such as "Donkeys doing neighs." Imagery may also be added to a poem. Here, a creative comparison is made such as "Clear skies in a dessert look as if *perfection reigns in the universe.*" "Clear skies" is compared with "perfection in the the universe." Pupils enjoy making creative comparisons when the concept of "imagery" is being emphasized in reading and writing poetry. Social studies teachers need to stress diverse poetry concepts when reading poems aloud as well as writing them as models for all to see clearly in the classroom (See Palinscar, *et al.*, 1986).

Free verse is easier to write with no rhyme, nor number of syllables, or number of lines per poem. One form of free verse is for pupils to write acrostic poems. For each poem, the social studies teacher needs to provide a good model and this may be done orally as learners listen and observe intently when the poem is printed. The writer when supervising university student teachers in the public schools notice a sixth grader who wrote the following acrostic choosing the word Jordan (printed vertically) a nation east of the Jordan River:

Jordan whose capital city is Amman
Olive trees produce well in the Mediteranean world
Rice is a leading food eaten.
Dead Sea water contains about 25% salt content
A land of many hills and valleys as well as dessert
Nomads herd sheep and goats within a modern nation.

The above acrostic poem indicates the pupil has learned much about the Middle East area of the world. Each line states important information about the nation of Jordan. Novel drawings may also be made of poetry written as well as of other creative works such as a short novel or short story.

REFERENCES

De Roche, and Susan Kostelay (2006), "An Adventure in Problem Based Learning," *Phi Delta Kappan,* 87 (9), 708.

Ediger, Marlow Ediger (2003), *Teaching Social Studies Successfully*. New Delhi, India: Discovery Publishing House.

Ediger, Marlow (2006), "Testing Versus Portfolios to Assess Achievement," *OASCD Journal,* 13 (1), 31-32.

Ediger, Marlow (2010), "Issues in the Social Studies," *International Journal of Educational Research, Development and Extension,* 1 (1), 43-49.

Palinscar, *et al.,* (1986), *Teaching Reading As Thinking*. Alexandria, Virginia: Association For Supervision and Curriculum Development.

Shanklin, N. L, and L. K. Rhodes (1989), "Comprehension Instruction in Sharing and Extending," *The Reading Teacher,* 42 (1) 496-500.

Tiedt, Iris M. (1982), *The Language Arts Handbook*. Englewood Cliffs, New Jersey: Prentice Hall, Inc.

20

CHAPTER

Student Notebooks and the Social Studies

Students need to do well in keeping notebooks with entries on the present unit of study being emphasized. These entries assist pupils to summarize what has been learned as well as review previous subject matter studied. They, also, help students to review main ideas and subordinate ideas gleaned from the ongoing lessons and unit. Writing skills in notebook development need adequate emphasis and these promote learner achievement, useful in school and in society. Different major objectives are then attained in the curriculum pertaining to the cognitive domain as well as skills in written work (Ediger, 2010).

Social Studies Notebooks and the Learner

Social studies notebooks may be stressed in electronic form or in traditional procedures. The content therein must be chosen carefully by the involved student. Only salient items should be recorded and dated. One daily entry should include major generalizations. Thus in a unit on the Middle East, the student might record that the Holy Land is very mountainous with one area being level and suitable for cultivation. This area is the Plains of Esdraelen, a triangle being thirty miles, by thirty miles, by forty miles for each side in dimension. It is located directly southeast of the modern city of Haifa. Depending upon the *developmental level* of the student, the written work may continue with cultivated crops raised here, such as wheat and barley (Ediger and Rao, 2010).

In the notebook, poetry related to the unit being studied may be recorded, such as the following unrhymed four line quatrain written by a talented sixth grader:

A Dairy Farm on the Kibbutz
Many Holstein cows wait to be milked and fed
With pipeline milking machines, the milk flows on
To the bulk holding tank waiting in the storage room
Where a truck will haul it away to a processing plant.

Many poems rhyme and pupils do enjoy writing this type of verse, written by a fifth grade pupil:

Tilling the Land on a Kibbutz
Tractors roar in disking and seeding the field
In hopes of growing crops with a high yield
The wheat and barley grew well and produce much
With feelings there was a magical touch.

In the above quatrain, lines one and two rhyme whereas lines three and four rhyme. Essential social studies content must be in each poem whether it be free verse, a couplet, triplet, quatrain, limerick, haiku, and/or tanka (See Tiedt, 1982, on poetry writing).

The notebook belongs to the involved learner with the teacher serving as a guide and stimulates achievement. The writer when supervising university student teachers in the public schools observed poetry writing as was emphasized in ongoing units of study, and as prerequisites, students must have experienced:

- listening to and reading the type of poetry to be stressed in social studies units of study

- analyzing what makes for each type of poem to be written such as a limerick or a haiku
- being ready for writing poetry. Learnings always should be developmental appropriate
- scaffolding used to achieve challenging objectives (See Risko and Dalhouse, 2010).

New vocabulary terms should be written in the notebook. Thus, students may experience the following pertaining to the Crusades in the Middle Ages:

- noblemen, serfs, hermits, and slaves
- the Church of the Holy Sepulchre, Mount Moriah, Synagogues, Muslims, monasteries, among other relevant terms
- castles, moats, peasants,and armies.

Each vocabulary item must be meaningful to the learner and make sense. Small illustrations (drawn; digital; and/or others) may be placed next to each entry in the social studies notebook. It also is good to have each vocabulary term be printed and placed on a classroom word wall. Many pupils will look at these words periodically and, thus, review and ask related questions. The notebook entries and the word wall are very important in assisting pupils in vocabulary development and retention of learnings (See NSTA Reports, May, 2010).

Assignments should also be included in a social studies notebook. Students should make it appoint to fulfil these requirements when due. Proper study habits must be encouraged a young age with sequential progress made in time. Note taking needs to be demonstrated by the teacher. A taped recording of discussion may provide the setting here. Students need to view the model carefully and be guided in note taking. Note taking skills are very poignant since students then might review and rehearse the content prior to each lesson. New subject-matter presented provides background information for ensuing main and subordinate subject-matter content. Notes also provide a salient basis in studying for an upcoming test. Summarizing information when taking notes is a relevant skill for attending university classes at a later time. The notes indicate what is perceived as being vital ideas from classroom presentations (See Medina and Costa, 2010).

The social studies notebook may also contain information in graphic form. Bar graphs, for example, showing population growth of nations studied provide content on trends and assist students to infer what might be likely to accrue in time. Line graphs might reveal growth in goods and serves produced yearly or during longer units of time by a specific nation or several countries studied in ongoing lessons and units of studies. Picture graphs may indicate the number of students attending school in a nation. When readiness is in evidence, circle graphs may be used to show relevant data on a certain topic (See Parker, 2001).

Charts made might well be incorporated into a notebook. Thus, the following charts, directly related to an ongoing unit of study may become a part of the notebook:

- a narrative chart with related illustrations and a brief description for each may contain sequential information on agricultural methods, i.e. disking the farm land, seeding the crop to be grown, harvesting the grain, and storing the harvested crops.
- a flow chart with related pictures showing change at a specific point, such as petroleum being refined and at different temperature readings providing kerosene, gasoline of different grades, diesel fuel, and home heating fuel.
- a foods chart showing traditional meals and delicacies eaten in the Middle East, i.e. Kousa (rice and lamb's meat cooked in an inside removed tomato, egg plant, among others), masche[1] (rice cooked inside of grape leaves), as well as baklava, a well known desert. Dates and figs are also eaten.

- a classification chart with categories and related illustrations pertaining to well known structures inside the walled city of Jerusalem such as (the Dome of the Rock, an octagonal mosque with a gold plaited dome, built in AD 691, covering Mount Moriah where the Patriarch Abraham was tempted to offer his son Ishmael according to devout Muslims); the Western Wall, holy to devout believers in Judaism, which is the only remnant of the ancient Jewish temple; the Church of the Holy Sepulcher, which contains the tomb of Christ, according to devout Christians. The classification chart might also include languages spoken, well known personalities, and digital pictures of art (See National Council for the Social Studies, 1997).

Children's literature containing informational books correlates well with ongoing units of study. A wide variety of selections need to be available on diverse reading levels to provide for individual differences. Different topics must, also, be there. For example, if a unit on the Middle East is being taught, then developmentally appropriate books need to be in the offing on topics such as urban living, the bedouin, village life, agriculture, manufacturing, desert life, and education. The social studies teacher needs to introduce selected library books enthusiastically with voice inflection. Also, social studies library books may be read aloud during story time. The teacher must evaluate if approaches used motivate pupils to read and achieve. Students may keep written reports of library books read. The reports need to be dated and a related bar graph kept to encourage more reading in time. The social studies teacher might well model writing a book report containing essential ideas gleaned. Students should pay careful attention to the model as it is presented sequentially. Students will be at diverse levels of accomplishments in reading library books and in writing reviews/summaries. High expectations, within reason, must be emphasized.

Digital illustrations of completed committee work might be included in the notebook. Also, a video tape would indicate the quality of oral interactions. Thus, the committee endeavors may reveal the following:

- how well each student stayed on the topic at hand
- contributions made by each member
- knowledge and skill presented which directly relate to the topic discussed
- respect and acceptance of others on the committee
- assisting the small group to move forward in the discussion setting.

The writer has presented selected ideas for learnings to become a part of a student's notebook. There are, of course, additional entries which may be included. The student's notebook should reveal what has been accomplished during a specific interval of time.

REFERENCES

Costa, Carmen I., and Maria del Rocio Costa, (2001), "Collaborative Voices Exploring Culturally and Socially Responsive Literacies," *Language Arts,* 87 (4), 263-276.

Ediger, Marlow (2010), "Constructivism in the Social Studies," *Edutracks*,9(7),13-14.

Ediger, Marlow, and D. Bhaskara Rao (2010), *The Effective School Curriculum.* New Delhi, India: Discovery Publishing House.

National Council for the Social Studies (1997), *Curriculum Standards for the Social Studies.* Edison, New York: Whitehurst and Clark.

NSTA Reports (May, 2010), "Enhancing Learning with Science Notebooks," Arlington, Virginia: National Science Teachers Association.

Parker, Walter C. (2001), *Social Studies in Elementary Education*. Upper Saddle River, New Jersey: Merrill, Prentice Hall.

Risko, Victoria, and Doris Walker-Dalhouse (2010), Reading Research into the Classroom," *The Reading Teacher*, 63(5), 420-423.

Tiedt, Iris M. (1982), *The Language Arts Handbook.* Englewood Cliffs, New Jersey: Prentice Hall, Inc.

21

CHAPTER

Reading in the Content Areas

Reading in the content areas is a basic in the curriculum. To learn and achieve optimally in any academic discipline, pupils need to be able to read well. The ability to read well involves a plethora of knowledge, skills, and attitudes. There are numerous components then to the act of reading. Teachers need to be aware of what is involved in pupils learning to read and be able to analyze its specific parts. Reading is a complex whole to describe and it may be analyzed in different ways depending upon the philosophy of the teacher.

Content Reading and the Measurement Movement

Measurement of instruction involves the use of highly specific objectives in reading instruction. These objectives are selected prior to instruction. Precision of objectives is necessary so that the teacher may measure, if after instruction, learners have/have not achieved the stated objectives. If the pupil has not achieved an objective, a different teaching strategy needs to be used. The learning activities in reading are closely aligned with the objectives of instruction. Measurement is emphasized in terms of the stated objectives. Thus, the teacher measures if the pupil has/has not achieved an objective.

With a measurement philosophy of instruction, the following are important to consider:

1. whatever exists, exists in some amount, and this amount then can be measured. The world of science stresses measurability of elements in the universe. The planet earth is made up of some 107 elements and these can be combined to form molecules. Any molecule can be expressed in numerical terms of the number of elements in each. Water, for example, contains two atoms of hydrogen and one atom of oxygen, resulting in the formula—Ha O. The smallest unit of measurement for an element is the atom.
2. achievement in student learning can be measured to determine what has been learned. For example, in state mandated tests, a pupil may be on the composite score of the fiftieth percentile, meaning that fifty percent are below and fifty percent are above that pupil from the total number of individuals who completed taking the test in the pilot study.
3. the standard error of measurement may be determined of the state mandated test. Thus, how consistently the test measures be it split half, alternative forms, or test/ retest reliability and may be ascertained statistically with a standard error of measurement from pilot study data. A pupil's percentile score might then vary plus or minus depending upon the size of the standard error of measurement. Pertaining to one state in the union's test results involving margin of error or standard error of measurement, Keller (Education Week, February 6, 2002) wrote the following:

   Montgomery County (Maryland), the State's largest district with 130,000 students, was the first to raise the alarm about the scores. The percentage of students in the district just outside Washington scoring at a satisfactory level dipped last year to 51 per cent, about four percentage points lower than the year before.

But state officials have stressed that the margin of error for the scores ranges from *two percentage points* for the state to as many as 14 for a small school.

They also have suggested that the lack of test-score increases may be linked to the fact that schools across the state have more disadvantaged students and fewer experienced teachers.

4. validity of the states' mandated test may be ascertained with pupils' results being correlated with results from the National Assessment of Educational Progress (NAEP). To increase validity, the teacher needs to align the local curriculum with the state standards or objectives of instruction.

It is quite obvious, from the above discussion, that testing pupil achievement stresses preciseness, statistical measurability, and quantification. With the testing and measurement movement, the teacher continually directs the reading activities for pupils in order that predetermined objectives are attained by learners. Wiersma (1991) wrote the following:

> The term statistics has multiple meanings in educational research but probably its simplest meaning is "bits of information." If one says that 632 students are enrolled in a specific school, this can be considered a statistic. The salary schedule and the number of teachers at each salary level for a district are sometimes called salary statistics.
>
> Statistics has a much broader meaning than simply bits of information, however. It also refers to the theory, procedures, and methodology by which data are summarized. It has been suggested that to some people, the terminology of statistics seems like a foreign language; although this may be true, the understanding and use of statistics is not so much a matter of

identifying new terminology and symbols for already known concepts as it is a way of reasoning and drawing conclusions. Although the lay person often views statistics as an accumulation of facts and figures, the researcher sees statistics as the methods used to describe data and make sense out of them.

Content Reading and Problem-solving

Problem-solving stresses flexible steps in the identification and finding solutions to a problem (See Dewey, 1916). In context, pupils in a committee setting identify a problem. The problem is open ended and requires a solution. Deliberation is involved in problem solving activities. The problem needs to be clearly defined so it is possible of being solved. This is done in a discussion setting. Reading is one avenue of securing information to solve the problem. The content chosen from reading must relate directly as a solution to the problem. An hypothesis or tentative answer to the problem is developed. The hypothesis is evaluated in a life like situation involving a variety of life like experiences, including reading. If the hypothesis stands up in the evaluation process, it is accepted. If not, a new hypothesis may be developed and evaluated. The steps of problem-solving given here are flexible, not an absolute.

Problem-solving approaches in learning are based on pupil's experiences, not externally determined objectives of instruction nor from testing. Thus, pupils with teacher guidance are heavily involved in determining and solving the identified problem.

Problem-solving emphasizes the following:

1. pupils with teacher guidance helping to determine the curriculum with flexible steps of identifying and securing solutions to problems.
2. pupils being assisted to obtain information to arrive at solutions.

3. pupils being involved in practical learning opportunities.
4. pupils having adequate chances to apply that which has been learned.

Throughout problem solving activities, reading is one experience for learning along with others. School and society are not to be separated, but integrated. What is useful in society provides objectives and experiences in the curriculum. In society, too, committees and groups are involved in problem solving experiences; thus, pupils need to learn to work harmoniously with others in the school setting.

In problem solving philosophy in reading, the teacher assists, encourages, and motivates pupils to engage in the identification and finding solutions to dilemma situations. Evelyn Dewey (1919), daughter of John Dewey, wrote the following:

> The development of a democracy demands that nothing be done to interfere with the fluidity of the population: there must be no barriers built between different groups and occupations; everything must be kept as open as possible to promote free and sympathetic communication. This demands common interests among all the people; and the strongest common interests among all the people; and the strongest common interest between people widely separated by space and occupation is the evolution of their government to the satisfaction of them all.

Content Reading and the Individual

Individualized instruction is advocated by selected educators in that optimal opportunities be given to the pupil to select and sequence his/her very own learning activities. Content reading may then be stressed in a personalized reading curriculum. Here, there are an adequate number of content or expository materials from which the pupil may select what to read in a sequential manner. Purposes for reading reside within the learner. The teacher may assist the learner to develop background information for reading by discussing a few illustrations in the library book or related pictures from a CD ROM. Otherwise, motivation for reading comes from within the pupil, not from externally imposed sources. The pupil may reveal comprehension from reading by choosing from the following procedures, among others:

1. writing a summary covering subject-matter read.
2. doing a related art project.
3. making objects, such as a diorama, to show main ideas acquired.
4. participating in a dramatization experience to reveal major concepts obtained.
5. video taping a personal research project based on subject matter read in the content areas.
6. cassette recording of expository selections from books being read aloud.
7. planning and implementing a bulletin board display pertaining to thematic books read.
8. having a conference with the teacher to appraise oral reading and comprehension quality.
9. choosing others to do a mural on collaborative reading completed.
10. self selecting a way to indicate comprehension such as journal writing of ideas apquired by the pupil (See Santman, 2002).

Individualized procedures of reading instruction emphasize the pupil as the major person in developing the curriculum. The teacher stimulates and assists in pupil learning and achievement. Individualizing the reading curriculum is open ended and is quite opposite of the measurement movement.

It stresses the importance of the learner being the focal point of instruction. Societal needs are of lesser importance than meeting the needs of the individual pupil. The interests and needs of the pupil come first in developing a reading curriculum. The teacher is a supporter of learning of the pupil. Pupils need to:

1. become skilful in the art of choosing and decision making.
2. assume responsibility for decisions made.
3. accept others as having extreme worth.
4. realize self fulfilment in terms of goals, learning opportunities, and evaluation procedures stressed in reading content (Ediger, 1995, p. 153)

Content Reading and Perennialism

Perennialism emphasizes pupils reading the classics to achieve knowledge, skills, and attitudinal objectives of instruction. The classics represent literature which has stood the test of time. Recently written literature does not come under the topical heading of the classics. The writings of Plato, Aristotle, Nathaniel Hawthorne, Henry Wadsworth Longfellow, Robert Louis Stevenson, among other examples, represent classical writings. Perennialism stresses a highly academic program of reading. Thus, a stimulating academic reading program needs to be in eyidence emphasizing vital, enduring ideas of the past. Cultivation of the intellect or mind becomes a major objective in reading instruction. Pupils need to read and reflect upon worthwhile ideas of great minds and writers of the past whose enduring ideas stimulate thinking. Perennialists believe in pupils reading the classics for the following reasons:

1. they have stood the test of time and place. These writings are still very salient presently.
2. they remain important today whereas recently written literature may not survive in terms of being salient.

3. they are written by the best of minds.
4. they provide pupils with common background information which all need as general education, before moving on to an area of specialization.

Pertaining to Mortimer Adler's Paideia Proposal (1990). Tanner and Tanner wrote the following:

> The perennialist's refusal to consider the nature of the learner in developing the curriculum is reflected in the *Paideia Proposal.* Instead of seeing childhood and youth as a distinct phase of human development requiring uniquely appropriate experiences for effective growth, childhood and youth are regarded as obstacles to be gotten over with as quickly as possible. "Youth itself is the most serious impediment- fact, youth is an inseparable obstacle to being an educated person," declares the Proposal. The Proposal goes on to call for twelve years of basic schooling for all, capped by the Socratic study of great literary works and other works of art. This kind of learning "aims at raising the mind up from a lesser or weaker understanding to a stronger and fuller one," and the "art of the teacher depends upon an understanding of how the mind learns by the exercise of its own power," declares Adler, as though the mind exists as a separate entity.

Perennialists advocate pupils studying the great ideas of the ancient world, the renaissance, and the age of the enlightenment. These ideas have endured as being worthwhile whereas recent writings may soon end up in oblivion. The changeless and the eternal are to be preferred to the transitory and changing ideas. A non-vocational curriculum needs to be in evidence. Vocational and professional training comes after the great ideas of the past have been studied. Reading and reflecting ocratically upon the classics provides pupils with what will remain in time and space. Reading in the content areas then emphasizes that which is vital and relevant subject matter.

With different philosophies of instruction, it behooves the teacher to study each diligently and come up with what will assist pupils individually to achieve as optimally as possible.

REFERENCES

Dewey, Evelyn (1919), *New Schools for Old: The Regeneration of the Porter School*. New York: E. P. Dutton and Company, p. 336.

Dewey, John (1916) *Democracy and Education*. New York: The Macmillan Company.

Ediger, Marlow (1995), *Philosophy in Curriculum Development*. Kirksville, Missouri: Simpson Publishing Company, p. 153.

Keller, Bess (February 6, 2002), "Controversy Surrounds Release of Maryland Test Results," *Education Week*, 21 (21), p. 19.

Santman, Donna (2002), "Teaching to the Test?: Test Preparation in the Reading Workshop," *Language Arts*, 79 (3), 203-211.

Tanner, Daniel, and Laurel Tanner (1990), *History of the School Curriculum*. New York: The Macmillan Publishing Company, p. 133.

Wiersma, William (1991), *Research Methods in Education*. Fifth Edition. Boston: Allyn and Bacon, pp. 306-307.

22

CHAPTER

Reading Aloud to Aid Pupil Achievement

There are numerous times for the teacher to read aloud to pupils to assist them to achieve more optimally. The teacher needs to plan carefully *when* pupils gain from the read alouds. He/she must also give much thought to *what* to read orally to pupils. The manner or method of reading aloud indicate• further necessary planning on the teacher's part. What might be selected relevant answers to these problems?

Reading Library Books Aloud to Pupils

There are a plethora of times for the teacher to read orally to pupils. Generally after lunch, teachers read aloud during story time which may be fifteen to twenty minutes in duration. The library books used here may pertain to all curriculum areas such as literature, social studies, science, and mathematics. But there are also excellent library books dealing with art, music, and physical education. The teacher may even choose a library book which correlates with what is being taught in science, for example. The book chosen for the read aloud needs to capture pupil attention. Little is gained if pupils become inattentive. For young children, the teacher should face the pupils being read to and read aloud peripherally, whereby he/she can observe the children as well as the print discourse. It is good, too, for these learners to see the illustrations clearly contained in the book in the ongoing read aloud. For intermediate grade pupils, the teacher should also observe pupils carefully during the read aloud to notice if interest is developed and maintained in the oral reading activity. There will be fewer illustrations in library books read to intermediate grade pupils. However, when feasible, they do need to be shared with pupils in the ongoing reading experience.

When library books are chosen for oral reading, the following criteria need to be adhered to:

1. the sequential library books read aloud need to capture and uphold pupil attention and interest.
2. the books read are on the understanding level of involved pupils.
3. the books help pupils to increase their listening vocabularies.
4. the books are meaningful to pupils and use can be made of their ideas and contents.
5. the books do provide for pupils of diverse reading and listening levels of achievement.
6. the books provide followup experiences to clarify ideas and build background information.
7. the books provide opportunities for higher levels of cognition such as critical and creative thinking as well as problem solving.
8. the books chosen for the read aloud may be a guidance source for pupils such as in bibliotherapy.
9. the books and their contents emphasize perceived purpose for pupils being read to.
10. the books selected foster a life long desire for reading on the part of pupils (Ediger and Rao, 2001, Chapter Eight).

Reading aloud to pupils should make for attentiveness on the part of listeners. A monotonous sounding voice destroys reading interest. The teacher then needs to use proper voice inflection including appropriate stress, pitch, and juncture in the read aloud. Clarity in oral reading to pupils is a must. The rate of reading speed needs to give pupils time to comprehend ideas read. Sometimes, teachers read aloud too rapidly and listeners cannot take in vital ideas as is necessary for quality comprehension. The rate of reading speed might also be too slow whereby pupils lose interest in the subject matter. Teacher enthusiasm needs to be manifested in the read aloud. Ideas gleaned by pupils should provide opportunities for application, retention and use of acquired subject matter (See Ediger, 2002, 20-21).

Beck and Me Keown (2002) indicate the following which assists read alouds to be successful:

- awareness of the distinction between constructing meaning of ideas in a text and simply retrieving information from the text;
- understanding the difficulty of the task young children face in gaining meaning from decontextualized language;
- designing questions that encourage children to talk about and connect ideas and developing followup questions that scaffold, building meaning from those ideas.
- helping students to meaningfully incorporate their background knowledge and reduce the kind of surface association of knowledge that brings forth a hodgepodge of personal anecdotes;
- awareness of how pictures can draw attention away from processing the linguistic content in a text, and thus attention to the timing of the use of pictures; and

- taking advantage of the sophisticated words found in trade books by using them as a source of explicit vocabulary activities.

Although reading a story to children is not a difficult task for a literate adult, taking advantage of the read aloud experience to develop children's literacy is a complex task. Even with awareness of what makes reading aloud most effective, it is difficult to keep discussions consistently focused on the most productive features. Especially for young children, there is much to manage in conducting a good read-aloud discussion. Key to the task is keeping important text ideas in focus while monitoring children's often limited responses and scaffolding their ideas toward constructing meaning.

Reading Aloud to introduce SSR and Individualized Reading

SSR (sustained silent reading) emphasizes that all pupils in a school, or even in the whole school building, choose a library book to read and have it ready for reading at a given designated time. The purpose of all reading at the same time, teachers included in a classroom, is to serve as a model for pupils.

Prior to pupils making selections for reading, the teacher needs to briefly introduce selected books to readers. The teacher may read aloud to pupils a paragraph from a few of these chosen library books. Good methods and procedures need to be used in these introductions. Readers are then to become motivated to choose and read library books.

Individualized reading goes one step beyond that of SSR in that pupils individually or in groups have conferences with the teacher after the completion of reading a library book. Group conferences may be held with the teacher if these pupils, for example, have read the same paperback. The teacher may then evaluate comprehension and oral reading skills of the learner involved in the conference. Thus, in the individualized reading program, the teacher may also introduce selected library books and read short selections therefrom aloud to whet pupil attitudes for reading. With individualized reading, the pupil:

1. owns the reading curriculum by choosing his/her very own library books to read.
2. may select books personally to read which are interesting and on his/her reading level.
3. may pace reading speed according to what can be readily comprehended.
4. appraises the self in terms of reading achievement in SSR, and in individualized reading with teacher assistance.
5. sequences his/her own reading achievement with personal selections of library books made.

The teacher in individualized reading monitors and assists pupils in word recognition and comprehension tasks. Here, the teacher's job is even more important that in large group instruction since each pupil needs to be on task and improving in reading skills.

Reading Aloud with Basal Textbooks Used

The teacher has important read aloud tasks, among a plethora of instructional decisions, in the basal text curriculum. Thus, the teacher may

1. read aloud a salient selection within a topic or theme which is deemed important for all to understand. The selection may have difficult words or ideas which, otherwise, may be difficult to read.
2. read aloud a few sentences which contain new words for pupils to recognize and understand. These sentences

come from the basal and may be written on the chalkboard, as the new unit or story is being introduced. Pupils are then aided in seeing the new words in print before reading silently.

3. read aloud paragraphs from the summary or conclusion, from the basal, to help pupils review that which had been learned previously. Comparisons may be made of pupils' versus the writer's summary/conclusions.
4. read the topical headings and subheads of an expository writing to be read by pupils. Learners should follow along in their own books as the teacher reads these aloud.
5. read aloud enumerated items in the text contained in the book as pupils follow along with the teacher doing the oral reading (See Ediger and Rao, 2001, Chapter Six).

If the textbook selection being read allows itself to being presented collectively in reader's theater, then the teacher should read aloud together with pupils each speaking part prior to giving the presentation to an audience. The narrator's part should also be read aloud cooperatively, initially, to practice excellence in pupil's presentation. Reader's theater can be an excellent way for pupils to read orally their respective role part with proper stress, pitch, juncture, and enthusiasm.

The Class/School Bulletin Board

There are important bulletin board items which need to e read aloud to pupils. These might be selected writings underneath an illustration which are complex to read. They may be read aloud by the teacher to pupils. The teacher here needs to observe pupils carefully if it appears that good listening is taking place. Periodically, sequential pupils may be asked to repeat and review what has been read aloud. The read aloud content is vital for pupils to understand so that meaning is attached to an ongoing unit of study.

Inservice Oral Reading for Parents and Paraprofessionals

Abilities and skills to do well in read alouds need to be learned and practised. The author has known school systems which have offered successfully inservice programmes for parents and paraprofessionals to do well in reading aloud effectively to children. Modelling and practising was used to assist parents and paraprofessionals to read well orally to pupils. In the inservice education approach, the following procedures were discussed and then practised by participants:

1. how to choose good literature for the read aloud. The reading materials need to be appealing to youngsters.
2. how to introduce the library book or reading selection to pupils.
3. how to obtain learner attention to what is being read.
4. how to use the illustrations for the good of the successful read aloud experience.
5. how to read aloud at a rate whereby a pupil will attach meaning to subject matter read (See Ediger, 1993, 4-6).

Much needs too be done in getting parents more involved in helping their offspring to achieve well. The school seemingly has increased responsibilities which, no doubt, the home should take care of. Kpehler and Banner (2002), as written in the February, 2000 issue of the Principal, published by the National Association of Elementary School Principals, stated the following:

> In November 2001, we held a series of four Parent Reading Connection sessions held at Kirksville Primary

from 6 to 7:30 PM Thursday evenings. Each evening event included a light supper for the family, child care, parent training sessions, and student monitoring.

In the parent training sessions, parents learned the best reading strategies to use with their children and practical training sessions, and student monitoring.

In the parent training sessions, parents learned the best reading strategies to use with their children, received materials to use at home, worked with other parents, and practiced using some of the strategies. In addition, students came for 12 one hour sessions after school, three times a week during November. Transportation home was provided through grant money. Six teachers, a high school student and an administrator worked with the students. The grant was funded by a Goals 2000 grant.

To determine which students qualified for the special services, each classroom teacher and the reading teachers conducted leveled reading assessments. Using previous data as a baseline, the scores were evaluated by the team of teachers, Title 1 specialists and an administrator to determine participants. Students who were reading more than one grade level below expected grade level were invited to participate. The administrator, Title 1 specialists, and classroom teachers met with parents individually to share information about the programme.

We were pleased with the results of the programme in its second year. Of the children invited to participate, 17 of 27 attended both the training sessions for one hour after school.

When retesting is done in January, it will determine whether each child still needs more assistance....

Reading aloud to children is a very valuable way of assisting pupils to enjoy reading and in learning to read (See Gupta, 2001).

REFERENCES

Banner, Coleen, and Marilyn J. Koehler (2002), "Parent Reading Connection," *Kirksville Daily Express*, February 17, 8.

Beck, Isabel L, and Margaret G. Me Keown (2002), "Text Talk: Capturing the benefits of read aloud experiences for young children," *The Reading Teacher*, 55 (1), 19.

Ediger, Marlow, and D. Bhaskara Rao (2001), *Teaching Social Studies Successfully*. New Delhi, India: Discovery Publishing House, Chapter Eight.

Ediger, Marlow (1993), The school counselor and achievement," *Manitoba Journal of Counseling*, 20 (2), 4-6. Published in Canada.

Ediger, Marlow (1994), "Satellite Systems of Instruction," *The Progress of Education*, 68 (10- 11), 226-228.

Ediger, Marlow (2002), "Writing Achievement in Technical Education," *ATEA Journal*, 29 (3), 20-21.

Ediger, Marlow, and D. Bhaskara Rao (2001), *Teaching Science Successfully*. New Delhi, India: Discovery Publishing House, Chapter Six.

Gupta, V. P. (2001), "Concept Learning in Science," *School Science*, 39 (3), 34-36.

23

CHAPTER

Factors Making Expository Reading Difficult

When supervising university student teachers in public school classrooms, the author's attention was brought, by the cooperating teacher, to selected pages in a social studies textbook. These pages had a plethora of new concepts. On one page, for example, sixth graders were to experience reading the following new terms: meridians, parallels, latitude, longitude, degrees, and polar regions. The cooperating teacher told about the difficulties pupils experienced in being able to identify each word in print, let alone knowing the meaning of these words.

The complexity of expository reading materials does increase tremendously in difficulty when an excessive number of new words are placed on a single page of print discourse. Teachers need to write to the publisher to state how textbooks may be improved so that more optimal pupil achievement is possible. To omit those pages of complexity does not work since future references are made sequentially to previous pages of content in the textbook (See Ediger, 1978, 412-416).

Introducing New Words in Reading

The manual section of a basal text may list the new words for pupils to read and understand in print. These can be a valuable resource for teachers to use in selecting new words to introduce to pupils prior to reading a selection. However, pupils are at different levels of achievement and important adjustments need to be made in which words to introduce. Thus, the teacher needs to study and attempt to realize at which level each pupil is reading. The teacher needs to list words, in a notebook, which pupils have difficulty with in identifying and provide needed help here.

The new words need to be printed in manuscript style on the chalk-board for all to see clearly. The teacher should point to each new word as it is being pronounced clearly. The new word may be printed within a sentence or in isolation. The latter helps pupils to focus upon the individual word only, whereas the former assists pupils to notice that words are used contextually. The author has noticed teachers who even have one new word visible at a time, printed on the chalkboard, to avoid pupils having too many stimuli to look at when being introduced to a new word! Selected teachers here would cover all new words on the chalk-board with the pull down map located directly above and then lift the map for the next word to be introduced. The point being, and wisely so, that pupils view a word carefully so that it will be identified accurately while reading the expository text. Learners may then make discoveries of selected phonics elements. These elements include noticing words which begin alike and/or end alike. How much time to take in teaching phonics at this point depends upon the needs of the learner (Ediger, 2000, Chapter Seventeen).

Phonics and Reading in the Content Areas

Reading expository materials should be done to secure ideas, vital facts, concepts, and generalizations. However, pupils may fail to glean important subject matter due to the inability to recognize words independently. Thus, not being able to identify words may hinder comprehension. This is true also if a pupil reads haltingly and struggles to make sense of the abstract symbols or graphemes. When being an elementary age pupil, the author was asked by the teacher to pronounce words orally to those who raised their hands when reading silently. Up to a point, this was OK, but he would also have liked to read to himself and not spend so much time pronouncing words to others. Each pupil likes to benefit optimally from a developmental appropriate reading curriculum. It is imperative then to assist pupils to become fluent readers and learn to use appropriate word attack skills in a language which is not as consistent in grapheme/phoneme relationships as are selected other languages. But there is considerable consistency in initial consonants in words being read. Where consistency is involved, the teacher should assist pupils to determine the unknown by "sounding out" the sound/symbol relationship in unknown words encountered. The following *initial* consonants are highly consistent between symbol and sound —b, d, f, h, k, I, m, n, p, r, s, t, v, w, y. The letter "h," for example, may lack as much consistency as desired with a common word such as "hour." However, there are a plethora of common words beginning with "h" which do have this consistency - heart, health, her, him, and so on. The teacher needs to help pupils make the grapheme/phoneme connection where feasible. Help only should be given as needed, not for the sake of doing so. If a pupil is competent in word recognition, he/she should not be drilled in phonics instruction. It makes sense, though, to help a pupil identify a word in context by having him/her sound out the initial consonant and, if possible, to notice other phonetic elements when needed, to identify the unknown (See also, Weaver, 2000).

Identifying important consistently used syllables may be taught to pupils as needed. A word may not be new to the pupil if he/she notices an important prefix such as "un" in a word such as *unimportant.* The unknown can become the known by identifying a prefix in a word.

The above learnings can be emphasized in expository reading and pupils can still focus upon ideas and subject matter. The word recognition techniques are stressed to help pupils read content, not for the sake of learning phonics and syllabication skills.

Context Clues in Expository Reading

A first intervention point in pupils facing problems in word recognition when redoing subject matter is to guide learners to use context clues. This is an holistic approach in identifying the unknown. The teacher or a peer may help pupils with the unknown by asking for that word which makes sense within the total framework of the sentence or sentences being read. If several words do fit in, then the first consonant letter may provide further clues for word recognition. Generally, the context and the initial consonant sound of the unknown word gives the needed information for word identification.

Meaning theory is involved when context clues are used to identify the unknown word. It is a very valuable approach to use. Thus, for meaning and understanding to accrue in reading, the learner needs to fit in a word for the unknown which will make sense.

Expository content must be understandable to the reader. Reading involves obtaining ideas; the mechanics of reading such as phonics and syllabication skills are there to assist pupils in attaching meaning to what is being read. When irregularly spelled words appear in print, phonics is not to useful to help in word recognition. These words should be introduced prior to pupil's reading the selection and learned as sight words. Words such as the following are irregularly spelled: through, bough, though, tough, cough, dough, rough. These words contain the "ough" letters and yet each is pronounced differently from the other. Learning words by sight means that the pupil meets up with the same words frequently and commits these to memory for immediate recall (See Gunning, 2000).

Writers for pupils' expository reading materials need to be:

1. appropriate for involved readers. Commonly used words based on research studies may provide clues as to which words to use in writing these materials. When viewing Dolch's (1955) research study of 220 most frequently used words by pupils, not all of these words are phonetically spelled. Thus, there are useful words in print which may not posses the grapheme/phoneme regularity in spelling, but pupils do read and write them due to their being functional.
2. in the speaking vocabulary of pupils. Pupils tend to learn selected words in oral communication due to their being relevant to personal needs. What is read also must meet needs of pupils.
3. have illustrations on the page directly related to the printed script. These illustrations assist pupils to attach meaning to the abstract ideas experienced in print. The Teacher's Manual shoujd provide assistance on how to help pupils attach meaning to print discourse and the related illustrations. Identifying unknown words can be done through an illustration, for example, an unknown word may be identified through looking at the related illustration, especially for young children. Perhaps, an increased number of illustrations should appear on pages for older age pupils also, than is presently the case. All illustrations should relate directly to the printed ideas.
4. on the reading level of the learner. In any classroom, the gap in reading achievement from high to low may

be great. For example, in a heterogeneously grouped fourth grade class, the range in reading achievement may be from the second grade level to the sixth or seventh grade level. The teacher here has a tremendous responsibility in assisting all pupils to achieve and learn. Audio tapes and CDs should be available to pupils who need to listen to the contents therein as they follow along in silent reading from their own texts. This will help to minimize gaps between the good reader and those needing more aid in reading achievement.

5. written on three reading levels, but contain the same subject matter and illustrations. By having developmentally appropriate texts for pupils, each should be able to learn from reading print discourse.
6. aware of the need for listing related library books in the manual. A pupil may learn much from reading a library book written on the same topic or by the same writer, as is contained in the text. The author noticed in selected classes while supervising university student teachers in the public schools that pupils could read library books, when available on the same topic as contained in the textbook, and contribute much there from, to the ongoing class discussion. Pupils, too, also need to be accountable for reading and achieving objectives of instruction.
7. have books available for young children containing large print to be used as a Big Book approach in teaching reading. The Big Book needs to be large enough for all to see in the group being taught. Thus, the teacher may discuss the related illustrations in the Big Book before the print discourse reading activity commences. The teacher then reads aloud the contents, pointing to each word, as the pupils follow along from

the Big Book. This assists pupils to notice the words contained therein and help to overcome word identification problems. Next, the pupils should read aloud together with the teacher the same printed words as the teacher again points to each. Rereading may occur as frequently as desired and is necessary. The Big Book approach should be used with pupils, in particular, who have problems in word recognition.

8. use a predictable approach in writing printed materials so that pupils may experience success in reading. Thus, the pupil has security in reading in that he/she may develop awareness of ensuing subject matter. Predictability in reading content assists pupils to make sense out of print discourse.
9. emphasize a variety of ways to help pupils attach meaning to words in context. One way is to give the meaning of a new word in context. Additional approaches are to provide a synonym or antonym for the new word or use the new word with a related appositive.
10. use imagery to make a word meaningful. Imagery includes both similes and/or metaphors (Ediger, 1986, 25- 33).

The new words should be spread out within a chapter, not be contained on a single page. The gradual sequence in presenting new words helps pupils in identifying and reading each new word meaningfully. Too many new words on a single page to read is frustrating and complex. To guide pupils in pronouncing a new word correctly, the writers of the book should use phonetic spelling, placed in parenthesis, for *selected* irregularly spelled words in context. It becomes annoying to the reader if too many of these words are spelled phonetically in parenthesis. To assist pupils in contextual word recognition skills, there needs to be repetition of vital words in the subject matter. What the author feels to be annoying in reading science and mathematics content is when every English given measurement also contains the related metric measurement in parenthesis. In addition to its annoyance, no learner can remember both systems simultaneously. Why not rather use one or the other, preferably the English system since it is used more commonly as compared to the metric system of measurement? The metric system has its important context too, in that there are excellent children's library books written about the metric system. In mathematics, if the metric system is being studied, then the metric system alone should be taught. In science, the metric system alone should be used since measures of atoms and molecules are in evidence. If pupils ask how a meter stick compares with a yard, the comparison can definitely be made by holding up the two sticks to make the comparison. It is ridiculous for pupils, however, to learn that a meter is 39.37 inches. The English and the metric system are two different systems used to measure length, area, and solids. The author well remembers when in the early 1950's, he taught two years on the West Bank of the Jordan and asked the carpenter in the Mennonite Central Committee woodshed, in Jericho, how many yards long the olive wood tray was which he was making. As the question was being raised, the carpenter was holding up a meter stick to measure lengths and widths. The carpenter looked up in amazement and asked, "What is a yard?" He had no concept, as a carpenter, what a yard was (See Ediger, 1981, 8- 12).

Syntactic and Semantic Considerations

Using appropriate syntactic structures which enhance pupil reading of a selection is a worthwhile consideration for writers of expository materials. These should adhere to stressing, *gradually,* more complex syntactic considerations. Easiest to read are those which contain the subject predicate pattern of sentence. Modifiers such as adjectives and adverbs, initially, should be few. An increased number of sentence patterns may be brought in as learners become more proficient in reading subject matter. Thus, the following may be added to the subject predicate sentence pattern: subject, predicate, direct object; subject, predicate, indirect object, direct object; subject, predicate, predicate nominative; and subject, predicate, predicate, predicate adjective pattern. In sequence complex sentences, compound sentences, and compound complex sentence patterns may be included. Dependent clauses should be placed in content as they provide enriched meanings for readers. They may be adjective, adverb, or noun dependent clauses. Sentences which increase in length make it necessary to understand syntax to increase comprehension and decoding skills.

Different purposes in reading need to be emphasized. Skimming and scanning, for example, might be stressed when pupils are locating information for problem solving. Thus, the need is there to skim/scan the table of contents, the index, the glossary, or the dictionary to locate what is needed in information. It is ridiculous to read every word when attempting to locate what is vital from the perviously mentioned reference sources (Parker, 2001).

Semantics deals with pupils determining proper meanings from content read. There will be, of course, differences in interpretation. These should be discussed and can even be debated. An exciting discussion is a motivator to learn for many pupils. Statements which are open ended need to be sorted out and elaborated upon. In depth study is important as compared to survey approaches. If pupils are reading the open ended sentence/paragraph that President Woodrow Wilson, toward the close of World War I, wanted to make the world safe for democracy, what did he mean? Critical thinking is involved in ascertaining what President Wilson meant by the concept *democracy*. Furthermore, pupils need to understand what is meant by "making the world safe (for democracy)." President George W. Bush wanted to free the world from terrorism; there are logical similarities between the two statements or goals. Perhaps, the writers of the text may provide several meanings and then the teacher may guide pupils to brainstorm for other learnings. Problem-solving, critical thought, as well as creative thinking are silent here. Semantics then involves interpretation of what is meant when there are oral or print utterances (Ediger, 2001, Chapter Nine).

REFERENCES

Dolch, Edward (1955), *Methods in Reading*. Champaign, Illinois: Garrard Publishing Company.

Ediger, Marlow (2000), *Teaching Reading Successfully*. New Delhi, India: Discovery Publishing House, Chapter Seventeen.

Ediger, Marlow (1978), "issues in Curriculum Development," *College Student Journal*, 12 (4), 412-416.

Ediger, Marlow (1981) "Problem Solving in the Curriculum," *Journal of the Institute of Educational Research*, 5 (1), 8-12).

Ediger, Marlow (1986), "Reading and the Language Arts," *Philippine Education Quarterly*, (17), 25-33.

Gunning, Thomas G. (2000), *Creating Literacy for all Children*. Boston: Allyn and Bacon, Chapter Three.

Parker, Walter S. (2001), *Social Studies in Elementary Education*. Columbus, Ohio: Merrill, Prentice-Hall, 284-317.

Weaver, B. (2000), *Leveling Books K-6: Matching Readers to* Texts. Newark, Delaware: International Reading Association.

24

CHAPTER

Pupil Decision-making in the Reading Curriculum

Being able to make important decisions is important for all pupils. Thus, pupils need to have opportunities to choose, from among alternative situations. Reading, as one curriculum area, provides a plethora of opportunities to choose and to select. Throughout life, individuals make choices in terms of criteria used, hoping for quality results. John Locke (1632-1704) believed the following facets of a person's development were in the ensuing order of importance:

1. being virtuous, such as living a decent life. There are numerous library books, for example, which may provide inspiration and models for pupil emulation.
2. possessing wisdom as in having foresight to determine appropriate choices to make in life. Pupils here may select and read library books on words of wisdom as in biographies of famous personalities, in proverbs, and in Aesop's Fables.
3. having good breeding such as in exhibiting good manners and working well with others. Library books on bibliotherapy are available to assist pupils in adjusting better to social situations and problems in life.

4. achieving knowledge. There are library materials available to help pupils acquire knowledge in all curriculum areas such as in social studies, science, mathematics, literature, art, music, and physical education (Ediger, 1995, 37-43).

Reading instruction can definitely make its many contributions in order that pupils may achieve each of the above named objectives. Decisions must be made by the learner as to which library books to read sequentially.

Sustained Silent Reading and Making Decisions

Sustained silent reading (SSR) has implications for pupil decision-making. From among alternatives, the pupil then needs to choose library books to read during the designated time in the classroom. Here, every one reads, including the classroom teacher. In selected schools, the total school reads a selection, including custodians and cafeteria workers. This, however, may be difficult to implement. The local classroom, with everyone reading silently a self chosen selection, is a more realistic implementation of SSR. The goal here being that pupils see models of adults and children reading a library book. To stress a successful SSR programme, the teacher may:

1. develop a bulletin board display of possibilities for library books to be chosen by pupils for reading.
2. introduce reading selections to children to stimulate interest in SSR.
3. have peers tell abbut certain library books which they found to be interesting.
4. guide pupils to develop a visible collage pertaining to fascinating library books read.
5. assist peers having read the same library book to develop a mobile to indicate interests and comprehension.
6. cassette record contents from a library book read aloud by a good reader to be used by those who need

assistance in reading the same book. The latter may listen to the cassette as he/she reads along silently from that same book.

7. video tape times when everyone in a classroom is actively engaged in SSR. The play back to pupils can be exhilarating.
8. have learners pantomime contents from a library book and have others guess what is being pantomimed.
9. help pupils draw illustrations of content read and post them on the bulletin board for all to see in the classroom.
10. arrange committees to engage pupils in telling about favorite incidences read in a library book (See also - Hatcher and Olson, 1984).

SSR provides ample opportunities for pupils to make decisions on selecting and reading library materials.

Personalized Reading and Decision-making

With personalized reading, the pupil chooses a library book to read. The book chosen, as is true of SSR, should be on the reading level of the learner, not the frustrational level. The chosen book should be of maximum interest to the reader. The learner is in control of what is selected and read. The teacher assists when the pupil is not able to make a selection. Personalized reading may replace or be added on to the regular reading curriculum involving basal reader use.

After completing the reading of a library book, the pupil may have a conference with the teacher to assess comprehension and reading skills. The pupil may use diverse ways to reveal comprehension of content (See Gardner, 1999). The teacher may record, date, and compare earlier with later conferences held with the pupil to notice the latter's progress.

Personalized reading stresses the importance of:

1. the learner making choices in terms of content to be read. External dictates are not in evidence such as state mandated objectives to be achieved. However, personalized reading should help pupils to do better on these kinds of externally devised tests.
2. the learner has input into the assessment process following the completion of reading a library book. He/she may then suggest ideas for discussion in the conference with the classroom teacher. The pupil may also choose which selection to read orally so that the teacher might appraise reading progress.
3. the pupil is heavily involved in sequencing his/her own reading experiences.
4. decision-making is a leading goal of personalized reading with the learner choosing sequential books to read.
5. accountability in reading should be emphasized. With accountability in reading, the pupil may
   (*a*) do journal writing covering content read or personal impressions gained in personalized reading.
   (*b*) draw sequential illustrations of what was read.
   (*c*) pantomime certain selections from the book read.
   (*d*) make a model pertaining to selected concepts contained in a completed library book.
   (*e*) complete a related bulletin board display on "My favorite library book."
   (*f*) write a poem or an essay on my favorite character in a narrative library book read.
   (*g*) keep a diary on daily reading activities in personalized reading.

(*h*) summarize the diary entries with writing a log.

(*i*) video-tape working with others in a collaborative activity involving personalized reading (Ediger and Rao, 2001, Chapter Eight).

The Psychology of Learning and Personalized Reading

Humanism, as a psychology of learning, is strongly in evidence in personalized reading. The focal point here is upon the pupil as being central in the reading curriculum. The pupil is a chooser. Thus, the learner selects, from among a variety of library books, the following kinds of reading materials:

1. those which are interesting.
2. those which possess intrinsic purpose or reasons for reading.
3. those which are related to personal background experiences possessed.
4. those which emphasize meaningful learning.
5. those which are perceived as being personally worthwhile.
6. those which are on the recreational or instructional level, not the frustrations!, level of reading.
7. those which stress either an individual or collaborative learning style. With collaboration, the pupil is the chooser of being a committee member in which all have read the same paperback (See Searson and Dunn, 2001).
8. those which emphasize personal choices in how to be evaluated (See Gardner, 1993).
9. those which have enduring values.
10. those which meet needs of pupils individually (Ediger and Rao, 2000, Chapter Six).

The psychology of learning is important to stress in that it does assist pupils to achieve more optimally in the classroom setting.

Philosophy of Reading Instruction

Measurement driven instruction (MDI) has become quite common with the many tests administered in the public schools for determining pupil achievement as well as teacher accountability. The concept of measurability of achievement has its roots in the manufacturing and business world. Here, profits and losses can be ascertained in terms of dollars and cents. Precision and accuracy are key terms to emphasize. If achievement is there, it can be measured precisely. Noll (1987) wrote the following:

> Mental measurement and scientifically grounded assessment instruments date back to the beginnings of the 20th century as part of a general movement to devise a "science of education."

Somewhat similarly, the current dispute over measurement concerns whether the art of teaching and the art of learning can be clearly assessed by the science of testing. W. James, an advocate of standardized testing, contends that high quality testing programs are essential to the survival of public schooling. The tax paying public has exerted great pressure for more concrete evidence of performance in light of what is seen as a decline in standards over recent decades.

Opponents raise the question about the quality of fairness of the current tests and about the effects of test-retest competition on both students and schools. Banesh Hoffman's 1962 book, The Tyranny of Testing, first posed these concerns. More recently, Andrew J. Strenio, Jr., in his book *The Testing Trap*, attacks meritocratic competitiveness, the perpetuation of the fear of failure, curricular manipulation by the test makers, the distortion of the teaching process, and the "branding" of children which emanate from an overemphasis upon standardized test results. Harold Berlak of the Public Information Network offers a case against the current heavy dependence upon standard examinations in an article entitled "Testing in a Democracy (Educational Leadership, October, 1985). He contends that such testing reduces learning to multiple choice test items which trivialize knowledge, that many of the tests are written by experts who are remote from the classroom and from the subject matter, and that teachers are spending more and more time teaching tests.

Testing and measuring has its role, along with other evaluation procedures, to ascertain pupil achievement. One, however, should not go overboard on a single procedure to ascertain what pupils have learned and achieved. Quality tests need to be written which are valid in that they cover what has been meaningfully taught. These tests should be reliable in that they measure consistently what pupils have acquired and imbibed.

Problem-solving, as a second approach to evaluation of pupil progress, stresses different tenets as compared to MDI. Problem solving stresses practical situations in life. Thus in context, pupils identify a problem area. The problem needs to be clear and distinct so it can be solved. Information is gathered in answer to the problem. Reading can be a major approach in the information gathering process. A tentative hypothesis should result. The hypothesis is an temporary answer to the problem. A reality based situation needs to accrue to evaluate the worth of the hypothesis. The hypothesis is then accepted or revised.

It would be impossible to give a numerical absolute score for the quality of each flexible step in problem solving. There are also diverse procedures to use in problem-solving; the above is one model. Problem-solving is open ended as an approach in teaching and learning situations. Pupils cooperatively select the problem. The teacher is a guide and stimulates pupil learning. From the total learning environment, pupils select a problem which possesses intrinsic motivation for solving. The interests of pupils are generally involved in problem selection. Interest provides for effort in learning and seeking possible solutions to problems. Pertaining to John Dewey and his problem solving emphasis in the curriculum, Good and Teller (1973) wrote the following:

> Dewey held that we think when we must, and that thinking originates in a perplexity, an obstacle, or a doubt. Some have regarded this as a great discovery but it is in fact only a truism. If thinking is defined as the effort to find the answer to a problem or to resolve a perplexity, then, naturally it cannot occur except in the presence of some difficulty. Like other truisms however, this one is worth stating. It says that situations can be set up to stimulate thinking.

The sources and varied nature of pupil's problems are themselves problems that closely concern the teacher. Children are active by nature, "spilling with activities," and from these practical concerns many problems arise. Getting out of this play pen is for the small child a problem that is about par with the problem of the cat in the cage. Rousseau and Froebel suggested many children's activities that involve problems, but they did not, like Dewey, consider the detailed ways in which the problems are solved by children. Dewey suggests a few somewhat more intellectual but still simple problems. From *How We Think* everyone will remember the case of the ferry boat with the white pole projecting from the front of the pilothouse, the soapy tumblers, and the problem in transportation.

Such examples are altogether appropriate as types of work for children; but they lead to the notion that problems usually or always arise from external conditions. This is not true. Philosophers including Dewey have often gone out in search of problems because they enjoyed thinking. Problems do not always arise from circumstances nor do they have to be assigned by a teacher. It is a fact of history that science has been created largely by pure scientists—Galilleo, Newton, Faraday, Darwin, and a host of others who went out to look for problems and investigated them for the love of it.

A third approach in reading, namely perennialism, has a definite philosophy to emphasize. Perennialists advocate pupils read library books stressing the great ideas of he past. There are books which have survived time and space. They contain the treasured ideas of the past. These Great Books are well known by title and author such as:

1. The Scarlet Letter by Nathaniel Hawthorne.
2. Treasure Island by Robert Louis Stevenson.
3. A Tale of Two Cities by Charles Dickens.
4. Romeo and Juliet by William Shakespeare.

Additional great writers, among others, who are from the past but well known presently are Edgar Alien Poe, Henry Wadsworth Longfellow, Leo Tolstoy, Sir Walter Scott, and Oliver Wendell Holmes. These writers have written the classics. Perennialists believe that good literature needs to be considered important over an extended period of years to notice if it remains salient, not temporary. There are a dearth of writings which may have been important within a short segment of time, but they are not well known today. Within a long period of time, writers can be identified who are considered to have written the classics and whose fame has remained important, significant, and unfaltering. Pertaining to Perennialism as a philosophy of literacy in good literature, Hutchins (1953) wrote the following in his essay "The Conflict in Education":

> Nor is it possible for a person to have too much liberal education, because it is impossible to have too much understanding and judgement. But it is possible to undertake

too much in the name of liberal education in youth. The object of liberal education in youth is not to teach the young all they ever need to know. It is to give them the habits, ideas, and techniques that they need to continue to educate themselves. Thus, the object of formal education in youth is to prepare the young to educate themselves throughout their lives. I would remind you of the impossibility of learning to understand and judge many of the most important things in life. The judgement and understanding of practical affairs can amount to little in he absence of experiences with practical affairs. Subjects that cannot be understood without experience should not be taught to those who are without experience; it should be clear that those subjects can be taught only by way of introduction and that their value to the student depends upon his continuing to study them as he acquires experience. The tragedy in America is that economics, ethics, politics, history and literature are studied in youth, and seldom studied again. Therefore the graduates of American universities seldom understand them.

Simplified versions of the Great Books can be purchased and read by pupils. This might well assist them to better understand the original writings when reading the classics at a later time. Recently, advocates of The Great Books have advocated that the teacher choose books for pupils to read if they are the classics or not. The book chosen needs to:

1. be highly interesting to children.
2. contain content pertaining to morality, ideally.
3. promote reading habits on the part of pupils.
4. encourage lively interaction among pupils when the teacher leads the discussion pertaining to contents in each library book.
5. promote wide reading of content by pupils, as well as promote lifelong reading habits.

A fourth reading philosophy is existentialism. Existentialists advocate a literature curriculum which focuses on

1. the human condition with its many uncertainties.
2. the dread and anxiety which individuals have when making decisions and choices.
3. freedom which individuals face when choosing from the many alternatives in life.
4. the realization that death is the ultimate for all persons.
5. feelings of loneliness in being by the self when facing life's dilemmas.

Harper (1955) wrote the following:

Existentialism is, as the word implies, a philosophy of human existence. It arose early in the nineteenth century in response to a cultural climate in which Soren Kierkegaard observed that men had forgotten what it means to exist. Men had learned what it means to be in a crowd, to be a mass- man; but they had forgotten what it means to be an individual, that is what it means to die, to suffer, to loye. They had forgotten what it means to stand apart, as each man is born to stand apart, from the rest of the universe and from one's fellows.

Library books emphasizing existentialism stress the following kinds of books for each pupil to select from:

1. those which contain problems faced in life by individuals.
2. those which stress handicaps faced by individuals.
3. those which reflect dread and awe faced by individuals in decision making.
4. those emphasizing loneliness and isolation from other human beings.
5. those stressing the human condition with its joys and sorrows.

REFERENCES

Ediger, Marlow (1995), *Philosophy in Curriculum Development*. Kirksville, Missouri: Simpson Publishing Company, 37-43.

Ediger, Marlow, and D. Bhaskara Rao (2000), *Teaching Reading Successfully*. New Delhi, India: Discovery Publishing House, Chapter Six.

Ediger, Marlow, and D. Bhaskara Rao (2001), *Teaching Social Studies Successfully*. New Delhi, India: Discovery Publishing House, Chapter Eight.

Gardner, Howard (1993), Multiple Intelligences: Theory into Practice. New York: Basic Books.

Gardner, Howard (1999), *The Disciplined Mind*. New York: Simon and Schuster.

Good, Harry G., and James D. Teller (1973), *A History of American Education*, Third Edition. New York: the Macmillan Company, p. 372.

Harper, Ralph (1955), "Significance of Existence and Recognition for Education," *Modern Philosophies of Education*. Chicago: The University of Chicago Press, p. 215.

Hatcher, Barbara, and Mary Olson (1984), "Sidewalk Social Studies," *Social Studies*, 48 (September/October), 473-474, 485.

Hutchins, Robert Maynard (1953), "The Basis Of Education," *The Conflict in Education*. New York: Harper and Row, p. 351.

Noll, James William (1987), *Taking Sides: Clashing Views on Controversial Educational Issues*. Guilford, Connecticut: The Dushkin Publishing Group, Inc., pp. 294-295.

Searson, Robert, and Rita Dunn (2001), "The Learning Styles Teaching Model," *Science and Children*, 38 (5), 22-36.

CHAPTER

The Substitute Teacher in Reading Instruction

Substitute teachers have a very important role to play in teaching reading. They are needed to fill vacancies when the regular, certified teacher is unable to be in school due to illness. Approximately eight school days on the average are missed by teachers each year due to illness. There is a need then to have well-trained substitute teachers for the public schools. It is necessary for the regular teacher to leave a listing of what has been covered in class previously and what the objectives are for the substitute teacher to pursue. This is good, but not adequate. The substitute teacher needs inservice education programs which prepare him/her to do a quality job of teaching pupils. They are not merely baby sitters, but actually do teach pupils to make as much progress as possible (See Ediger, 2001, 129-134).

Inservice Education for Substitute Teachers

Having been a university teacher educator for over 30 years, it seems as if there never is enough time to do a good job of preparing teachers for the public schools. Thus, a four or five-year teacher education programme appears short in duration to educate future teachers in what is necessary to function well in teaching pupils. For the substitute teacher, the duration of time is very short for inservice education in developing high quality instruction. The following are essential reading skills to develop within certified substitute teachers:

1. word recognition skills such as phonetic analysis, syllabication, and contextual clues, to assist pupils to unlock unknown words.
2. structural analysis to help pupils understand word order in reading sentences.
3. syntactical analysis to guide pupils to understand meanings of sentences in reading discourse.
4. comprehension of ideas be it narrative, expository, or creative content.
5. higher levels of cognition in questioning including those stressing creative and critical thinking, as well as problem solving (Ediger, 2001, 183-187).

Developing a Love for Reading

One of the most salient objectives for pupils to achieve is to love learning and to make it a life long venture. The substitute teacher needs to understand and implement strategies whereby the affective dimension in reading is implemented and in evidence among pupils. Affective objectives, emphasizing a love for reading, may be emphasized with basal reader use. For any reading selection to be read, background information needs to be developed within pupils. Illustrations in the basal, directly related to the selection to be read, may be used here. The teacher needs to encourage pupils to ask questions pertaining to these illustrations. The resulting questions should be listed on the chalkboard and may be used to establish pupil purpose for reading. The questions come from pupil's interests and should then be used to gather necessary information from reading. Following the reading activity, answers to the previously identified questions may be brainstormed. Brain storming does aid in achieving higher levels of thinking. Both creative (developing additional possible answers) and critical thought (not duplicating on what has been listed) are then being stressed in reading comprehension. In an atmosphere of respect, brain storming can be challenging and enjoyable.

To achieve good attitudes toward phonics in reading, pupils may give words which begin with the same initial consonant, end with the same consonant, or rhyme with a word in the reading selection. Words may also be found having the same vowel sound, regardless of spelling, from the content read. Thus, a word search game may be used here.

To make use, developmentally, of what has been read from the basal, pupils may choose from the following, among other ways:

1. drawing sequential pictures covering content read.
2. writing one or more poems.
3. making a model.
4. developing a different beginning or ending to the story read.
5. redoing the characterization, the setting, or the plot.
6. dramatizing what has been read such as in pantomime, in formal dramatizations, or in creative dramatics. Collaboration among learners is necessary here.
7. arranging and doing a reader's theater within a committee of pupils.
8. writing a set of test questions pertaining to what was read.
9. reading additional stories written by the author(s) or on the same/similar topic read from the basal.
10. keeping a journal on what was experienced from basal reading (See Parker, 2001).

Developing a love for reading is a key component of the curriculum. Hopefully, the love of reading will be a life long adventure for the learner. The substitute teacher needs to be aware of multiple strategies for reading instruction which assist pupils to enjoy and participate actively in the reading curriculum.

In addition to the basal, the substitute teacher may also stress individualized reading in the classroom. Individualized reading emphasizes pupils individually choosing sequential library books to read. Generally, library books are chosen on the basis of being interesting. The reader completes reading the entire book and then has a conference with the teacher. In the conference, the pupil with substitute teacher guidance discusses the contents read. The pupil also reveals skills by reading aloud a particular selection from the chosen library book. The teacher records pupil achievement during/after the conference. Individualized reading may be used along with the basal approach. There is no manual to accompany individualized reading whereas the basal does have a manual to provide suggestions for teaching. These suggestions need to be used creatively to provide a curriculum of excellence in reading.

If time is too short for a conference in individualized reading, sustained silent reading (SSR) may be used. The SSR emphasizes pupils choosing a library book to read, as does individualized reading, but without a followup conference. With SSR, all in a classroom, or even in a school building including custodians and cafeteria workers, read at a designated time. Here, pupils may see models of people reading to themselves. It might well be impossible for all of these individuals to read at one time, but in a single classroom, pupils and the teacher may engage in SSR. The substitute teacher then serves as a role model for children. Reading for enjoyment and pleasure is a key goal for pupils to achieve in affective objectives in reading instruction (Ediger, 2002, 16-19).

Word Recognition Techniques and the Substitute Teacher

There are a plethora of word recognition techniques which may be used by teachers in reading instruction. Substitute teachers need to have structural ideas in mind as to what needs to be emphasized in reading instruction. Gunning (2000) wrote the following:

1. the ultimate goal of phonics is to enable students to become independent readers. Functional practice and extensive reading are recommended to help them reach the goal.
2. words can be read in a number of ways: predicting, decoding, analogizing, or retrieving sight words. How a word is read depends, in part, on the stage that a reader is in ..... Instruction should be geared to student's stage.
3. the two main approaches to teaching phonics are analytic (whole word) and synthetic (sound by sound).
4. consonants are generally taught before vowels because their sounds have fewer spellings and because they are more useful in helping students sound out unfamiliar words.
5. consonant elements to be taught include single consonants, digraphs, and clusters. Vowel elements include short- and long-vowel correspondences, other vowels, r vowels, and schwa. Phonics generalizations have limited usefulness.
6. along with phonics, students should use semantic and syntactic clues and their general knowledge to decode words. Along with context clues, students should be taught how to use two powerful word identification strategies: pronounceable word parts and analogy.
7. as children invent spellings, they make important discoveries about their language's writing system.

Invented spellings can also give the teacher insight into a child's grasp of the writing system.

8. sight words are frequently appearing words that cannot be easily sounded out or that require advanced decoding skills. They are learned through memorization and frequent use and are expected to be recognized instantly. If possible, phonics should be used to supply additional memory pegs for storing and retrieving sight words.
9. in syllabication, words are broken into parts primarily based on sound patterns. Syllabication may be taught through generalizations or patterns or some combination of the two.

Each substitute teacher needs to experience inservice education pertaining to the above generalizations to be emphasized in the teaching of reading.

Comprehension Skills to be Emphasized

The reading teacher needs to possess a repertoire of skills for pupils to use in increasing compression abilities. Comprehension skills for substitute teachers to implement in the reading curriculum are the following:

1. reading for facts. There are vital facts which need to be sorted out from those of lesser values.
2. reading to follow directions. Pupils need to read and follow directions to do a task correctly. Not being able to follow directions correctly makes for wasted time in attempting to pursue a task.
3. reading to obtain relevant concepts. Concepts are made up of facts and provide valuable information in dealing with the mass maze of available knowledge. Knowledge becomes increasingly valuable as it becomes an inherent part of a concept. Concepts are single words or phrases which provide categories for acquired information.

4. reading to secure main ideas. Main ideas consist of concepts. Related concepts in sentence form make for a main idea.
5. reading to apply or use information. Main ideas become functional as they can be applied in a new situation. The level of application is practical in that ideas can be useful and utilitarian.
6. reading to analyze. When information is analyzed, it is separated into component parts. The practical from the non-practical, the relevant from the irrelevant, the salient from the non-salient, as well as the important from the unimportant, in terms of subject matter read need to be analyzed.
7. reading to assess information. Here, the pupil judges the wroth or value of what has been read. The reader, too, needs to detect bias, bandwagon approaches, and "popularity" contests.
8. reading for recreational purposes. Here, the pupil should select reading materials for relaxation and sheer enjoyment. Reading can, indeed, be a highly pleasurable experience.
9. reading to extend information. Reading to accrue ideas and knowledge for its very own sake can be highly valuable to the involved individual. Thus, reading to attain general education and be a more highly informed person in and of itself has intrinsic values.
10. reading for utilitarian purposes is a practical kind of reading which assists the individual to achieve more optimally in the vocational and avocational arenas (Ediger, 1998, 74-77).

The substitute teacher when growing and developing as a professional incorporates the above named objectives to guide optimal pupil comprehension in reading. Achieving professionally is ongoing and continuous. It is never completed, but there is more to learn as knowledge/skills presently are in evidence as well as trends in reading instruction change. From where the substitute teacher is presently in attainment to something that represents a more ideal situation is what needs to be achieved.

Managing Reading Instruction

The substitute teacher needs to be well versed in management strategies when teaching pupils. First, large group instruction may be used when background information is being provided to pupils for reading a given selection. Audio visual aids and discussions need to be used to assist pupils to activate and obtain subject matter directly related to what will be read. Pupils also need to jean upon their own individual experiences to achieve this needed information. It is good, too, to have pupils raise questions for the ensuing reading activity. The questions may be recorded on the chalk-board for pupils to notice to secure answers as the reading experience progresses. By obtaining new content, discussing ideas presented for clarification purposes, and relating personal experiences to the background information en toto, in large group instruction, pupils individually should be ready to read the ongoing lesson to obtain necessary information (See, for example, Bruner, 1986).

Second, small groups may then be formed, after the actual reading of the selection has commenced. Within small groups, pupils may discuss ideas read. Meaning needs to be established for that which lacks understanding by learners within the committee setting. Culminating activities need to be discussed so that pupils individually or in a collaborative endeavour may reveal what has been learned. The culminating experience may cover one lesson or a larger segment of reading instruction. The summarizing activities might well include the following:

(*a*) developing a chart indicating main ideas gleaned from reading.

(*b*) making a collage, mural, or frieze containing illustrations of ideas read.

(*c*) drawings, using diverse media, might reveal learnings obtained. The media may include colored pencils and/or chalk, water color, and magic markers, among others.

(*d*) construction experiences to indicate major concepts or generalizations achieved through reading. Models, realia, and creative work may be made by pupils using wood and cardboard, among other materials.

(*e*) doing a pantomime, creative dramatics, formal dramatization, or role play (See also Clay, 1982).

Creativity is important when small groups have purposes, plan to achieve these purposes or reasons, carry out each purpose, and then assess each in terms of quality standards.

Third, individual endeavours also should be in the offing. These might well include the following:

(*a*) reading a library book by the same author or a book covering similar content.

(*b*) developing an experience chart expressing creative ideas pertaining to subject matter contained in the completed reading lesson.

(*c*) writing diary entries, doing journal writing, developing logs, among other written experiences, might well assist the learner to focus upon salient ideas gleaned from reading.

(*d*) completing an art project encompassing main ideas read.

(*e*) a creative self-chosen method of showing pupil achievement, growth, and development. This might include peer teaching and assistance, dyads working together on a reading task, as well as intergrade grouping in cooperation with another teacher (Devine, 1986).

The substitute teacher then needs to have a repertoire of planned activities to assist pupils to indicate what has been learned within diverse culminating activities.

Assessing Pupil Reading Achievement

The substitute teacher needs to have quality knowledge of and implement evaluation techniques which are valid and reliable. Thus, to ascertain what pupils have learned, the substitute teacher may use the following approaches of assessment:

(*a*) teacher observation based on updated criteria.

(*b*) teacher written test items.

(*c*) teacher supervised portfolios developed by individual pupils.

(*d*) teacher developed/used checklists and rating scales of pupil achievement.

(*e*) teacher written anecdotal statements, diary entries, logs, and journal writing, pertaining to episodes/instances of pupil achievement.

(*f*) teacher application of multiple intelligences theory to assist in assessing pupil achievement (See Gardner, 1993).

Assessment procedures need to be based on the objectives of instruction. A variety of procedures need to be used to ascertain pupil achievement and progress. The substitute teacher needs to lean upon the self and trust his/her thinking to come up with innovative procedures of teaching reading to pupils.

REFERENCES

Bruner, Jerome (1986), *Actual Minds, Possible Worlds*. Cambridge, Massachusetts, Harvard University Press.

Clay, Marie M. (1982), *Observing Young Readers*. Portsmouth, New Hampshire: Heinemann.

Devine, T. G. (1986), *Teaching Reading Comprehension: From Theory to Practice*. Boston: Allyn and Bacon.

Ediger, Marlow (1998), "Reading Poetry in the Language Arts," *The Progress of Education*, 73 (4), 74-77.

Ediger, Marlow (2001), "Assessing Student Achievement in Spelling," *Reading Improvement*, 38 (4), 183-187.

Ediger, Marlow (2001), "Punctuation in the Reading/ Writing Curriculum," *Experiments in Education*, 29 (7), 129-134.

Ediger, Marlow (2002), "Developing a Reading Community," *Edutracks*, 1 (4), 16-19.

Gardner, Howard (1993), *Multiple Intelligences: Theory Into Practice*. New York: Basic Books.

Gunning, Thomas (2000), *Creating Literacy Instruction for All Children*. Needham Heights, Massachusetts: Allyn and Bacon, p. 145.

Parker, Walter S. (2001), *Teaching Social Studies in Elementary Education*. Eleventh Edition. Upper Saddle River, New Jersey: Merrill, Prentice Hall, Chapter Ten.

26

CHAPTER

Listening and the Language Arts

There are a plethora of reasons why pupils should become good listeners. These reasons include the following:

1. politeness is involved when listening carefully to the thinking of others.
2. much can be learned from others through careful listening.
3. learning can become increasingly sequential with the involvement of good listening habits.
4. embarrassment results when one is asked to respond but has not listened carefully to the identified question.
5. actiye participation is not possible in a discussion when a person's listening has been inadequate.
6. time is wasted when directions have not been followed carefully and the inaccurate product/process has to be done over.
7. inadequate oral communication is in evidence with poor quality listening between and among individuals.
8. listening needs to be stressed across the curriculum in order that a pupil may become a good listener.

9. quality listening habits result when pupils integrate school and society. Thus, good listening in school is not separated from quality listening in the societal arena.
10. improved human relations result when people listen politely to each other (Ediger, 1971, 14, 82).

The Psychology of Learning and Listening

There are selected guidelines from the psychology of learning which are truly applicable to improving listening skills on the part of pupils. These guidelines include the following:

1. improved listening occurs when content for pupils captures their attention.
2. improved listening occurs when pupils attach meaning to what is being learned.
3. improved listening occurs when pupils perceive purposes or reasons for learning selected content.
4. improved listening accrues when pupils' individual learning styles are in emphasis in teaching and learning situations.
5. improved listening occurs through accepted reasons for review and practice.
6. improved listening occurs when a school environment stresses a caring/nurturing set of interactions among learners and teachers (Ediger, 1986, 15-19).
7. improved listening occurs when there are classroom standards developed by pupils with teacher assistance as reference points for pupil behavior.
8. improved listening occurs when individual differences among pupils are considered in teaching and learning situations. Thus, differences in learning styles need implementation to guide more optimal pupil achievement in listening (See Searson and Dunn, 2001).

9. improved listening occurs when pupils have choices as to how they are to evaluated in terms of achievement (Gardner, 1993).
10. improved listening occurs when mutually accepted goals in listening are in evidence with parental involvement and assistance.

The psychology of learning is highly important to consider in guiding optimal learner achievement when listening across the curriculum is being emphasized. Following the tenets of educational psychology in teaching is a motivator for pupils to achieve and learn.

Philosophy of Education in the Listening Curriculum

The philosophy of education needs adequate consideration when developing the listening across the curriculum concept. First, Measurement driven instruction (MDI) emphasizes the importance of establishing predetermined objectives for pupils to achieve. There is no input from learners here. Teachers and the state department of education might then have selected objectives for pupil achievement, prior to instruction. With MDI, the objectives are highly precise. It can then be measured if a pupil has/has not achieved an objective after instruction. Either the pupil has/has not attained the stated objective. If an objective has not been achieved by a pupil, a different teaching strategy then needs to be in evidence. The objectives should be arranged in a sequential manner so that a previously attained objective assists the learner to achieve the ensuing end. Thayer (1970) wrote the following:

> The early years of the twentieth century were conspicuous in their applications of science to all phases of business and industry. It was applied not merely to the invention of new products and processes but to the details of organization and management designed to promote economy and efficiency. Experts trained in "scientific

management" studied carefully the performance of workers on the job with results so fruitful in economy and efficiency that many came to be seen in "job analysis" possibilities of application not only to vocational education but also the reform of other aspects of education as well. All that was need, it seemed, was to identify the scientific outcomes by insuring that pupils engage in the activities to eventuate the proper habits and skills, information, attitudes, ideals, and the like.

To become a good listener, the researcher determines specific sequential steps involved in pupils becoming those who listen well, and describe these behaviors in measurable terms. With continuous research and study, good listeners can be identified and their ways analyzed what it is, which was done, to be able to listen effectively. Designing a related curriculum which incurs quality listening is then an end goal.

Second, a problem-solving philosophy may be implemented. Here, pupils with teacher guidance identify a problem contextually in the curriculum. The problem needs to be clearly stated so that it can be solved. Information in its solution needs to be gathered by pupils. An hypothesis should result which is tentative. By gathering more information, the hypothesis is evaluated in a practical situation. The hypothesis may then be accepted as is or may be modified if necessary. The MDI is not possible in problem solving since each of the flexible involved steps are subjective to those involved in arriving at solutions. There are no predetermined objectives in problem solving since pupils are involved in choosing the problem, gathering related information, and evaluating the hypothesis. New problems may arise at any point during the problem solving process. Problem solving emphasizes group and committee endeavors. In society, collective decisions are made in a democracy; thus in the school setting, pupils should also work in groups to identify and solve problems (Ediger,1977, 269-270).

A third philosophy of education stresses humanism. Humanists strongly believe the individual with teacher assistance should be heavily involved in decision making as to what to learn. Choices need to be made and the pupil is the chooser. The teacher motivates, encourages, and guides pupils to stay on task. Objectives, within flexible bounds, then come from the pupil and are subjective to the learner. Self evaluation is important here including portfolio development and use. The teacher here is one who helps pupils to achieve, grow, and learn (See Stumpf, 1971).

Learning Opportunities to Achieve Objectives

There are a plethora of good learning opportunities for pupils, to achieve objectives. These learning opportunities need to be provided in manner which involves using the best of research findings and educational thought. What might the teacher do to guide optimal listening among pupils? First, the teacher needs to evaluate the self to ascertain if selected facts, concepts, and generalizations are repeated top frequently, resulting in pupils coming to depend on repetition if they fail to secure these ideas the first time. Rather, in a discussion, for example, the teacher through observation can ascertain what pupils know, what they have left to learn, and where they might find the needed information. To be sure, there needs to be adequate opportunities for pupils to review what has been learned so that forgetting does not occur. But repetition should be cut down in amount so that each pupil becomes a better listener. If a pupil did not "get it," due to faulty listening, the teacher may ask another pupil what had just been said. As university supervisor of student teachers, the author noticed that pupils tend to not listen carefully enough to oral directions given by the teacher, resulting in a product/process done incorrectly. The directions need to be given clearly and concisely. Too avoid repeating directions excessively, the teacher may need to write them on the chalk-board for pupil reference purposes.

As a second learning opportunity to foster quality listening, time spent on developing cooperatively, with pupils, standards for good behaviour in the classroom is time well spent. Here, pupils learn about quality behavior standards and why these are salient. Evaluation in terms of these standards is a must! The teacher may then notice which standards are violated and help pupils to understand how to overcome these weaknesses. Diagnosis and remediation are important.

Third, special class sessions may be devoted in guiding pupils to become improved listeners. Tape recording of different sounds might be listened to so that pupils may determine the cause(s) of each sound or noise. Or, pupils may put their heads face down, securely, upon the desk top. The teacher then makes individual sounds for learners to guess their sources. These kinds of activities might be perceived as a game approach in teaching and learning situations.

Fourth, a good learning environment needs to minimize/ eliminate unnecessary noises. Too be sure, a busy classroom will have some noise which indicates that pupils are at work and achieving to attain objectives. Certainly, pupils with teacher guidance are aware of unnecessary distractions which occur in the classroom. These need identification and elimination. Continuous heed must be given to these kinds of irritations. Pupils should hot be exposed to concentrate on the unnecessary (Ediger, 1993, 368-371).

Fifth, the physical conditions in the classroom need assessment to notice if weaknesses here may be downgraded. Excessively high temperature readings can make pupils drowsy and results in poor listening. Conversely, low temperature readings may make for pupils concentrating excessively on the discomfort in the classroom rather than listening to the discussion. Equally important to proper temperature readings in the classroom is appropriate ventilation.

Sixth, a variety of learning activities need to be provided for pupil engagement. Using printed materials, AV aids, excursions, construction experiences, and dramatizations, among many others, as developmentally appropriate experiences, may well avoid boredom situations among learners. Activities may be changed by the teacher, when observing pupils in class, to develop and maintain careful listening and interest in learning (Ediger, 1987, 9-11).

Seventh, the teacher needs to present a good example for pupils in the area of listening. He/she listens carefully to pupils comments, questions, and goals. The teacher must show interest in each pupil and not shun individuals. Each pupil regardless of income level, interests possessed, physical appearance, and abilities has tremendous intrinsic worth as a human being. Pupils individually need to be assisted to achieve as much as possible. Thus, pupil esteem needs must be met so that a positive self concept emerges.

Eighth, pupils need to experience learning opportunities possessing purpose for listening carefully. Thus, the teacher may briefly explain reasons for listening carefully to an ongoing lesson presentation. Quality listening is salient across the curriculum (Ediger, 1980, 38-41).

Ninth, each learner needs to receive praise for good listening. Receiving honest praise, periodically, should encourage better pupil listening.

Tenth, pupils should be seated in a place whereby optimal listening is possible. Thus, pupils with hearing impairment need to be seated as close to the spoken voice as possible.

Assessing Listening Achievement

Numerous quality approaches may be used to assess pupil achievement in listening. Procedures used need to be valid and reliable. The teacher may write dated diary entries on pupils' achievement in listening. When viewing each pupil's diary entries, a trend may be noticed in how well a pupil is doing in the area of listening. Analysis of the entries might well indicate what needs exist for helping pupils individually to improve listening skills. Second, the teacher may do journal writing to obtain an overall observation of how well pupils are achieving sequentially in listening. This helps the teacher to recall how well each pupil is achieving in listening when content in journal writing is reviewed. Third, self evaluation by the pupil, in terms of standards, may be stressed to ascertain how well the learner feels he/she is achieving in listening. These self-evaluation procedures may be used each six weeks of schooling. Fourth, an informal listening test may be given to pupils. Here, the teacher clearly reads aloud a short story to pupils. Then questions are raised by the teacher covering the subject matter read. If the whole class is involved in the discussion, then the teacher needs to make judgments pertaining to how well individual pupils listened. Should pupils respond on paper to these questions, then a better indication of how well each person listened can be ascertained. However, there are pupils who have difficulty in putting ideas down on paper and this needs to be considered.

There are certainly numerous situations in which the teacher may assess pupils informally in listening across the curriculum. These include the following situations for listening within the framework of oral communication experiences:

1. discussions and committee work.
2. directions followed in doing a product or process.
3. conversations in the lunchroom and at recess time.
4. peer teaching and peer collaboration endeavors.
5. project methods of teaching and activity means of instruction.

Fifth, portfolios may be developed by pupils individually with teacher guidance. The portfolio may contain the following suggested items as examples, among others:

(*a*) graded answers to questions on listening to stories on cassettes.

(*b*) a video tape pertaining to the pupil interacting with others in developing a project in which listening is inherent.

(*c*) self assessment of listening quality experienced within a group or committee. Definite criteria are used in the self evaluation instrument.

Continuous evaluation by the pupil and by the teacher pertaining to the former's achievement in listening is important. Carefully developed standards need to be used in the assessment. The pupil needs to change from what is presently in listening achievement to a selected achievable ideal (Ediger, 2000, Chapter Fifteen). Parental involvement is very important in assisting their offspring to achieve more optimally. In an article on "An education evening out," Corso, Funk, and Gaffney (2002) wrote the following:

> We wanted to provide parents with ways they could support their children on the path to literacy. As the first literacy evening was being perceived, surveys were being sent out asking families if they would be interested in learning more about helping children learn to read. The parents were also asked what time and day of the week they would prefer a literacy night. The response was tremendous...

The above movement started the ball rolling in involving parents to assist their offspring to achieve more optimally in reading. Good listening is very salient and inherent in helping pupils improve in listening.

REFERENCES

Corso, Laurie, Sue Funk, and Janet S. Gaffney (2002), "An education evening out," *The Reading Teacher*, 55 (4), 326-329.

Ediger, Marlow (1971), "Learning to Listen," *School and Community*, 58 (3), 14, 82.

Ediger, Marlow (1977), "Problem Solving, the Teacher, and Society," *College Student Journal*, 11 (3), 269-270.

Ediger, Marlow (1986), "Human Relations and the Curriculum," *Comment on Education*, 16 (4), 15-19.

Ediger, Marlow (1980), "Philosophy, the Pupil, and the Curriculum," *Secondary Education Today*, 21 (4), 38-41.

Ediger, Marlow (1987), "Learning Activities in the Curriculum," *Alberta Learning Resources Journal*, 8 (3), 9-11.

Ediger, Marlow (1993), "The Student and the Curriculum," *College Student Journal*, 27 (3), 368-371.

Ediger, Marlow (2000), *Teaching Reading Successfully*. New Delhi, India: Discovery Publishing House, Chapter Fifteen.

Gardner, Howard (1993), *Multiple Intelligences: Theory into Practice*. New York: Basic Books.

Searson, Robert, and Rita Dunn (2001), "The Learning Styles Teaching Model," *Science and Children*, 38 (5), 22-26.

Stumpf, Samuel Enoch (1971), *Philosophy, History and Problems*. New York: Me Graw Hill Book Company, 96-143.

Thayer, V. T. (1970), *Formative Ideas in American Education*. New York: Dodd, Mead and Company, p. 224.

27

CHAPTER

Philosophical Implications in Choosing Learning Activities

There salient implications for philosophy in selecting learning activities for pupils. Each activity is based upon a selected school of thought in the philosophy of education. Then too, philosophies might well overlap; some may not be as clearly defined as others. Teachers, supervisors, and school administrators must study, evaluate, and then appraise different schools of thought. Being highly knowledgeable assists the decision making process in providing for individual differences among learners be it in interests, talents, and intelligences. Learning styles, too, differ when emphasizing one style of learning as compared to others.

Learning Opportunities in the Curriculum

Perhaps, the oldest type of activity is for the younger children to observe adults in hunting and gathering societies. Direct observation was involved in securing adequate wild life and plants for food. The adult helped the young to become increasingly proficient in obtaining enough food. Knowledge and skill was stressed here, and success in endeavors was salient to prevent hunger/starvation.

In present day schools many educators stress selected direct experiences for pupils. Pupils, for example, with teacher guidance are engaged in gardening experiences. Even elementary age pupils are learning techniques of being gardeners. In a recent issue of the Hutchinson, *Kansas News* (July 15, 2010), intermediate grade pupils with teacher guidance in selected local schools were growing radishes and peppers, in cooperation with Kansas State University School of Agriculture, on an experimental basis. Newton, Kansas Public Schools supervises their Rural Life School at nearby Walton, in which meals are served using the school's homegrown fruits and vegetables.

There are diverse beliefs in selecting activities for pupils to attain objectives of instruction. E. L. Thorndike (1874-1949) was instrumental in advocating precisely stated objectives. The specificity of these objectives made it so the teacher could determine if pupils had/had not achieve an objective after instruction. Thus, Thorndike receives much credit for starting the measurement movement in education, "Whatever exists, exists in some amount, and if it exists in some amount, it can be measured." With the measurement movement, many tests were developed to measure pupil achievement in different academic areas. The present day accountability movement has built upon measuring learner achievement with teachers being held accountable for pupils doing well on mandated tests in emphasizing measurement philosophy of education, objectives must be stated with clarity so no doubt exists in terms of their meaning. Teachers then know what exact target to aim toward in teaching pupiis With mandated objectives, the teacher chooses the learning activities, but not the objectives of instruction. Nor does the teacher ascertain tests to be used in measuring teacher success. The tests as well as the objectives are written on the state/national levels (Ediger and Rao, 2003).

With teacher designed classroom objectives and tests, he/she has more control over the curriculum. The learning activities, too, are teacher chosen The measurement movement tended to advocate using:

- standardized tests to measure achievement. There is uniformity here in test items, directions given for test taking, time limits in taking the test, the same scoring key for multiple choice test items, for pupils in any age level.
- aligning learning activities with the objective. This stressed the importance in not straying from the objectives of instruction.
- testing to determine if the objectives have been achieved. Test results may be compared state by state and/or compare school districts within a state when published in the news media. This may be labelecj as the nation's score card.

There are plethora of weaknesses in the mandated testing approach of instruction. It places much faith in choosing the right objectives by those specialists removed from the local school, prior to instruction. There is little leeway for input from teachers in terms of *what* to teach or for pupils to identify problems to solve. What is tested is what will be taught has become a slogan. This omits content from academic disciplines not being a part of the test. Then too, it omits qualities which are difficult to test such as good attitudes, caring for others, and being considerate. When making comparisons among teachers based on their pupils test results, there are differences in the makeup of learners within a classroom. Pupils tend to receive iower test results if they come from low income homes and/or come from minority groups. These pupils have not had the opportunities to iearn which learners have had from favorable income levels. Money buys reading materials for the home, travelling to see distant places from home base, iessons for extra curricuiar ieamings such as inslrumenlai and dance, among others (See Stiggins. 1997).

Somewhat toward the other end of the continuum from the measurement moment is constructivism. Constructivists have much less confidence in testing to notice achievement. They believe that pupils create their own knowledge and skills As the learning activity continues within an ongoing unit of study, the pupil sequences learnings and reveals questions which need answers. The answers are not provided by the teacher, rather he/she pupils to what is needed such as in a reference source, or the teacher may ask a question in return whereby the pupil may learn the necessary content inductively. The teacher must be well-versed in subject matter and reference sources to use constructivism as a philosophy of instruction. The questions need to be sequential to assist pupils to achieve inductively Learning by discovery is a key component of constructivism. The teacher not only enables, but also encourages pupil achievement (Ediger, 2010).

With constructivism, the teacher does not lecture, unless it amounts to a brief explanation in helping learners move forward. Criticism and rudeness interfere with learning and the classroom environment must be very supportive and encouraging. The teacher's role is not to be "a sage on the stage," but rather one who facilitates and motivates iearner progress. Teacher observation is utilized to appraise pupil achievement by noticing progress and assisting when needed This leaves ample room for problem solving and projects where pupils individually and collectively order their very own sequences. Modeling by the teacher may be necessary at different points in using either method.

Problem-solving and the Project Method

Problem-solving approaches was advocated by John Dewey (1859-1953). late professor of education at Columbia University. Dr. Dewey believed that school and society not be separated from each other, and problem solving emphasized life itself, individuals/groups are always identifying and solving problems where change is paramount. Certainly, this is true in:

- selecting a vocation/job or position.
- attending higher education or entering the work place.
- choosing a marriage partner.
- buying/renting a house or an automobile.
- securing finances to purchase needed housing and transportation.
- purchasing groceries and living within one's budget.

There are problems then which take considerable time in solving whereas others may be solved rather quickly. Dr. Dewey in his laboratory school at the University of Chicago stressed problem solving with flexible steps involved here such as clearly selecting a problem so that capability exists in its possible solving. Vague, hazy problems do not lend themselves to further action. Once the problem possesses clarity, then an hypothesis is developed. The hypotheses is tentative and subject to modification. Data are gathered from a variety of reference sources, be they concrete, semi-concrete, or abstract. The information gathered must be in answer to the problem and might well lead to refuting, modifying, or accepting the original hypothesis. The accepted hypothesis must be tried out in a real live situation. New problems might well arise along the way. Problem solving emphasizes pupils with teacher guidance selecting the problem as well as the teacher being a helper in guiding problem solving experiences. Dr. Dewey stressed experimentalism as a philosophy of education, Thus the following principles are followed in the instructional arena:

- the pupil is an active learner, not a passive recipient of knowledge.
- problem solving is a lifelong endeavour.

- absolute knowledge is not possible, but tentative solutions are. They are continually tested in action and lead to more certainty.
- the consequences of any action need to be evaluated before progressing to a new endeavor (Dewey, 1916).

Dewey lived in an era of rapid change. He was born in 1859 with automobiles arriving on the scene in the early 1900s. During the 1930s, cars already came out with electric lights, starters, hydraulic brakes, and heaters. This made for rapid changes in society such as traveling for recreation purposes, more restaurants and hotels, and car agencies selling automobiles. Farming changed rapidly from using draft horses in pulling implements to tractors on steel wheels to those with rubber tires, lights, starters. Combines increasingly were in number to harvest grain in a single operation, replacing grain binders which cut grain and made bundles which were hauled to a stationary threshing machine. Here, the grain was separated from the straw and chaff as well as being augured into a trailer and then shoveled by hand into a grain bin. During the 1940s, grain augurs powered by gasoline engines augured the grain from the truck into a grain bin with no shoveling by hand involved. By the time, Dewey died in 1953, society was heavily mechanized and doing much of the work with the use of machines.

A project method was developed by William Heard Kilpatrick (1871-1964), late professor at Columbia University. He used as a model that students in agriculture classes had projects such as swine, cattle, sheep, among others, and applied these examples to the public schools. Thus in an ongoing unit in the school setting, pupils with teacher guidance identified projects to be developed. The project might stress making a solar collector in science. Generally, pupils worked collectively since social development of pupils was held in high esteem. They needed to follow up in developing a plan in making the model. Pupils needed to perceive purpose in the planning and doing the model. The teacher served as a guide and facilitator and it was up to learners to engage wholeheartedly in this endeavor. Involved pupils then carried through with the carefully designed plan. Pupils then sequenced their very own learnings under teacher supervision. Criteria were devised to evaluate the model. The project method stressed the importance of:

- securing pupil interests in making the model.
- utilizing a variety of learning activities in doing the model such as reading, writing, listening, and oral communication.
- pupils working harmoniously with quality interaction on the project.
- learners being meticulous in planning and doing.
- responsibility on the learner's part.
- pupils being cooperative when working with others.
- a child/pupil centered curriculum (See Bowyer, 1970).

Dr. Kilpatrick's method may be contrasted with textbook usage in that the teacher selects and implements content deemed to be important in teaching from the basal. The teacher is solely in control of the class and may fear relinquishing this method for fear of pupils misbehaving. The interest of pupils is felt to be relatively unimportant and purpose for learning resides within the teacher, not pupils. Sequence, too, also resides in the thinking of the teacher; a teacher centered curriculum is in the offing with the textbook determining what is to be taught.

During the early 20th century with much debate on educational philosophy, there were educators who emphasized a strict subject centered approach in teaching such as William Chandler Bagley (1874-1946). Bagley believed there were basics or essentials for all pupils to acquire. Each academic discipline should be taught as a separate subject, not fused or integrated with other disciplines. Correlating different academic disciplines weakened inherent subject matter to be taught in the public school setting. Bagley opposed lax discipline in schools and this was stressed in his opposing the interest factor in learning. Discipline should emphasizing learning content and not catering to the child's whims. In society, work needs to be completed if the interests are there or not. Bagley believed in a stable curriculum, not one of continual change. Activity centred curricula such as those advocated by Dewey and Kilpatrick should be replaced with solid academic learnings. A properly certified, competent teacher should select objectives, learning opportunities, and evaluation procedures. This procedure was opposite than teacher/pupil planning of the curriculum. Instructional decisions involve the responsibility of the teacher, not pupils, according to Bagley.

Essentialists like Bagley believed strongly in passing on the basics to future generations. There were educators involved in identifying the basics in literature, history, geography, science, and mathematics. The present day trend of mandated objectives certainly emphasizes that there is a body of knowledge and skills which all pupils should master (See Thayer, 1970).

There are also educators who recommend an activity centered approach in teaching, somewhat related to Dewey and Kilpatrick. A learning centers procedure emphasizes decision making by pupils in an ongoing unit of study. Thus, a classroom may provide four centers with suggested tasks listed for each. For example, four to five tasks may be listed on a card at each center, and after the learning centers have been introduced, pupils may choose the center and task to work on, be it individual or committee endeavors. There are more tasks than what any pupil can complete so that choices truly exist. The teacher is a supervisor and helps pupils to be on task. If a pupil fails to do so, the teacher assists the learner to pursue and accomplish. Pupils sequence their own achievement and teacher observation is used to assess progress. Pupils here are active learners and seek out their very own interests in sequential task selection.

At the different learning centres, there are attempts at providing for individual differences with the following kinds of activities available for pupil choice:

- hands on experiences as well as learning academic content
- art activities directly related to the unit being emphasized
- oral and written work
- reading experiences such as library book and internet content
- listening experiences such as following directions in constructing a model (See Joyce, *et al.*, 1983).

The Standards Movement in Education

The No Child Left Behind (NCLB) federal mandate of 2002 emphasized each state develop standards or objectives for all pupils to achieve within their respective borders. Aligned tests measured achievement in grades three through eight in reading, arithmetic, and science, as well as an exit test in high school. Pupils needed to pass the tests to be promoted to the next higher grade level. The exit test on the secondary level must be passed to receive a high school diploma. The standards were the same for all pupils on a specific grade level as well as the standards for measurement. Thus, for testing, the directions were the same, the time limits for test taking, as well as the key for scoring the results were also the same. Test results for special education results as well as for English Language Learners (ELL) were disagraggated to notice if adequate progress had been made here. Schools were also required to meet Adequate Yearly Progress (AYP) by the year 2014.

Measurement Theory was certainly in evidence here in that learner and school performance can be measured, using standardized tests (Ediger, 2006).

The Common Core Standards, no doubt, will replace NCLB in time. Common Core Standards stress the same standards for all states within each grade level. The complaints with NCLB standards were the following:

- it was anarchic in that each state determined standards regardless of what other states were doing.
- there were great differences among the states in terms of what was required and measured.
- differences existed in terms of percentage of pupils passing tests for promotion.
- states differed in percentage meeting adequate yearly progress (See Ray, 2006).

With common core standards, there will be disadvantages with regions differing on what is salient to be taught. The standards may be uniform nationwide, but pupils differ from each other in achievement. Should all pupils attain the same standards when learners may differ much from each other in interests, aptitudes, and abilities? Can the teacher make up for these differences with stimulating learning activities? Is it possible to develop high quality standards nationwide? These are questions which need answers from advocates of common core standards.

To achieve common core standards, the teacher needs to select learning opportunities which engage and are of interest to pupils. Diverse levels of achievement need to be provided for in the classroom. Thus, the chosen activities need to harmonize with the learning styles of pupils. They also need to be perceived as

- being relevant and purposeful

- meaningful and on the developmental level of the pupil
- being aligned with the standards as well as leave room for pupil's questions.

There are issues in the testing movement which certainly do need resolving. Which curriculum areas should should be tested? NCLB was narrow in scope here, in that reading and mathematics were requirements initially; this was broadened to include science. Social studies was omitted as were physical education, music, and art. Also, there was criticism of moral/ethical dimensions being ignored such as good citizenship and the caring person. Methods of teaching, too frequently, emphasized studying for NCLB tests through rote learning and memorization.

Each school of thought may be appraised in terms of the traditional four philosophical classifications. The curriculum will be discussed in analyzing through the lens of realism, idealism, experimentalism, and existentialism.

Realism traditionally has stressed that human beings can know reality as it truly is. Thus, a pupil secures a replica of the natural and social environment. Realism has science as its basis and rests upon the concepts of precision and exactness. Numerals are generally used to describe observations as is true of test scores - percentiles, grade age equivalents, stanines, standard deviations, and percentages. The world of science such as chemistry stresses precision in describing the number of electrons, protons, neutrons, elements, and compounds within different kinds of matter.

For the classroom teacher, the objectives of instruction must possess clarity and stated in measurable terms. Learning activities are aligned with the stated objectives. Progress is measured if a pupil has/has not secured the correct answer, generally in a multiple choice or word problem solving format. Either the learner was/Was not correct in responding. A pupil's score may be compared with others in the classroom. The achievement of one classroom may be compared with others.

School districts and states might well be compared also to perceive progress. Teachers may be evaluated on pupil success in test results, such as in merit pay proposals.

With realism, teachers teach toward ends (objectives) and pupil test scores reveal the degree of success of the classroom teacher (See, National Research Council, 1995).

Idealism, a second philosophy, emphasizes an idea/ideal centered curriculum for pupils and has the social sciences as a foundation. The ideas are broader than those of the precision based realism. Literature and history, in particular, may be used as illustrations. Morality and universal ethics might well be discussed in viewing pros and cons of actions taken by nations, states, regions, as well as of individuals. For example, immanuel Kant in the eighteenth century, emphasized the Categorical Imperative, which stressed a universal standard. Here, the individual should want as an ethical/moral principle for all as he/she desires for the self. The Golden Rule rule, "Do unto others as you would want them to do to you." This indicates that idealism is not only idea, but also ideal centered. Ideals in life form the basis in interacting with others. History and literature lend themselves well to analyzing actions in terms of the Categorical Imperative.

Each academic discipline may be discussed in terms of being idea centered. Pythagoras an ancient Athens philosopher emphasized ultimate reality as being a number for each entity. Thus in geometry a point may be represented by the abstract "one." Two points represented a line whereas three points indicated a triangle and four points a square. Mathematical ideas may be discussed in the abstract completely in an idealist's thinking. Plato (424-344 BC) was a true idealist. He emphasized the sensible world of objects that human beings see every day like a chair, table, a door, among many other things in one's surroundings, inferior to the Forms. The Forms existed above the world of sense and was represented by perfection. Thus the things in the here and the now are an imperfect representation of the perfect, chair, table, door, and so on. The Forms represented the ideal and not the temporary sensible things on this planet earth. Plato's idealism is further stressed when he divided workers in the economic world into three categories. Each person then was born/educated into one of three categories - leaders in government who ruled his ideal republic. These individuals had the most talent and ability for their role in society. On a lower level were the guardians of the state whose duty it was to defend the republic against all enemies. The third and lowest level were the *workers* who provided goods and services for all members in the republic. These three categories made for balance in the republic whereby talents were used which were possessed. In present day thinking of idealists, the following major generalizations in curriculum development might well be emphasized:

- mental development of pupils come first with diverse academic disciplines providing challenging content to pupils.
- pupils might then become increasingly motivated to reach ideals in learning.
- an academically inclined teacher needs to select and teach subject matter which involves pupils. Indepth knowledge and skills must be taught.
- the teacher is a model for pupils to emulate in the subject centered curriculum.
- thought provoking subject matter needs to be taught with the ideals of the good, the true, and the beautiful as broad goals.
- character development should assist pupils to move in the direction of the ideal or the Absolute. Individuals are perceived to be finite and moving toward the Infinite. A process is involved here.

- the learner must be perceived holistically intellectually, socially, emotionally, and physically, as well as morally/ ethically (See Ozman and Cramer, 1990).

Existentialism, a third philosophy, emphasizes the individual first of all exists or is, and then attempts to find his/her purposes in life. These are not given, but must be sought in time. There are no absolutes in life and truth resides within the learner. Constructivists emphasize the saliency of the individual developing truths as he/she progresses in education. The teacher is a guide and stimulates pupils to achieve, but does not lecture as "a sage on the stage." Rather, the teacher assists pupils to raise questions pertaining to what is not understood, and then assists learners to find necessary information. Thus, knowledge is subjective, rather than objective as the realist contends. The teacher helps pupils to find freedom in learning. Morality and ethics are key components in the curriculum and each pupil needs to take a position on relevant purposes in life. To let others make the choices robs the individual of being human. He/she must do the choosing. The learner chooses his/her own destiny in an open ended world. The inner directed person makes choices and decisions; however, these choices are made on the basis of much thought and background information. The inner directed person looks at the consequences of choices/ decisions made. How do these affect others? They may make for personal unhappiness, joy, or contentment but one cannot escape from choosing; life demands that one chooses, from among alternatives. Morality and ethics are salient in decision making, not personal self gratification. No other person is responsible for what transpires as a result of making decisions, but the one making the choice.

The curriculum must be quite open ended according to existentialists. Pupils need to be heavily involved in choosing objectives, learning opportunities, and appraisal procedures with learners choosing their destiny. The existentialist curriculum emphasizes:

- individual rather than group endeavors unless a pupil chooses to work with others.
- subjectivity, rather than objectivity. Creative experiences are very important for learners.
- the feeling dimension in choosing activities and experiences. The teacher is a facilitator and assists each pupil to achieve his/her goals in learning.
- the individual makes the self rather than living a predetermined life.
- to be human is to choose and choices made need to be ethical. Individuals act in a way which stresses responsibility.

Each person acts in situations in relationship to others and must be a responsible person for choices made.

A fourth philosophy to be discussed is experimentalism. Experimentalists emphasize that one cannot know ultimate reality, but each person experiences reality in a changing world in society. Experimentalism is a practical philosophy in that it deals with decision making in every day situations. Decisions involve problem-solving; absolutes do not exist. To deal with problems, individuals identify the problem, clearly. An hypothesis is developed which is a tentative solution. Information from a variety of sources need to be used with selected problems being difficult to solve, whereas others need an on the spot solution. With information, the hypothesis is tested in a life like situation, not a paper/pencil test. The consequences of each act must be noticed to reflect upon its consequences. Changes, in courses of action, may need to be made in terms of possible consequences. The test reveals the quality of the hypothesis. New problems might arise in problem solving and these should have hypotheses and and evaluation of the hypotheses based in information secured. One can only know what is experienced which is not based on a predetermined standard. Thus, problems and situations differ in time and place; old "tried and`true" answer may not work in the new problem being considered in daily living.

There is an active and a passive side to experimentalism. The active side pertains to problem identification and solution seeking; the passive side is undergoing the consequences of choices made.

Experimentalists believe that schools should not be separated from society. Too frequently, the school curriculum stresses subject matter learnings, largely or only. The subject matter taught may have nothing to do with problems in society or with problem-solving. Authentic problems, then, must be chosen for solving. There can be problem solving activities in academic subject-matter when the teacher invites questions from students and these lend themselves to developing an hypotheses, information gathering, and hypotheses testing. Lecturing to students does not lend itself to this complete act of thought in problem solving.

REFERENCES

Bowyer, Carlton (1970), *Philosophical Perspectives for Education.* Glenview, Illinois: Scott, Foresman and Company.

Dewey, John (1916), *Democracy and Education.* New York: the MacMilan Company.

Ediger, Marlow (2010), "Issues in the social Studies," International Journal of Educational Research, Development and Extension, 1 (1), 43-49.

Ediger,Marlow (2006), "Testing Vs. Portfolios to Assess Achievement," *OASCD Journal,* 31-32.

Ediger, Marlow, and D. Bhaskara Rao (2003), *Philosophy and Curriculum.* New Delhi, India: Discovery Publishing House.

Joyce, Bruce, et.al. (1983), *The Structure of School Improvement.* New York: Longman's, Inc.

National Research Council (1995), *National Science Education Standards.* Washington, DC: National Academy Press.

Ozman, Howard A., and Samuel M. Cramer (1990), *Philosophical Foundations of Education.* Columbus, Ohio: Merrill Publishing Company.

Ray, K. W. (2006), "What Are You Thinking?" *Educational Leadership,* 64 (2), 58-62.

Stiggins, Richard J. (1997), *Student Centered Classroom Assessment.* Upper Saddle River, New Jersey: Merrill.

Thayer, V. T. (1970), Formative Ideas in American Education. New York: Dodd, Mead and Company.

Philosophical Implications in Selecting Objectives of Instruction

Teachers, curriculum directors, and school administrators need to study and appraise objectives for pupil achievement in terms of philosophical implications in order to improve the quality of objectives for pupil attainment. Mandated objectives also leave leeway for additional, quality objectives in the school curriculum. Mandated objectives are stated quite precisely and in measurable terms. Either pupils do/do not achieve them as a result of learning activities provided in the school/classroom setting. Additional philosophical schools of thought also might well serve to enrich the learnings provided for pupils. Philosophy of mandated objectives will be analyzed first in this manuscript (Ediger and Rao, 2003).

Objectives of Instruction

Measurably stated objectives with accompanying aligned tests represent a popular approach presently in teaching and learning situations. Mandated objectives, be they district state, or nation wide tend to emphasize the use of standardized tests which should possess accompanying objectives for teachers to use in gauging teaching and learning in the direction of measurably stated ends. These precise objectives lend themselves to having aligned learning experiences chosen by teachers in the classroom. With multiple choice test items on the standardized tests taken by pupils, machine scoring may be used to score large numbers of tests. Test results may then reveal, numerically, a percentile, age/grade equivalent, and/or stannic for each pupil. The results may also indicate class, school, district, state, and national comparisons for a news media report card evaluation.

Mandated objectives stress Stimulus/Response theory of learning in that there is a learner connection to each knowledge item acquired. The stimulus then brings on a pupil response with previously acquired content which bridges the new learning or knowledge taught. Multiple choice test items, for example, may have a stem and the test taker locates the correct answer from four distractors, e.g. Which is the capital city of Austria? (A) Berlin; (B) Vienna; (C) Budapest; (D) Prague. There are no clues given as to the correct response. The test taker is to connect/associate the stimulus (Austria) with the response (Vienna). Stimulus/response theory of learning has a long history with E. L. Thorndike (1874-1949) stating that "whatever exists, exists in some amount, and if it exists in some amount, it can be measured." Many standardized tests were developed in Thorndike's day and later to measure pupil achievement in different academic disciplines. These tests contained:

- the same directions to be given to test takers, prior to taking the standardized test.
- the same test items for each age or grade level.
- the same key for test scoring (Ediger, 2010).

Present-day standardized tests still follow the above-named standards and are used for accountability purposes; they are used once each school year. Teachers are then held accountable for pupils doing well on the test in order to be promoted to the next grade level in grades three through eight. Also, an exit test must be taken and passed to receive a high school diploma.

Decision-making philosophy represents a second school of thought in the school and classroom setting. Individual decision making, for example, may be emphasized with individualized reading. Here, an adequate number of library books on different genre need to be available. They ateo must be on diverse reaching levels to provide for individual differences. The teacher needs to introduce new titles at selected intervals. An attractive bulletin board display assists pupils to choose reading materials. The learner then chooses an interesting library book to read. The selection is up to the individual with the teacher helping those who cannot decide. The teacher monitors the classroom reading environment and guides learners who need assistance with word pronunciation. The library books chosen should help to engage pupils in desiring to read. After the completion of reading a library book, the pupil has a conference to indicate comprehension and word recognition growth. The learner chooses which selection from the library book to read aloud to the teacher as well as being encouraged to raise questions for discussion during the conference. The teacher records information and dates it making comparisons with the next conference. Growth and achievement are to be noted within each conference. Individualized reading programs are based upon:

- pupils vary from each other in reading skills and knowledge interests which call for library books of different levels of complexity and subject matter content.
- pupils need to choose in order to select library books sequentially which meet personal needs.
- pupil interest is a powerful factor in learning to read proficiently.

- pupils possess diverse purposes in choosing library books to read (Ediger, 2010).

Basal textbook use represents a third approach in a philosophical procedure in curriculum development. Here in the school or district setting, teachers, among other professionals, have selected a basal series of textbooks in terms of desired criteria. The textbook then, becomes the foundational setting in selecting objectives of instruction. The accompanying Manual contains a list of objectives for teachers to emphasize in teaching. Also, objectives may need additions/ deletions, depending upon the philosophy of the school. Thus, the teacher may rigidly follow the Manual or add/ modify objectives.

If objectives are added/modified, they serve to broaden the scope of what is taught, as well as possibly increasing objectives which deal with higher level cognitive objectives. Generally textbook content is highly condensed and needs a wider scope such as in the social studies where the Middle East area of the world receives a narrow focus in textbook content. The nation of Jordan might receive short shrift. Also, a social science discipline such as sociology may need to be incorporated to provide a model for how culture affects human behavior.

Relying upon the basal text for teaching pupils may make for a rigid, formal curriculum. Whereas, a teacher must be creative in using a Manual and other methods of teaching to meet the needs of individual learners. Too frequently, too, large group class as a whole instruction predominates. To provide for individual differences, small group and individual tasks must also be in the offing. Objectives must stress what is meaningful, interesting, possess purpose, and challenge. Basal textbooks have certain advantages in teaching use in that:

- there is a structure for teachers to follow which then may be broadened in scope by the teacher.

- the Manual presents teaching suggestions for consideration and new ideas may also be incorporated to provide for individual differences.
- they are written by specialists in the field (See Stiggins, 1997).

A fourth philosophy of education to emphasize is constructivism. Constructivists do not believe in the testing movement. Rather, pupils construct their own knowledge as a lesson or unit of study progresses. The rote of the teacher is to encourage and assist pupils to achieve sequentially. Here, the teacher does not lecture nor tell correct answers when pupils have questions. Rather, the teacher helps pupils to find answers to their questions. If, for example, a pupil has a question, the teacher may raise questfons(s) leading the pupil to an answer. The learner is control of the curriculum and sequences his/her own knowledge and skills. Thus, if a pupil or committee is working on a project, they may proceed with a minimal amount of assistance. The project possesses a purpose since pupils have in inward desire to pursue. Careful planning is needed to develop the project. As pupils follow through with the plans, they largely work independently with minimal teacher guidance. Sequence resides within the mind of the pupil, not the teacher, although the latter carefully observes learner achievement to provide encouragement when deemed necessary. Teacher observation is a major procedure to use in evaluating pupil progress with assistance given as needed to make for continual progress. The pupil eventually develops criteria and appraises his/her project in terms of these desired criteria. Constructivists emphasize the following tenets:

- pupils being independent, not teacher dependent in teaming.
- pupils being active learners, not passive recipients of knowledge.
- the role of the teacher is not to be "the sage on the stage," but rather a helper in assisting pupils to achieve objectives of instruction.

- pupils are actively involved in ordering their very own experiences.
- self evaluation by pupils is salient with teacher observation also being involved.
- pupils have much input into developing the curriculum (See Gardner, 1993).

There are differences in the four philosophies discussed. Each has its own generalizations with the teacher having different roles and responsibilities. Pupils also are perceived to have differences in relating to the curriculum (See Shanklin and Rhodes, 1989). The following then are issues asa educators continue to develop/modify a new philosophy.

- is the learner a passive or active being in securing knowledge and skills?
- who should have ownership of the curricula, the teacher/and or the pupil?
- should the teacher or the pupil basically sequence learnings?
- what is the role of academic subject matter in learning?
- should objectives be predetermined or should they arise within a lesson or unit of study?
- how and by whom should pupil progress be assessed?

Teachers and others in the school setting must appraise the objectives, learning opportunities, and the evaluation section of the curriculum to notice what might be modified or changed. The best of each philosophical school of thought needs to be utilized in formulating the curriculum (De Roche and Kostelny, 2006).

REFERENCES

De Roche, and Susan Kostelny (2006), "An Adventure in Problem Based Learning," *Phi Delta Kappan*, 87 (9), 708.

Ediger, Marlow, and D. Bhaskara Rao (2003), *Philosophy and Curriculum.* New Delhi, India: Discovery Publishing House.

Ediger, Marlow (2010), "Issues in Social Studies," *International Journal of Educational Research, Development, and Extension*, 1 (1), 43-49.

Ediger, Marlow (2010), "Sequence in the Social Studies," *Edutracks*, 9 (11), 9-10.

Gardner, Howard (1993), Multiple Intelligences. Theory into Practice. New York: Basic Books.

Shanklin, N. L, and L. K. Rhodes (1989), Comprehension Instruction as Sharing and Extending," *The Reading Teacher*, 42 (5), 496-500.

Stiggins, Richard (1997), *Student Centered Classroom Assessment*. Upper Saddle River, New Jersey: Merrill.

Psychology in the Selection of Objectives of Instruction

It is of utmost importance in choosing vital objectives for pupil attainment. What is salient to teach should be contained in these relevant ends. Objectives have changed in time but not always for the good of the learner. A study of important objectives is necessary in order to choose the best for pupils. There, of course, is subjectivity in the selecting of objectives. Educators are human beings who choose what pupils are to learn. They use reason, societal trends, recommendations from learned societies, academicians, and curriculum specialists in making these choices.

Many statements of objectives have been written and published to indicate what is considered salient. The writer will trace selected sets of objectives to indicate their importance.

Objectives and the Learner

An important set of progressive objectives was published by the Commission to Reorganize Secondary Education, of the National Education Association in 1918 (See Bibliography).

These are equally salient for the elementary school level. The categories were the following:

- *health:* Proper nutrition, exercise, suitable clothing, meeting medical and dental needs, among others.
- *command of fundamental processes:* This includes vital subject matter learnings as well as skills needed in school and in society.
- *worthy home membership:* These learnings which include knowledge and skills which may be integrated into many units of study and are certainly needed in an era of recession, economically, which affects any involved family.
- *ethical character:* One must learn to deal fairly and truthfully in relating to others.
- *vocational competence:* This objective emphasizes being interested in and becoming knowledgeable about relevant jobs, careers, and professions.
- *citizenship:* The person develops those attitudes as well as knowledge, and skills to function well as a member in society.
- *worthy use of leisure time:* The individual finds positive ways to use spare time wisely.

The above Seven Cardinal Principles provide a broad framework in educating the whole child. These objectives represented, indeed, a progressive education curriculum. The total development of the child is emphasized and extends well beyond acquiring subject matter content. Holism in the curriculum is definitely in evidence. Each broad goal may be changed to specific objectives for teaching and learning situations in many units of instruction.

The National Education Association, again, issued a set of broad educational objectives with four broad, major areas of concern developed by the Educational Policies Commission in 1938:

- an educated person in school and social setting
- human relationships in the family, community, and larger social setting.
- economic well being as a consumer and producer.
- quality citizenship as a worthy member in society.

Subgoals are stated in this report for each of the above four asterisked areas (Educational Policies Commission, 1938). The broadly stated objectives as well as the sub-objectives may be stated as relevant ends for pupil attainment and, if relevant, become inherent in daily lesson plans. In selected cases, the 1918 and the 1938 statement of objectives are important today and can be updated with included statements of objectives in vogue presently.

There are objectives, presently, for pupil achievement which are mandated and have aligned tests. Pupils take these standardized tests once a year to reveal progress. Thus, in grades three through eight, pupils are tested in reading and mathematics, as well s in science. Pupils need to pass these tests to be promoted to the next higher grade level, as in the No Child Left Behind (NCLB) law of 2002. High school students also need to pass an exit test for graduation purposes. These tests are written by specialists and are then available in different states in the union. Each state has their own standardized test, making it difficult to make comparisons among test scores in comparing one state with another. The results are printed and announced in the media, being referred to as the nation's report card. Comparisons are also made among school districts and within schools. Competition is emphasized here in having school districts as well as individual schools meet challenging standards. Schools also need to meet Adequate Yearly Progress (AYP) so that students may achieve "proficiency" by 2014. There are difficulties involved in using NCLB standards:

- the scope of the curriculum is too narrow with pupils being tested in reading, mathematics, and science

- pupils are tested once a year only, to indicate if they should be promoted
- multiple choice test items are generally used to test pupils, making it difficult to evaluate higher levels of learner cognition
- knowledge and skills objectives predominate, leaving out measuring quality attitudes of pupils
- salient objectives are omitted as in good human relations and caring for others (Ediger, 2003).

For domain specific frameworks in developing broadly stated purposes, the National Council for the Social Studies (NCSS, 1992) developed the following themes, with elaboration by the author, as organizing strands for social studies programmes:

1. *culture, this theme brings in the academic disciplines of anthropology and sociology:* The society in which people live affects human behavior such as languages spoken, foods eaten, patterns in recreation, types of music available, and means of transportation.
2. *time, continuity, and change:* In units stressing history, learners should attain objectives emphasizing how changes occur in society such as the Great Depression of the 1930s and how the different levels of government dealt with grave problem areas.
3. *people, places, and environment:* Among other things, pupils need to learn about the kinds of occupations and jobs individuals/groups perform within a specific geographical region and how natural resources are used/preserved.
4. *individual development and identity:* Here, pupils among other, items, need to acquire knowledge and skills pertaining to human growth and maturation, as well as what makes for personal achievement.
5. *power, authority and governance:* Understandings must be acquired pertaining to different levels of

government in political science such as local, state, and federal levels as well as how they are affected, as citizens, by these different levels of governance.

6. *production, consumption, and distribution:* Pupils learn about goods and services produced for human use. Goods and services are distributed through a long list of processes in order to reach where they are needed.
7. *science, technology, and society:* Objectives in science need to be carefully selected so that pupils might learn to think objectively and scientifically. Science then provides necessary content for life, living, and technological advances such as use of cyber space, computers, and other inventions which assist in providing for quality endeavors.
8. *individuals, groups, and institutions:* The human being and membership in groups such as the family, clubs, organizations, and as a member in society must be salient in the curriculum.
9. *global connections:* People, nations, and cultures interact in an era of rapid transportation and communication systems.
10. *civic ideals and practices:* Active participation in the community by citizens needs to be emphasized as in "no person is an island unto itself."

Each of the above structure may be incorporated into ongoing units of study. They might also be planned as an entire unit. The Task Force for NCSS (2010) has also produced standards for each of these ten areas. Thus, for example, pertaining to civic ideals and practices, the following sample of knowledge goals is significant: Learners will understand

- the theme of civic ideals and practices helps us to know how we can have influence on how people live and act together.
- concepts such as individual dignity, fairness, freedom, the common good, rule of law, civic life, rights and responsibilities.

- key practices in a democratic society include civic participation based on studying community issues, planning, decision making, voting, and cooperating to promote civic ideals.
- democratic ideals and practices are often represented in excerpts from contemporary and historical sources, quotations, and stories.
- the importance of gathering information as the basis for informed civic action.

These more specific objectives may be stated behaviorally so that achievement can be measured. However, selected objectives may need to be broadly stated due to the difficulties of writing civics objectives very precisely.

Objectives need careful study and revision, when warranted. Periodically, new objectives need to be incorporated, but this is to be done only when definite needs exist, not for the sake of doing so. Society changes and so does what is salient to teach. Change is one of the facts of life and a curricula must be relevant for each pupil. Outdated curricula make for learners who will lack motivation to attain vital objectives. They must perceive a purpose for learning so that reasons are in evidence for achievement. Outdated objectives have made for situations whereby pupils wonder why these leanings are taught. Interest certainly will then be lacking when objectives are irrelevant and pupils fail to be actively involved in learning. Active engagement is needed with interesting objectives for pupils to achieve. When supervising university student teachers, the writer, too frequently, has noticed learners who are turned off in achieving. It is no wonder when viewing objectives for lessons and units of study being taught. Teachers, supervisors, and school administrators must observe to see if pupils are fully involved in what is being taught. Lessons and units of study need changes when pupils see little/no purpose in learning. From purposeless to purposeful objectives are modifications which must be made in any academic discipline. Faculty meetings, diverse forms of inservice education, as well as conferences must focus upon developing salient objectives for learner attainment. Faculty members and school administrators have as an obligation to continually seek the best objectives possible for pupils. The objectives become targets for teachers to aim toward in teaching and learning situations. Room is left for learner input into curriculum development (See Hedin and Conderman, 2010).

Constructivism

Constructivism as a psychology of teaching and learning emphasizes pupils establishing what is *reasonable* within ongoing activities. Thus, there objectives which pupils have in mind as they engage in learning. As pupils learn, they continually modify what is being accepted as being correct. With these modifications, pupils individually are more accurate in ultimate content and skills secured. The focus is upon the pupil achieving inductively. Lecture definitely is not a part of instructional procedures. Instead, the pupil learns through inquiry, not by the teacher aiming toward predetermined objectives. If pupils have questions and problems, the teacher assists in finding answers by asking questions of the learner which lead to the correct answer. The teacher must have a good subject matter knowledge base to use inquiry methods of teaching. Pupils acquire and form their own knowledge and skills in context, but these concepts are modified as needed. This is not anarchy, but it is the way pupils learn. Each one fashions his/her own truth and then modifies within a contextual setting.

Teacher observation is used to appraise progress. When observing learner achievement, he/she notices how energetic pupils are in learning and the desire that exists to' achieve. Motivation to learn is also observed with learner interests in mind. The interest factor is highly salient in learning since this does determine the direction of learning and how to channel intrinsic interests. Learning by discovery makes for enthusiasm and excitement in achieving and yet measurement of achievement is not emphasized; rather the pupil provides impetus in sequential learnings. The teacher is a resource person and encourages pupil achievement.

Conclusion

In the selection of objectives, the following criteria need to be followed:

- they need to be achievable with high expectations involved, but success in learning for the pupil is salient
- scaffolding must be used in certain situations so that optimal achievement is possible
- behaviorism emphasizes the use of measurably stated objectives in teaching whereas constructivism stresses the use of open ended goals
- measurably stated objectives may provide impetus for learning in that pupils realize that these need achieving in order to be promoted to the next grade level whereas constructivism stresses that learning is its own reward.

REFERENCES

Commission on the Reorganization of Secondary Education (1918). Washington, DC: Department of the Interior, Bureau of Education Bulletin, #35.

Ediger, Marlow (2003), Teacher Involvement to Evaluate Achievement," *Education*, 12 (1),137-142.

Educational Policies Commission (1938), *The Purposes of Education in American Democracy*. Washington, DC: National Education Association.

Hedin, Laura R., and Greg Conderman (2010), Teach Students to Comprehend Through Rereading," *The Reading Teacher*, 63 (7), 556- 565.

NCSS (1992), *Expectations of Excellence: Curriculum Standards for the Social Studies*. Washington DC: National Council for the Social Studies.

NCSS Task Force (2010), *"The Revised Social Studies Standards,"* as stated in Social Education, 74 (4), 204-209.

Bibliography

Aggarwal, J.C. (1993). *Development and Planning of Modern Education*, 4th Edition. New Delhi: Vikas Publishing Pvt. Ltd.

Aggarwal, J.C. (1994). *Essentials of Educational Psychology*. New Delhi: Vikas Publshing House Pvt. Ltd.

Aggarwal, J.C. (1999). *Essentials of Educational Technology*, Teaching Learning Innovations in Education. New Delhi: Vikas Publishing House Pvt. Ltd.

Aggarwal, J.C., Aggarwal, S.P. (1989). *National Policy on Education*. New Delhi: Concept Publishing Compnay.

Atkinson, J., Berna, E. anad Woodworth, R.S. (1988). *Dictionary of Psychology*, 4th Edition. New Delhi: Goyal Saab Publishers.

Baskara Rao, Digumarti (1997). *Scientific Attitude*. New Delhi: Discovery Publishing House.

Baskara Rao, Digumarti (2004). *Scientific Attitude, Scientific Aptitude and Achievement in Biology*. New Delhi: Discovery Publishing House.

Baskara Rao, Editor (1998). *Reforming School Education*. New Delhi: Discovery Publishing House.

Best, John W. and James V. Khan (2005). *Research in Education*, 9th Edition. New Delhi: Prentice-Hall of India Private Limited.

Bhatia and Bhatia (1984). *The Philosophical and Sociologial Foundations of Education*, 5th Edition. Delhi: Doaba House.

Bhatia, B.D. and Safaya, R.N. *Educational Psychology and Guidance*. Delhi : Dhanpat Rai and Sons.

Bhatiya and Bhatiya (1996). *A Text Book of Educational Psychology*. New Delhi: Doaba House.

Bhatiya, H.R. (1977). *A Text Book of Educational Psychology*. New Delhi: MacMillan India Ltd.

Bipin Asthana and Agarwal (1991). *Measurement and Evaluation in Psychology and Education*, 4th Edition. Agra: Vind Prakash Mandir.

Buch, M.B., (Editor) (1974). *A Survey of Research in Education*. Baroda: M.S. University.

Buch, M.B., Editor (1978-1983). *Third Survey of Research in Education*. Baroda: CASE, M.S. University of Baroda.

Buch, M.B., Editor (1983-1988). *Fourth Survey of Reseach of Education*. New Delhi: NCERT.

Chaube, S.P. (1983). *Educational Psychology*. Agra: Printsman.Chaube, S.P. (1983). *Educational Psychology*. Agra: Printsman.

Chauhan, S.S. (1978). *Advanced Educational Psychology*. New Delhi: Vikas Publishing House.

Crow, L.D. and Crow, A. (1991). *Educational Psychology*. New Delhi: Eurasia Publishing House Pvt. Ltd.

Dosajh, N.L. (1982). *Advanced Educational Psychology*. New Delhi: Allied Publishers Pvt. Ltd.

Garret, M.E. *Statistical in Psychology and Education*. Hyderabad: International Book Bureau.

Hariss, Chester W. (1960). *Encyclopaedia of Educational Research*, 3rd Edition. New York: The MacMillan Co.

Hurlock, Elizabeth (1992). *Development Psychology, A Life-span Approach*, Fifth Edition, Bombay: Tata McGraw-Hill Publishing Co. Ltd.

Husen Torsten, Neville Postlethwaite (1985). *The International Encyclopaedia of Education*, Vol. 3 D.E., Vol.4, F-H. England: Pergamon Press Ltd.

Jagannath, Mohanty (2004). *Modern Trends in Educational Technology*. Hyderabad: Neelkamal Publications Pvt. Ltd.

Jyosthana, M. and Nageswara Rao (2010). *Methods of Teaching English*. Guntur : Sri Nagarjuna Publishers, master minds.

Kulbir Singh Siddhu (1990). *Methodology of Research in Education*. New Delhi: Sterling Publishers Pvt. Ltd.

Kuppu, Swami (2003). *Advanced Educational Psychology*. New Delhi: Sterling Publishers Pvt. Ltd.

Lokesh, Koul (1984). *Methodology of Educational Research*. New Delhi: Vikas Publishing House Pvt. Ltd.

Mangal, S.K. (1989). *Abnormal Psychology*. New Delhi: Sterling Publishers Pvt. Ltd.

Mangal, S.K. (1998). *Psychological Foundations of Education*. Ludhiana: Prakash Brothers.

Mangal, S.K. (2004). *Statistics in Educational and Psychology*, 2nd Edition. New Delhi: Prentice-Hall of India Pvt. Ltd.

Mathur, S.S. (1983). *Educational Psychology*. Agra: Vinod Prakash Mandir.

Murthy, S.K. (1983). *Essentials of Educational Psychology*. Ludhiana: Prakash Brothers.

Murthy, S.K. (1984). *Educational Technology*. Ludhianan: Prakash Brothers.

Safaya, R.N. and Bhatia, B.D. *Educational Psychology and Guidance*. New Delhi: Dhanpat Rai and Sons.

Sharma, R.N. (1992). *Principles and Techniques of Education*. New Delhi: Surjeet Publications.

Siddhu, Kulbir Singh (1990). *Methodology of Research in Education*. New Delhi: Sterling Publishers Private Limited.

Srinivastava, D.M. (1985). *Abnormal Psychology*. Agra: Vinod Pustak Mandir.

Srinivastava, D.N. (1985). *General Psychology*. Agra: Vinod Pustak Mandir.

Usha Rao (1997). *Educational Technology*. Mumbai: Himalaya Publishing House.

Withing Arno, F. and Gurney, Williams III (1984). *Psychology - An Introduction*. New York: Fony and Sons Prentery Private Limited.

Yakaiah, P. and Bhatiya, K.E. (2003). *Introduction to Educational Psychology*. New Delhi: Kalyani Publications.

Young, Pauline V. (1988). *Scientific Social Surveys and Research*, 4th Edition. New Delhi: Prentice-Hall of India Pvt. Ltd.

Additional Reading

Amala, P. A. and Anupama, P., Authors and Digumarti Bhaskara Rao, Editor (2004). *History of Education*. New Delhi: Discovery Publishing House. ISBN 81-7141-860-0.

Appala Naidu, P.Ch., Author and Digumarti Bhaskara Rao, Editor (2007). *Feedback Methods and Students Performance*. New Delhi: Discovery Publishing House. ISBN 81-8356-284-1.

Bhaskara Rao, Digumarti (1994). *Scientific Aptitude*. New Delhi: Ashish Publishing House. ISBN 81-7024-658-X.

Bhaskara Rao, Digumarti (1995). *Animal Kingdom*. New Delhi: Discovery Publishing House. ISBN 81-7141-274-2.

Bhaskara Rao, Digumarti (1995). *Batracology*. New Delhi: Discovery Publishing House. ISBN 81-7141-279-3.

Bhaskara Rao, Digumarti (1997). *Scientific Attitude*. New Delhi: Discovery Publishing House. ISBN 81-7141-381-1.

Bhaskara Rao, Digumarti (1996). *Scientific Attitude vis-à-vis Scientific Aptitude*. New Delhi: Discovery Publishing House. ISBN 81-7141-308-0.

Bhaskara Rao, Digumarti (2004). *Scientific Attitude, Scientific Aptitude and Achievement*. New Delhi: Discovery Publishing House. ISBN 81-7141-781-7.

Bhaskara Rao, Digumarti (2004). *Educational Administration*. New Delhi: Discovery Publishing House. ISBN 81-7141-842-2.

Bhaskara Rao, Digumarti (2004). *Issues in School Education*. New Delhi: Discovery Publishing House. ISBN 81-8356-025-3.

Bhaskara Rao, Digumarti, Editor (1996). *Encyclopaedia of Education For All*, 5 volumes. New Delhi: APH Publishing Corporation. ISBN 81-7024-759-4 (set).

Vol. I *Education For All: The World Conference*. ISBN 81-7024-760-8

Vol. II *Education For All: The EPA-9 Summit*. ISBN 81-7024-761-6.

Vol. III *Education For All: Quality Education For All*. ISBN 81-7024-762-6.

Vol. IV *Education for All: Planning and Monitoring*. ISBN 81-7024-763-4.

Vol. V *Education For All: The Indian Scenario*. ISBN 81-7024-764-0.

Bhaskara Rao, Digumarti, Editor (1999). *International Encyclopaedia of AIDS*, 11 volumes. New Delhi: Discovery Publishing House. ISBN 81-7141-522-6 (set).

Vol. 1 *Introduction to HIV/AIDS*. ISBN 81-7141-523-7.

Vol. 2 *HIV/AIDS – Issues and Challenges*, 2 parts. ISBN 81-7141-524-5.

Vol. 3 *HIV/AIDS – Socio Economic Realities*. ISBN 81-7141-524-3.

Vol. 4 *HIV/AIDS – Law Ethics and Human Rights*, 2 parts. ISBN 81-7141-526-1.

Vol. 5 *AIDS and NGOs*. ISBN 81-7141-527-X.

Vol. 6 *AIDS and Home Care*. ISBN 81-7141-528-8.

Vol. 7 *STD Case Management*. ISBN 81-7141-529-6.

Vol. 8 *HIV/AIDS Prevention and Care – Teaching Modules for Nurses and Midwives*. ISBN 81-7141-530-X.

Vol. 9 *HIV Prevention Education for Educational Institutions*. ISBN 81-7141-531-8.

Vol. 10 *Instructional Modules for AIDS Education*. ISBN 81-7141-532-6.

Vol. 11 *School Health Education to prevent AIDS and STD – A Package for Curriculum Planners*. ISBN 81-7141-533-4.

Bhaskara Rao, Digumarti, Editor (2000). *International Encyclopaedia of Human Rights*, 7 volumes in 13 parts. New Delhi: Discovery Publishing House. ISBN 81-7141-567-9 (set).

Vol. 1 *International Instruments of Human Rights*, 2 parts. ISBN 81-7141-569-4.

Vol. 2 *Regional Instruments of Human Rights.* ISBN 81-7141-604-7.

Vol. 3 *Human Rights and the United Nations*, 2 parts. ISBN 81-7141-605-5.

Vol. 4 *Fact Files of Human Rights*, 3 parts. ISBN 81-7141-606-3.

Vol. 5 *Study Stories of Human Rights*, 3 parts. ISBN 81-7141-607-3.

Vol. 6 *International Meetings on Human Rights*, 2 parts. ISBN 81-714-608-X.

Vol. 7 *Professional Training in Human Rights.* ISBN 81-7141-609-8.

Bhaskara Rao, Digumarti, Editor (2000). *International Encyclopaedia of Science and Technology Education*, 11 volumes. New Delhi: Discovery Publishing House. ISBN 81-7141-548-2 (set).

Vol. 1 *Science and Technology Education.* ISBN 81-7141-568-7.

Vol. 2 *Science Education in Developing Countries.* ISBN 81-7141-569-9.

Vol. 3 *Organizational Structure of Science.* ISBN 81-7141-570-9.

Vol. 4 *Science Education in Asia and the Pacific.* ISBN 81-7141-571-7

Vol. 5 *Science and Technology Education For All.* ISBN 81-7141-572-5.

Vol. 6 *Values, Ethics, Talent and Girls in Science and Technology Education.* ISBN 81-7141-573-3.

Vol. 7 *Popularization of Science and Technology Education.* ISBN 81-7141-574-1.

Vol. 8 *Science, Power and Society.* ISBN 81-7141- 575-X.

Vol. 9 *Information Technology.* ISBN 81-7141-576-8.

Vol. 10 *Teacher Training in Science and Technology Education.* ISBN 81-7142-577-6.

Vol. 11 *Teacher Training in Science and Technology: A Curriculum Framework.* ISBN 81-7141-578-4.

Bhaskara Rao, Digumarti, Editor (2000). *Education For All: Achieving the Goal*, 3 Volumes. New Delhi: APH Publishing Corporation. ISBN 81-7648-152-1 (set).

Vol. I *The Global Consensus.* ISBN 81-7648-155-6.

Vol. II *Mid-Decade Review Reports of Regional Seminars.* ISBN 81-7648-154-8.

Vol. III *Issues and Trends.* ISBN 81-7648-155-6.

Bhaskara Rao, Digumarti, Editor (2004). *International Encyclopaedia of Learning to Live Together,* 4 Volumes. New Delhi: Discovery Publishing House. ISBN 81-7141-848-1.

Vol. 1 International Conference on Learning to Live Together.

Vol. 2 Globalization and Living Together.

Vol. 3 Curriculum for Learning to Live Together.

Vol. 4 Science Education for the Contemporary Society.

Bhaskara Rao, Digumarti, Editor (1996). *National Policy on Education,* 2 Volumes. New Delhi: Anmol Publications Pvt. Ltd. ISBN 81-7488-323-1.

Bhaskara Rao, Digumarti, Editor (1996). *Global Perceptions on Peace Education,* 3 volumes. New Delhi: Discovery Publishing House. ISBN 81-7141-319-6.

Bhaskara Rao, Digumarti, Editor (1997). *Education for the 21st Century.* New Delhi: Discovery Publishing House. ISBN 81-7141-389-7.

Bhaskara Rao, Digumarti, Editor (1997). *Reflections on Scientific Attitude.* New Delhi: Discovery Publishing House. ISBN 81-7141-319-6.

Bhaskara Rao, Digumarti, Editor (1997). *Success Story of a Primary Education Project.* New Delhi: APH Publishing Corporation. ISBN 81-7024-850-7.

Bhaskara Rao, Digumarti, Editor (1997). *World Food Summit.* New Delhi: Discovery Publishing House. ISBN 81-7141-386-2.

Bhaskara Rao, Digumarti, Editor (1997). *Care the Child,* 2 volumes. New Delhi: Discovery Publishing House. ISBN 81-7141-394-3.

Bhaskara Rao, Digumarti, Editor (1998). *Earth Summit,* 2 volumes. New Delhi: Discovery Publishing House. ISBN 81-7141-435-4.

Bhaskara Rao, Digumarti, Editor (1998). *Adolescence Education.* New Delhi: Discovery Publishing House. ISBN 81-7141-432-X.

Bhaskara Rao, Digumarti, Editor (1998). *Community and School Nutrition Education.* New Delhi: Discovery Publishing House. ISBN 81-7141-435-4.

Bhaskara Rao, Digumarti, Editor (1998). *District Primary Education Programme.* New Delhi: Discovery Publishing House. ISBN 81-7141-396-X.

Bhaskara Rao, Digumarti, Editor (1998). *National Policy on Education: Towards an Enlightened and Humane Society.* New Delhi: Discovery Publishing House. ISBN 81-7141-426-5.

Bhaskara Rao, Digumarti, Editor (1998). *Reforming School Education.* New Delhi: Discovery Publishing House. ISBN 81-7141-403-6.

Bhaskara Rao, Digumarti, Editor (1998). *Teacher Education in India.* New Delhi: Discovery Publishing House. ISBN 81-7141-406-0.

Bhaskara Rao, Digumarti, Editor (1998). *World Summit for Social Development.* New Delhi: Discovery Publishing House. ISBN 81-7141-420-6.

Bhaskara Rao, Digumarti, Editor (2001). *Nuclear Materials: Issues and Concerns,* 2 volumes. New Delhi: Discovery Publishing House. ISBN 81-7141-611-X.

Bhaskara Rao, Digumarti, Editor (2001). *Distance Education in Different Countries.* New Delhi: APH Publishing Corporation. ISBN 81-7648-229-3.

Bhaskara Rao, Digumarti, Editor (2001). *Decentralised Management of Education: Management of Education in Panchayati Raj and Municipal Bodies.* New Delhi: Discovery Publishing House. ISBN 81-7141-617-9.

Bhaskara Rao, Digumarti, Editor (2001). *Electrochemistry for Environmental Protection.* New Delhi: Discovery Publishing House. ISBN 81-7141-619-5.

Bhaskara Rao, Digumarti, Editor (2001). *Global Educational Studies.* New Delhi: Discovery Publishing House. ISBN 81-7141-616-0.

Bhaskara Rao, Digumarti, Editor (2001). *Global Synthesis of Educational Assessment.* New Delhi: Discovery Publishing House. ISBN 81-7141-613-6.

Bhaskara Rao, Digumarti, Editor (2001). *Jomtein Decade of Education.* New Delhi: Discovery Publishing House. ISBN 81-7141-618-7.

Bhaskara Rao, Digumarti, Editor (2001). *World Conference on Education for All.* New Delhi: APH Publishing Corporation. ISBN 81-7141-274-9.

Bhaskara Rao, Digumarti, Editor (2001). *World Conference on Higher Education.* New Delhi: Discovery Publishing House. ISBN 81-7141-610-1.

Bhaskara Rao, Digumarti, Editor (2001). *World Conference on Science.* New Delhi: Discovery Publishing House. ISBN 81-7141-612-8.

Bhaskara Rao, Digumarti, Editor (2003). *Inspiring Experiences in Teacher Education.* New Delhi: Discovery Publishing House. ISBN 81-7141-656-X.

Bhaskara Rao, Digumarti, Editor (2003). *International Studies in Education,* 3 volumes. New Delhi: Discovery Publishing House. ISBN 81-7141-647-0.

Bhaskara Rao, Digumarti, Editor (2003). *Military Conversion: Impact on Science and Technology.* New Delhi: Discovery Publishing House. ISBN 81-7141-578-4.

Bhaskara Rao, Digumarti, Editor (2003). *United Nations Millennium Summit.* New Delhi: Discovery Publishing House. ISBN 81-7141-632-2.

Bhaskara Rao, Digumarti, Editor (2003). *World Assembly on Aging.* New Delhi: Discovery Publishing House. ISBN 81-7141-637-3.

Bhaskara Rao, Digumarti, Editor (2003). *World Conference on Human Rights.* New Delhi: Discovery Publishing House. ISBN 81-7141-661-6.

Bhaskara Rao, Digumarti, Editor (2003). *World Education Forum.* New Delhi: Discovery Publishing House. ISBN 81-7141-639-X.

Bhaskara Rao, Digumarti, Editor (2003). *Education, Employment and Human Resource Development.* New Delhi: Discovery Publishing House. ISBN 81-7141- 681-0.

Bhaskara Rao, Digumarti, Editor (2003). *Successful Schooling.* New Delhi: Discovery Publishing House. ISBN 81-7141-677-2.

Bhaskara Rao, Digumarti, Editor (2003). *European Education and Teachers.* New Delhi: Discovery Publishing House. ISBN 81-7141-702-7.

Bhaskara Rao, Digumarti, Editor (2003). *Teachers in a Changing World.* New Delhi: Discovery Publishing House. ISBN 81-7141-694-2.

Bhaskara Rao, Digumarti, Editor (2004). *International Guidelines on Open and Distance Teacher Education.* New Delhi: Discovery Publishing House. ISBN 81-7141-777-9.

Bhaskara Rao, Digumarti, Editor (2004). *Adult Learning in the 21st Century.* New Delhi: Discovery Publishing House. ISBN 81-7141-797-3.

Bhaskara Rao, Digumarti, Editor (2004). *Educational Practices: Research and Recommendations.* New Delhi: Discovery Publishing House. ISBN 81-7141-835-X.

Bhaskara Rao, Digumarti, Editor (2004). *General Secondary Education In the 21st Century.* New Delhi: Discovery Publishing House.

Bhaskara Rao, Digumarti, Editor (2004). *Reforming Secondary Education.* New Delhi: Discovery Publishing House. ISBN 81-7141-843-0.

Bhaskara Rao, Digumarti, Editor (2004). *Human Rights Education.* New Delhi: Discovery Publishing House. ISBN 81-7141-882-1.

Bhaskara Rao, Digumarti, Editor (2004). *United Nations Decade for Human Rights Education.* New Delhi: Discovery Publishing House. ISBN 81-7141- 887-2.

Bhaskara Rao, Digumarti, Editor (2004). *Technical and Vocational Education and Training in the 21st Century.* New Delhi: Discovery Publishing House. ISBN 81-7141- 984-4.

Bhaskara Rao, Digumarti, Editor (2005). *Encyclopaedia of Education For All,* 3 volumes. New Delhi: Discovery Publishing House.

Bhaskara Rao, Digumarti, Editor (2005). *Encyclopaedia of Education For All*, 3 volumes. New Delhi: Discovery Publishing House. ISBN 81-7141-647-0 (set).

Bhaskara Rao, Digumarti, Editor (2007). *Encyclopaedia of Teacher Education*, 4 volumes. New Delhi: Discovery Publishing House. ISBN 81-8356-306-6 (set).

Bhaskara Rao, Digumarti, Editor (2007). *Encyclopaedia of Edeucation for Living Together*, 4 volumes. New Delhi: Discovery Publishing House. ISBN 81-7141-848-1 (set).

Bhaskara Rao, Digumarti, Editor (2011). *Right to Education*. Hyderabad: Neel Kamal Publishers.

Bhaskara Rao, Digumarti, Editor (2011). *International Encyclopaedia of Educational Policies*. Hyderabad: Neel Kamal Publishers.

Bhaskara Rao, Digumarti, Editor (2011). *International Encyclopaedia of Educational Practices*. Hyderabad: Neel Kamal Publishers.

Bhaskara Rao, Digumarti and B.S.V. Dutt, Editors (2003). *Education: Programmes and Policies*. New Delhi: APH Publishing Corporation. ISBN 81-7648-470-9.

Bhaskara Rao, Digumarti, C.A.P. Swamy and B.S.V. Dutt (1997). *Self-Evaluation in Student Teaching*. New Delhi: Discovery Publishing House. ISBN 81-7141-374-9.

Bhaskara Rao, Digumarti and C. D. Swarna Lattha, Editors (2006). *Encyclopaedia of Biotechnology*, 5 volumes. New Delhi: Discovery Publishing House. ISBN 81-8356-168-3 (set).

Bhaskara Rao, Digumarti, C. Sridevi and K. Vijaya (1995). *Achievement in Social Studies*. New Delhi: Discovery Publishing House. ISBN 81-7141-281-5.

Bhaskara Rao, Digumarti and D. Naresh Kumar (2004). *School Teacher Effectiveness*. New Delhi: Discovery Publishing House. ISBN 81-7141-782-5.

Bhaskara Rao, Digumarti and D. Sridhar (2002). *Job Satisfaction of School Teachers*. New Delhi: Discovery Publishing House. ISBN 81-7141-652-7.

Bhaskara Rao, Digumarti and Digumarti Pushpa Latha, Editors (1998). *International Encyclopaedia of Women*, 5 volumes. New Delhi: Discovery Publishing House. ISBN 81-7141-410-9 (set).

Vol. 1 *Status of World's Women*. ISBN 81-7141- 494-X.

Vol. 2 *Women, Education and Empowerment*. ISBN 81-7141-498-1.

Vol. 3 *Women Challenges and Advancement*. ISBN 81-7141-497-4.

Vol. 4 *Women and Family Health.* ISBN 81-7141- 497-4.

Vol. 5 *Women and International Action.* ISBN 81-7141-498-2.

Babu, P.C., Author and Digumarti Bhaskara Rao, Editor (2004). *Flowers of Wisdom.* New Delhi: Discovery Publishing House. ISBN 81-7141-695-0.

Bhagya Lakshmi, L., Author and Digumarti Bhaskara Rao, Editor (2000). *Reading and Comprehension.* New Delhi: Discovery Publishing House. ISBN 81-7141-543-1.

Bhasha, S.A., Author and Digumarti Bhaskara Rao, Editor (2004). *Methods of Teaching Geography.* New Delhi: Discovery Publishing House. ISBN 81-7141-807-4.

Bhaskara Rao, Digumarti and D. Naresh Kumar (2004). *School Teacher Effectiveness.* New Delhi: Discovery Publishing House. ISBN 81-7141-782-5.

Bhaskara Rao, Digumarti and Digumarthi Harshitha (2004). *Adjustment of Adolescents.* New Delhi: APH Publishing House. ISBN 81-7648-836-8.

Bhaskara Rao, Digumarti and Digumarthi Harshitha, Editors (2001). *Education in India.* New Delhi: APH Publishing House. ISBN 81-7648-207-2.

Bhaskara Rao, Digumarti and Digumarti Pushpa Latha (1994). *Achievement in Biology.* New Delhi: Discovery Publishing House. ISBN 81-7141-264-5.

Bhaskara Rao, Digumarti and Digumarti Pushpa Latha (1994). *Achievement in Science.* New Delhi: Discovery Publishing House. ISBN 81-7141-280-70.

Bhaskara Rao, Digumarti and Digumarti Pushpa Latha (1995). *Achievement in English.* New Delhi: Discovery Publishing House. ISBN 81-7141-283-1.

Bhaskara Rao, Digumarti and Digumarti Pushpa Latha (1995). *Achievement in Mathematics.* New Delhi: Discovery Publishing House. ISBN 81-7141-278-5.

Bhaskara Rao, Digumarti and Digumarti Pushpa Latha (2004). *Education for Women.* New Delhi: Discovery Publishing House. ISBN 81-7141-873-2.

Bhaskara Rao, Digumarti and E. Sreekanth Babu (2004). *Educational Interests of School Students.* New Delhi: Discovery Publishing House. ISBN 81-7141-837-6.

Bhaskara Rao, Digumarti and K. Vijaya (1995). *A Text Book Evaluation.* Ambala Cantt: The Associated Publishers.

Bhaskara Rao, Digumarti and K.R.S. Sambasiva Rao, Editors (1996). *Current Trends in Indian Education.* New Delhi: Discovery Publishing House. ISBN 81-7141-311-0.

Bhaskara Rao, Digumarti and M.A. Fayaz (2004). *Problems of Primary School Drop-outs.* New Delhi: Discovery Publishing House. ISBN 81-7141- 834-1.

Bhaskara Rao, Digumarti and N.V.M. Mohana Rao (2002). *Problems of Mentally Handicapped Children.* New Delhi: Discovery Publishing House. ISBN 81-7141- 645-4.

Bhaskara Rao, Digumarti and S. Chandra Mohan (2002). *Sports Management.* New Delhi: APH Publishing House. ISBN 81-7648-467-9.

Bhaskara Rao, Digumarti and S.A. Khader (2004). *Problems of Private School Teachers.* New Delhi: Discovery Publishing Corporation. ISBN 81-7141-838-4.

Bhaskara Rao, Digumarti and S.A. Khader (2004). *School Education in India.* New Delhi: Discovery Publishing Corporation. ISBN 81-7141-849-X.

Bhaskara Rao, Digumarti and Sk. Johni Basha (2004). *Teachers' Population Education Awareness.* New Delhi: Discovery Publishing House. ISBN 81-7141-832-5.

Bhaskara Rao, Digumarti, Digumarthi Harshitha and K.R.S. Sambasiva Rao, Editors (1999). *Advanced Biotechnology.* New Delhi: Discovery Publishing House. ISBN 81-7141-516-4.

Bhaskara Rao, Digumarti, Digumarti Pushpa Latha and Digumarthi Harshitha, Editors (2001). *Biological Warfare.* New Delhi: Discovery Publishing House. ISBN 81-7141-597-0.

Bhaskara Rao, Digumarti, Digumarti Pushpa Latha and Digumarthi Harshitha, Editors (2001). *Women As Educators.* New Delhi: Discovery Publishing House. ISBN 81-7141-602-0.

Bhaskara Rao, Digumarti, Digumarti Pushpa Latha and Digumarthi Harshitha, Editors (2001). *Assessing Learning Achievement.* New Delhi: Discovery Publishing House. ISBN 81-7141-601-2.

Bhaskara Rao, Digumarti, Digumarti Pushpa Latha and Digumarthi Harshitha, Editors (2001). *Energy Security.* New Delhi: Discovery Publishing House. ISBN 81-7141-598-9.

Bhaskara Rao, Digumarti, V.V. Rao, V.V. Lakshmi and V.V. Krishna, Editors (1999). *Status and Advancement of Women.* New Delhi: APH Publishing Corporation. ISBN 81-7648-169-6.

Bhuvaneswara Lakshmi, G. and K. Subba Rao, Authors and Digumarti Bhaskara Rao, Editor (2004). *Methods of Teaching Biology.* New Delhi: Discovery Publishing House. ISBN 81-7141-914-3.

Bhuvaneswara Lakshmi, G., Author and Digumarti Bhaskara Rao, Editor (2004). *Methods of Teaching Life Science.* New Delhi: Discovery Publishing House. ISBN 81-7141-804-X.

Bhuvaneswara Lakshmi, Gadde, Author and Digumarti Bhaskara Rao, Editor(2000). *Attitude Towards Science.* New Delhi: Discovery Publishing House. ISBN 81-7141-541-6.

Bujji Babu, K., Author and Digumarti Bhaskara Rao, Editor (2007). *Teaching Aptitude of Primary School Teachers.* New Delhi: Sonali Publications. ISBN 81-8411-083-9.

Chary, K.V.N.B., Author and Digumarti Bhaskara Rao, Editor (2006). *Techniques of Teaching Physics.* New Delhi: Sonali Publications. ISBN 81-8411-046-4.

Chowdary, S.B.J.R. and Naga Raju, Authors and Digumarti Bhaskara Rao, Editor (2004). *Mastery of Teaching Skills.* New Delhi: Discovery Publishing House. ISBN 81-7141-861-9.

Dayakara Reddy, V. and Digumarti Bhaskara Rao, Editors (2006). *Value-Oriented Education.* New Delhi: Discovery Publishing House. ISBN 81-8356-051-2.

Devraj, T.A.S., Author and Digumarti Bhaskara Rao, Editor (1997). *Trace Analysis of Uranium and Thorium.* New Delhi: Discovery Publishing House. ISBN 81-7141-375-7.

Durga Rani, K., Author and Digumarti Bhaskara Rao, Editor (2000). *Educational Aspirations and Scientific Attitudes.* New Delhi: Discovery Publishing House. ISBN 81-7141-555-5.

Dutt, B.S.V. and Digumarti Bhaskara Rao (2001). *Empowering Primary Teachers.* New Delhi: Discovery Publishing House. ISBN 81-7141-615-2.

Dutt, B.S.V., Author and Digumarti Bhaskara Rao, Editor (2004). *Comparative Education.* New Delhi: Discovery Publishing House. ISBN 81-7141-912-7.

Ediger, Marlow and Digumarti Bhaskara Rao (1996). *Science Curriculum.* New Delhi: Discovery Publishing House. ISBN 81-7141-321-8.

Ediger, Marlow and Digumarti Bhaskara Rao (2000). *Teaching Mathematics Successfully.* New Delhi: Discovery Publishing House. ISBN 81-7141-552-0.

Ediger, Marlow and Digumarti Bhaskara Rao (2001). *Teaching Science Successfully.* New Delhi: Discovery Publishing House. ISBN 81-7141-600-4.

Ediger, Marlow and Digumarti Bhaskara Rao (2001). *Teaching Social Studies Successfully.* New Delhi: Discovery Publishing House. ISBN 81-7141-596-2.

Ediger, Marlow and Digumarti Bhaskara Rao (2002). *Elementary Curriculum.* New Delhi: Discovery Publishing House. ISBN 81-7141-658-6.

Ediger, Marlow and Digumarti Bhaskara Rao (2002). *Improving School Administration.* New Delhi: Discovery Publishing House. ISBN 81-7141-633-0

Ediger, Marlow and Digumarti Bhaskara Rao (2002). *Philosophy and Curriculum.* New Delhi: Discovery Publishing House. ISBN 81-7141-631-4.

Ediger, Marlow and Digumarti Bhaskara Rao (2003). *Elementary Curriculum Improvement.* New Delhi: Discovery Publishing House. ISBN 81-7141-740-X.

Ediger, Marlow and Digumarti Bhaskara Rao (2003). *Language Arts Curriculum.* New Delhi: Discovery Publishing House. ISBN 81-7141-657-8.

Ediger, Marlow and Digumarti Bhaskara Rao (2003). *Psychology and Curriculum.* New Delhi: Discovery Publishing House. ISBN 81-7141-691-8.

Ediger, Marlow and Digumarti Bhaskara Rao (2003). *School Curriculum and Administration.* New Delhi: Discovery Publishing House. ISBN 81-7141-709-4.

Ediger, Marlow and Digumarti Bhaskara Rao (2003). *School Curriculum and Administration.* New Delhi: Discovery Publishing House. ISBN 81-7141-709-4.

Ediger, Marlow and Digumarti Bhaskara Rao (2003). *Teaching Language Arts Successfully.* New Delhi: Discovery Publishing House. ISBN 81-7141-

Ediger, Marlow and Digumarti Bhaskara Rao (2003). *Teaching Mathematics in Elementary Schools.* New Delhi: Discovery Publishing House. ISBN 81-7141-687-X.

Ediger, Marlow and Digumarti Bhaskara Rao (2003). *Teaching Science in Elementary Schools.* New Delhi: Discovery Publishing House. ISBN 81-7141-698-5.

Ediger, Marlow and Digumarti Bhaskara Rao (2004). *Relevancy in Elementary Curriculum.* New Delhi: Discovery Publishing House. ISBN 81-7141-845-9.

Ediger, Marlow and Digumarti Bhaskara Rao (2004). *School Organisation.* New Delhi: Discovery Publishing House. ISBN 81-7141-843-0.

Ediger, Marlow and Digumarti Bhaskara Rao (2005). *Quality School Education.* New Delhi: Discovery Publishing House. ISBN 81-8356-022-9.

Ediger, Marlow and Digumarti Bhaskara Rao (2006). *Administration of Schools.* New Delhi: Discovery Publishing House. ISBN 81-8356-244-2.

Ediger, Marlow and Digumarti Bhaskara Rao (2006). *Community College – Curriculum and Teaching.* New Delhi: Discovery Publishing House. ISBN 81-8356-053-9.

Ediger, Marlow and Digumarti Bhaskara Rao (2006). *Curriculum of School Subjects.* New Delhi: Discovery Publishing House. ISBN 81-8356-207-8.

Ediger, Marlow and Digumarti Bhaskara Rao (2006). *Curriculum Organisation.* New Delhi: Discovery Publishing House. ISBN 81-8356-205-1.

Ediger, Marlow and Digumarti Bhaskara Rao (2006). *Issues in School Curruculum.* New Delhi: Discovery Publishing House. ISBN 81-8356-052-0.

Ediger, Marlow and Digumarti Bhaskara Rao (2006). *Reading Curriculum and Instruction.* New Delhi: Discovery Publishing House. ISBN 81-8356-266-3.

Ediger, Marlow and Digumarti Bhaskara Rao (2006). *Successful School Education.* New Delhi: Discovery Publishing House. ISBN 81-8356-054-7.

Ediger, Marlow and Digumarti Bhaskara Rao (2006). *Successful School Administration.* New Delhi: Discovery Publishing House. ISBN 81-8356-046-6.

Ediger, Marlow and Digumarti Bhaskara Rao (2007). *Language Arts Education.* New Delhi: Discovery Publishing House. ISBN 81-8356-333-3.

Ediger, Marlow and Digumarti Bhaskara Rao (2007). *School Science Education.* New Delhi: Discovery Publishing House. ISBN 81-8356-352-X.

Ediger, Marlow and Digumarti Bhaskara Rao (2010). *Effective Schooling.* New Delhi: Discovery Publishing House. ISBN 978-81-8356-613-1.

Ediger, Marlow and Digumarti Bhaskara Rao (2010). *Effective School Curriculum.* New Delhi: Discovery Publishing House. ISBN 978-81-8356-585-1.

Ediger, Marlow and Digumarti Bhaskara Rao (2010). *Essays on Teaching Science.* New Delhi: Discovery Publishing House. ISBN 978-81-8356-882-1.

Ediger, Marlow and Digumarti Bhaskara Rao (2010). *Essays on Teaching Social Studies.* New Delhi: Discovery Publishing House. ISBN 978-81-8356-883-8.

Ediger, Marlow and Digumarti Bhaskara Rao (2010). *Essays on Teaching Reading.* New Delhi: Discovery Publishing House. ISBN 978-81-8356-881-4.

Ediger, Marlow and Digumarti Bhaskara Rao (2010). *Essays on Teaching Mathematics.* New Delhi: Discovery Publishing House. ISBN 978-81-8356-880-7.

Ediger, Marlow and Digumarti Bhaskara Rao, Editors (2006). *Encyclopaedia of School Education,* 5 volumes. New Delhi: Discovery Publishing House. ISBN 81-8356-308-2 (set).

Ediger, Marlow and Digumarti Bhaskara Rao, Editors (2006). *Encyclopaedia of School Administration,* 4 volumes. New Delhi: Discovery Publishing House. ISBN 81-8356-307-4 (set).

Ediger, Marlow and Digumarti Bhaskara Rao, Editors (2007). *Encyclopaedia of School Curriculum,* 10 volumes. New Delhi: Discovery Publishing House. ISBN 81-8356-305-8 (set).

Ediger, Marlow and Digumarti Bhaskara Rao, Editors (2007). *Encyclopaedia of Teaching,* 8 volumes. New Delhi: Discovery Publishing House. ISBN 81-8356-305-8 (set).

Ediger, Marlow, B.S.V. Dutt and Digumarti Bhaskara Rao (2003). *Teaching English Successfully.* New Delhi: Discovery Publishing House. ISBN 81-7141-707-8.

Elizabeth, M.E.S., Author and Digumarti Bhaskara Rao, Editor (2004). *Methods of Teaching English.* New Delhi: Discovery Publishing House. ISBN 81-7141-809-0.

Elizabeth, M.E.S., Author and Digumarti Bhaskara Rao, Editor (2004). *Acquisition of English Vocabulary.* New Delhi: Discovery Publishing House. ISBN 81-8356-075-X.

Fatima, Sk. and Digumarti Bhaskara Rao (2008). *Reasoning Ability of Adolescent Students.* New Delhi: Discovery Publishing House. ISBN 978-81-8356-315-4.

Fatima, Sk. Author and Digumarti Bhaskara Rao, Editor (2007). *Reasoning Ability of School Students.* New Delhi: Discovery Publishing House. ISBN 81-8356-330-9.

Gopala Krishna, M., Author and Digumarti Bhaskara Rao, Editor (2007). *Techniques of Teaching Physical Education.* New Delhi: Sonali Publications. ISBN 81-8411-044-8.

Gopala Krishna, M., Author and Digumarti Bhaskara Rao, Editor (2007). *Techniques of Teaching Education.* New Delhi: Sonali Publications. ISBN 81-8411-062-6.

Harshitha, Digumarthi, Author and Digumarti Bhaskara Rao, Editor (2004). *Methods of Teaching Information Technology.* New Delhi: Discovery Publishing House. ISBN 81-7141-805-8.

Harshitha, Digumarthi, Author and Digumarti Bhaskara Rao, Editor (2007). *Techniques of Teaching Computer Science.* New Delhi: Sonali Publications. ISBN 81-8411-036-7.

Indira Devi, Author and J. Prasanth Kumar and Digumarti Bhaskara Rao, Editors (2004). *Values in Language Text Books.* New Delhi: Discovery Publishing House. ISBN 81-7141-833-3.

Jalaja Kumari, C., Author and Digumarti Bhaskara Rao, Editor (2004). *Methods of Teaching Educational Technology.* New Delhi: Discovery Publishing House. ISBN 81-7141-810-4.

Jalaja Kumari, C., Author and Digumarti Bhaskara Rao, Editor (2007). *Job Satisfaction of Teachers.* New Delhi: Discovery Publishing House. ISBN 81-8356-329-5.

Janardhan Reddy, B., Author and Digumarti Bhaskara Rao, Editor (2006). *Techniques of Teaching Sociology.* New Delhi: Sonali Publications. ISBN 81-8411-042-1.

Jayasree, K., Author and Digumarti Bhaskara Rao, Editor (1999). *Correlates of Socialisation.* New Delhi: Discovery Publishing House. ISBN 81-7141-517-2.

Jayasree, K., Author and Digumarti Bhaskara Rao, Editor (2004). *Methods of Teaching Science.* New Delhi: Discovery Publishing House. ISBN 81-7141-801-5.

John Babu, C., Author and T.J.R. Prasad, G.M. Madhukar and Digumarti Bhaskara Rao, Editors (2004). *Problem Solving in Mathematics.* New Delhi: APH Publishing Corporation. ISBN 81-7648-273-0.

Joseph Raju, B and G.A. Anitha, Authors and Digumarti Bhaskara Rao, Editor (2004). *Population Education.* New Delhi: Sonali Publications. ISBN 81-88836-31-3.

Jyosthana, M., Author and Digumarti Bhaskara Rao, Editor (2011). *Achievement Motivation and Achievement in English of School Students.* New Delhi: Discovery Publishing House.

Krishna, G., Author and Digumarti Bhaskara Rao, Editor (2006). *Techniques of Teaching Physical Education.* New Delhi: Discovery Publishing House. ISBN 81-8411-044-8.

Kumar Raja, G., Author and Digumarti Bhaskara Rao, Editor (2007). *Principles of Primary School.* New Delhi: Sonali Publications. ISBN 81-8411-054-5.

Lakshmi Kumari, V., Author and Digumarti Bhaskara Rao, Editor (2006). *Techniques of Teaching Home Science.* New Delhi: Discovery Publishing House. ISBN 81-8411-048-0.

Lalitha, T., Author and K.S. Prabhakaram, D.S.N. Sastry and Digumarti Bhaskara Rao, Editors (2004). *Educational Philosophic Beliefs.* New Delhi: Discovery Publishing House. ISBN 81-7141-765-5.

Madhava, K., Author and Digumarti Bhaskara Rao, Editor (2008). *Personality of Adolescent Students.* New Delhi: Sonali Publications. ISBN 978-81-8356-262-1.

Madhu Bala, Jampala, Author and Digumarti Bhaskara Rao, Editor (2004). *Methods of Teaching Exceptional Children.* New Delhi: Discovery Publishing House. ISBN 81-7141-802-3.

Mallikarjuna Reddy, V., Author and Digumarti Bhaskara Rao, Editor (2011). *Teaching Aptitude, Social Adjustment and Job Satisfaction of Science Teachers.* New Delhi: Discovery Publishing House.

Marja, Talvi and Digumarti Bhaskara Rao, Editors (1996). *Educational Leadership and Social Changes.* New Delhi: Discovery Publishing House. ISBN 81-7141-320-X. ISBN 81-7141-320-X.

Marlow Ediger and Digumarti Bhaskara Rao, Editors (2006). *Encyclopaedia of School Education,* 5 volumes. New Delhi: Discovery Publishing House. ISBN 81-8356-308-2 (set).

Marlow Ediger and Digumarti Bhaskara Rao, Editors (2006). *Encyclopaedia of School Administration,* 4 volumes. New Delhi: Discovery Publishing House. ISBN 81-8356-307-4 (set).

Marlow Ediger and Digumarti Bhaskara Rao, Editors (2007). *Encyclopaedia of School Curriculum,* 10 volumes. New Delhi: Discovery Publishing House. ISBN 81-8356-305-8 (set).

Marlow Ediger and Digumarti Bhaskara Rao, Editors (2007). *Encyclopaedia of Teaching,* 8 volumes. New Delhi: Discovery Publishing House. ISBN 81-8356-305-8 (set).

Naga Kumari, U., Author and Digumarti Bhaskara Rao, Editor (2008). *Science Process Skills of School Students.* New Delhi: Sonali Publications. ISBN 978-81-8356-263-8.

Nageswara Rao, S. and M. Srihari, Authors and Digumarti Bhaskara Rao, Editor (2004). *Guidance and Counselling.* New Delhi: Discovery Publishing House. ISBN 81-7141-840-6.

Nageswara Rao, S. and P. Sridhar, Authors and Digumarti Bhaskara Rao, Editor (2004). *Methods and Techniques of Teaching.* New Delhi: Sonali Publications. ISBN 81-88836-33-8.

Nageswara Rao, S., Author and Digumarti Bhaskara Rao, Editor (2006). *Techniques of Teaching Psychology.* New Delhi: Discovery Publishing House. ISBN 81-8411-040-5.

Nirmala Jyothi, M., Author and Digumarti Bhaskara Rao, Editor (2003). *Non-detention System in School Education.* New Delhi: Discovery Publishing House. ISBN 81-7141-654-3.

Padma Tulasi, G., Author and Digumarti Bhaskara Rao, Editor (2004). *Methods of Teaching Elementary Science.* New Delhi: Discovery Publishing House. ISBN 81-7141-871-6.

Pala Prasada Rao, V., Author and D. Bhaskara Rao, Editors (2008). *Functioning of Autonomous Colleges.* New Delhi: Sonali Publications. ISBN 978-81-8356-258-4.

Pala Prasada Rao, V., Author and K. N. Rani and D. Bhaskara Rao, Editors (2004).*India Pakistan: Partition Perspectives in Indo English Novels.* New Delhi: Discovery Publishing House. ISBN 81-7141-871-6.

Pitchi Reddy, M., Author and Digumarti Bhaskara Rao, Editor (2007). *Techniques of Teaching Social Sciences.* New Delhi: Sonali Publications. ISBN 81-8411-066-X.

Prabhakaram, K.S., Author and Digumarti Bhaskara Rao, Editors (1998). *Concept Attainment Model in Mathematics Teaching.* New Delhi: Discovery Publishing House. ISBN 81-7141-424-9.

Prasad Babu, B., Author and M.V.R. Raju and Digumarti Bhaskara Rao, Editors (2006). *Behavioural Problems of School Children.* New Delhi: Discovery Publishing House. ISBN 81-8356-206-X.

Prasad Babu, B., Author and P. Madhu and Digumarti Bhaskara Rao, Editors (2006). *Psychological Adjustment and Well-being.* New Delhi: Discovery Publishing House. ISBN 81-8356-204-3.

Prasanth Kumar, J., Author and Digumarti Bhaskara Rao, Editor (1998). *Effectiveness of Distance Education System.* New Delhi: Discovery Publishing House. ISBN 81-7141-437-0.

Prasanth Kumar, J., Author and Digumarti Bhaskara Rao, Editor (2004). *Methods of Teaching Civics.* New Delhi: Discovery Publishing House. ISBN 81-7141-806-6.

Prasanth Kumar, J., Author and G. Sundara Rao and Digumarti Bhaskara Rao, Editors (2000). *Open University Student Support Services.* New Delhi: Discovery Publishing House. ISBN 81-7141-550-4.

Raja Kumari, M.A. and D.R.S. Sundari, Authors and Digumarti Bhaskara Rao, Editor (2004). *Special Education.* New Delhi: Discovery Publishing House. ISBN 81-7141-846-5.

Raja Kumari, M.A. and D.R.S. Sundari, Authors and Digumarti Bhaskara Rao, Editor (2004). *Methods of Teaching Educational Psychology.* New Delhi: Discovery Publishing House. ISBN 81-7141-820-1.

Rama Krishna Prasad and P. Vide Sagar, Authors and Digumarti Bhaskara Rao, Editor (2004). *Methods of Teaching Physical Education.* New Delhi: Discovery Publishing House. ISBN 81-7141-868-6.

Rama Krishnaiah, D., Author and Digumarti Bhaskara Rao, Editor (1998). *Job Satisfaction of College Teachers.* New Delhi: Discovery Publishing House. ISBN 81-7141-438-9.

Rama Kumar Ratnam, M.V., Author and Digumarti Bhaskara Rao, Editor (1998). *Dukkha: Suffering in Early Buddhism.* New Delhi: Discovery Publishing House. ISBN 81-7141-653-5.

Rama Seshaiah, P. Author and Digumarti Bhaskara Rao, Editor (2004). *Methods of Teaching Home Science.* New Delhi: Discovery Publishing House. ISBN 81-7141-916-X.

Rama Swamy, K., Author and Digumarti Bhaskara Rao, Editor (2007). *Techniques of Teaching Environmental Science.* New Delhi: Sonali Publications. ISBN 81-8411-035-9.

Ramatulasamma, K., Author and Digumarti Bhaskara Rao, Editor (2002). *Job Satisfaction of Teacher Educators.* New Delhi: Discovery Publishing House. ISBN 81-7141-655-1.

Ramesh, A.R., Author and Digumarti Bhaskara Rao, Editor (2006). *Techniques of Teaching Commerce.* New Delhi: Sonali Publications. ISBN 81-8411-043-X.

Ramesh, Ghanta and Digumarti Bhaskara Rao, Editors (1998). *Environmental Education: Problems and Prospects.* New Delhi: Discovery Publishing House. ISBN 81-7141-423-0.

Ranga Rao, B., Author and Digumarti Bhaskara Rao, Editor (2007). *Techniques of Teaching Economics.* New Delhi: Sonali Publications. ISBN 81-8411-056-1.

Ranga Rao, R., Author and Digumarti Bhaskara Rao, Editor (2004). *Methods of Teacher Teaching.* New Delhi: Discovery Publishing House. ISBN 81-7141-812-0.

Rani, S.S., Author and Digumarti Bhaskara Rao, Editor (2006). *Techniques of Teaching Botany.* New Delhi: Discovery Publishing House. ISBN 81-8411-037-5.

Rathaiah, Lavu and Digumarti Bhaskara Rao (1997). *Achievement Correlates.* New Delhi: Discovery Publishing House. ISBN 81-7141-385-4.

Rathaiah, Lavu and Digumarti Bhaskara Rao, Editors (1996), *International Innovations in Education.* New Delhi: Discovery Publishing House. ISBN 81-7141-359-5.

Ravi Krishna, M., Author and Digumarti Bhaskara Rao, Editor (2004). *Examination System*. New Delhi: Discovery Publishing House. ISBN 81-7141-824-4.

Ravi Kumar, M., Author and Digumarti Bhaskara Rao, Editor (2004). *Methods of Teaching Computer Science*. New Delhi: Discovery Publishing House. ISBN 81-7141-823-6.

Rudramamba, B. and V. Lakshmi Kumari, Authors and Digumarti Bhaskara Rao, Editor (2004). *Methods of Teaching Economics*. New Delhi: Discovery Publishing House. ISBN 81-7141-900-3.

Rudramamba, B., Author and Digumarti Bhaskara Rao, Editor (2003). *Problems of Teaching*. New Delhi: APH Publishing Corporation. ISBN 81-7648-462-8.

Sambasiva Rao, P., Author and Digumarti Bhaskara Rao, Editor (2007). *Techniques of Teaching Psychology*. New Delhi: Sonali Publications. ISBN 81-8411-040-5.

Sanjeeva Rao, P.C., Author and Digumarti Bhaskara Rao, Editor (1996). *A Text Book of Geology*. New Delhi: Discovery Publishing House. ISBN 81-7141-313-7.

Santhanam, T., B. Prasad Babu and S. Sugandhi, Authors and Digumarti Bhaskara Rao, Editor (2007). *Children with Learning Disabilities*. New Delhi: Sonali Publications. ISBN 81-8411-077-4.

Santhanam, T., B. Prasad Babu and S. Sugandhi, Authors and Digumarti Bhaskara Rao, Editor (2008). *Learning Disabilities and Remedial Programmes*. New Delhi: Discovery Publishing House.

Sarala, M.M.O., Author and Digumarti Bhaskara Rao, Editor (2006). *Techniques of Teaching English*. New Delhi: Sonali Publications. ISBN 81-8411-047-2.

Satya Narayana, G., Author and Digumarti Bhaskara Rao, Editor (2008). *Attitude Towards Social Studies and Achievement in Social Studies*. New Delhi: Discovery Publishing House. ISBN 978-81-8356-261-4.

Satya Narayana, P.V.V. and G. Krishna, Authors and Digumarti Bhaskara Rao, Editor (2004). *Curriculum Development and Management*. New Delhi: Discovery Publishing House. ISBN 81-7141-813-9.

Satya Narayana, V., Author and Digumarti Bhaskara Rao, Editor (2001). *Physical Education, Social Attitudes and Leadership Qualities*. New Delhi: Discovery Publishing House. ISBN 81-7141-593-8.

Shamsuddin, Sk. and V. Dayakara Reddy, Authors and Digumarti Bhaskara Rao, Editor (2007). *Values and Academic Achievement*. New Delhi: Discovery Publishing House. ISBN 81-8356-283-3.

Singh, Y.C., Author and Digumarti Bhaskara Rao, Editor (2006). *Techniques of Teaching Science.* New Delhi: Sonali Publications. ISBN 81-8411-041-3.

Sirisha Rani, S., Author and Digumarti Bhaskara Rao, Editor (2007). *Techniques of Teaching Botany.* New Delhi: Sonali Publications. ISBN 81-8411-037-5.

Siva Lakshmi, G.V. and G.L. Subbaiah, Authors and Digumarti Bhaskara Rao, Editor (2004). *Methods of Teaching Environmental Science.* New Delhi: Discovery Publishing House. ISBN 81-7141-839-2.

Sivaratnam Reddy, M., Author and Digumarti Bhaskara Rao, Editor (2004). *Creativity in College Students.* New Delhi: Discovery Publishing House. ISBN 81-7141-697-7.

Srihari, M., Author and Digumarti Bhaskara Rao, Editor (2003). *Values of Prospective Teachers.* New Delhi: Discovery Publishing House. ISBN 81-8356-328-7.

Srinivas Rao, P., Author and Digumarti Bhaskara Rao, Editor (2007). *Principles of Secondary School.* New Delhi: Sonali Publications. ISBN 81-8411-058-8.

Srinivas, G. and Digumarti Bhaskara Rao (2007). *Anxiety of Prospective Teachers.* New Delhi: Sonali Publications. ISBN 81-8411-084-7.

Srinivas, G. and Digumarti Bhaskara Rao (2011). *Intelligence and Personality of Prospective Teachers.* New Delhi: Discovery Publishing House.

Srinivas, M. and I. Prasada Rao, Authors and Digumarti Bhaskara Rao, Editor (2004). *Methods of Teaching History.* New Delhi: Discovery Publishing House. ISBN 81-7141-803-1

Srinivasa Rao, Mandalapu, Author and Digumarti Bhaskara Rao, Editor (2003). *Achievement Motivation and Achievement in Mathematics.* New Delhi: Discovery Publishing House. ISBN 81-7141-674-8.

Srinivasulu Reddy, M. and K.R.S. Sambasiva Rao, Authors and Digumarti Bhaskara Rao, Editor (1999). *A Text Book of Aquaculture.* New Delhi: Discovery Publishing House. ISBN 81-7141-482-6.

Srinivasulu, K., Author and Digumarti Bhaskara Rao, Editor (2011). *Achievement Motivation and Academic Achievement of Alcoholic and Non-alcoholic College Students.* New Delhi: Discovery Publishing House Pvt. Ltd.

Subba Rao, K., Author and Digumarti Bhaskara Rao, Editor (2007). *School Education Policy.* New Delhi: Discovery Publishing House. ISBN 81-8356-285-X.

Subba Rao, K., Author and Digumarti Bhaskara Rao, Editor (2007). *Education Planning.* New Delhi: Sonali Publications. ISBN 81-8411-053-7.

Subramanyam, N.R., Author and Digumarti Bhaskara Rao, Editor (2011). *Effectiveness of In-service Training Programmes.* New Delhi: Discovery Publishing House.

Sudhakar Reddy, Y., Author and Digumarti Bhaskara Rao, Editor (2003). *Creativity in Adolescents.* New Delhi: Discovery Publishing House. ISBN 81-7141-659-4.

Suneetha, G., Author and Digumarti Bhaskara Rao, Editor (2004). *Environmental Awareness of School Students.* New Delhi: Sonali Publications. ISBN 81-8411-085-5.

Sunil Kumar, K. and K. Rama Krishana, Authors and Digumarti Bhaskara Rao, Editor (2004). *Methods of Teaching Chemistry.* New Delhi: Discovery Publishing House. ISBN 81-7141-913-5.

Sunita, E. and R. Sambasiva Rao, Authors and Digumarti Bhaskara Rao, Editor (2004). *Methods of Teaching Mathematics.* New Delhi: Discovery Publishing House. ISBN 81-7141-915-1.

Surya Madhava, I., Author and Digumarti Bhaskara Rao, Editor (2006). *Techniques of Teaching Geography.* New Delhi: Discovery Publishing House. ISBN 81-8411-034-0.

Surya Madhava, I., Author and Digumarti Bhaskara Rao, Editor (2007). *Techniques of Teaching Political Science.* New Delhi: Discovery Publishing House. ISBN 81-8411-061-8.

Swamy, K.R., Author and Digumarti Bhaskara Rao, Editor (2006). *Techniques of Teaching Environmental Science.* New Delhi: Discovery Publishing House. ISBN 81-8411-035-9.

Swarna Jyothi, K., Author and Digumarti Bhaskara Rao, Editor (2007). *Educational Research.* New Delhi: Sonali Publications. ISBN 81-8411-063-4.

Swarna Latha, C.D., and Digumarti Bhaskara Rao, Editors (2006). *Encyclopaedia of Biotechnology,* 5 volumes. New Delhi: Discovery Publishing House. ISBN 81-8356-168-3.

Swarupa Rani, T. and J.R. Priyadarshini, Authors and Digumarti Bhaskara Rao, Editor (2004). *Educational Measurement and Evaluation.* New Delhi: Discovery Publishing House. ISBN 81-7141-859-7.

Valeri V. Koustiouk, Author and Digumarti Bhaskara Rao, Editor (2002). *A Text Book of Cryogenics.* New Delhi: Discovery Publishing House. ISBN 81-7141-642-X.

Vamsi Krishna, V., Author and Digumarti Bhaskara Rao, Editor (2004). *School Psychology.* New Delhi: Discovery Publishing House. ISBN 81-7141-880-5.

Vanaja, M., Author and Digumarti Bhaskara Rao, Editor (1999). *Inquiry Training Model.* New Delhi: Discovery Publishing House. ISBN 81-7141-515-6.

Vanaja, M., Author and Digumarti Bhaskara Rao, Editor (2004). *Methods of Teaching Physics.* New Delhi: Discovery Publishing House. ISBN 81-7141-867-8.

Veena Kumari, Balusu and Digumarti Bhaskara Rao (1996). *Operation Black Board.* New Delhi: Discovery Publishing House. ISBN 81-7024-711-X. ISBN 81-8356-354-6.

Veena Kumari, Balusu, Author and Digumarti Bhaskara Rao, Editor (2004). *Methods of Teaching Social Studies.* New Delhi: Discovery Publishing House. ISBN 81-7141-899-6.

Veena Kumari, Balusu, Author and Digumarti Bhaskara Rao, Editor (2000). *Psycho-Social Correlates of Achievement.* New Delhi: Discovery Publishing House. ISBN 81-7141-547-4.

Venkata Rao, B., Author and Digumarti Bhaskara Rao, Editor (2007). *Techniques of Teaching Chemistry.* New Delhi: Sonali Publications. ISBN 81-8411-057-X.

Venkata Rao, P. and Digumarti Bhaskara Rao (1989). A *Text Book of Zoology – Junior Intermediate.* Guntur: Vignan Publishers.

Venkata Rao, P. and Digumarti Bhaskara Rao (1989). A *Text Book of Zoology – Senior Intermediate.* Guntur: Vignan Publishers.

Venkateswara Rao, V., Author and Digumarti Bhaskara Rao, Editcr (2004). *Problems of Education.* New Delhi: Discovery Publishing House. ISBN 81-7141-841-4.

Venkateswara Rao, V., V. Vijaya Lakshmi and V. Vamsi Krishna, Authors and Digumarti Bhaskara Rao, Editor (2004). *Education For All.* New Delhi: Sonali Publications. ISBN 81-88836-30-3.

Venkateswara Rao, V., V. Vijaya Lakshmi and V. Vamsi Krishna, Authors and Digumarti Bhaskara Rao, Editor (2004). *Education in India.* New Delhi: Sonali Publications. ISBN 81-88836-858-9.

Venkateswara Reddy, L. and Narayana, M. L, Authors and Digumarti Bhaskara Rao, Editor (2004). *Methods of Teaching Rural Sociology.* New Delhi: Discovery Publishing House. ISBN 81-7141-811-2.

Venkateswara Reddy, L. and Narayana, M. L., Authors and Digumarti Bhaskara Rao, Editor (2004). *Education for Dalits.* New Delhi: Discovery Publishing House. ISBN 81-7141-872-4.

Venkateswarlu, K. and S.J. Basha, Authors and Digumarti Bhaskara Rao, Editor (2004). *Methods of Teaching Commerce.* New Delhi: Discovery Publishing House. ISBN 81-7141-808-2.

Venugopala Rao, K., Author and Digumarti Bhaskara Rao, Editor (2000). *Teacher Morale in Secondary Schools.* New Delhi: Discovery Publishing House. ISBN 81-7141-551-2.

Venugopala Rao, K., Author and Digumarti Bhaskara Rao, Editor (2007). *Techniques of Teaching History.* New Delhi: Sonali Publications. ISBN 81-8411-059-6.

Vidya, C., Author and Digumarti Bhaskara Rao, Editor (1996). *A Text Book of Nutrition.* New Delhi: Discovery Publishing House. ISBN 81-7141-309-9.

Vijaya Bharathi, D., Author and Digumarti Bhaskara Rao, Editor (2000). *Educational Philosophies of Swami Vivekananda and John Dewey.* New Delhi: APH Publishing House. ISBN 81-7648-309-9.

Vijaya Bharathi, D., Author and Digumarti Bhaskara Rao, Editor (2005). *Educational Philosophy of John Dewey.* New Delhi: Discovery Publishing House. ISBN 81-8356-024-5.

Vijaya Bharathi, D., Author and Digumarti Bhaskara Rao, Editor (2005). *Educational Philosophy of Swami Vivekananda.* New Delhi: Discovery Publishing House. ISBN 81-8356-023-7.

Vijaya Kumar, S.J., Author and Digumarti Bhaskara Rao, Editor (2006). *Techniques of Teaching Mathematics.* New Delhi: Sonali Publications. ISBN 81-8411-039-1.

Vijaya Lakshmi, D., Author and Digumarti Bhaskara Rao, Editor (2004) *Basic Education.* New Delhi: Discovery Publishing House. ISBN 81-7141-881-3.

Vijaya Lakshmi, V., Author and Digumarti Bhaskara Rao, Editor (2006). *Techniques of Teaching Music.* New Delhi: Discovery Publishing House. ISBN 81-8411-038-3.

Vimala, T.D., B. Prasad Babu and Digumarti Bhaskara Rao, Editors (2007). *Stress, Coping and Management.* New Delhi: Sonali Publications. ISBN 81-8411-086-3.

Visalakshi, V., Author and Digumarti Bhaskara Rao, Editor (2006). *Techniques of Teaching Biology.* New Delhi: Sonali Publications. ISBN 81-8411-045-6.

Visalakshi, V., Author and Digumarti Bhaskara Rao, Editor (2007). *Techniques of Teaching Zoology.* New Delhi: Sonali Publications. ISBN 81-8411-055-3.

Books in Telugu Language

Bhaskara Rao, Digumarti (1986). *Dhrushya Sravana Bodhanapakaranalu* (Audio Visual Teaching Aids). Guntur: Nagarjuna Publishers.

Bhaskara Rao, Digumarti (1993). *Jeevasashtra Bodhana* (Teaching of Biology). Guntur: Nagarjuna Publishers.

Bhaskara Rao, Digumarti (1994). *Vidya Manovignana Sastram* (Educational Psychology). Guntur: Nagarjuna Publishers.

Bhaskara Rao, Digumarti (1995). *Vignanasasthra Bodhana* (Teaching of science) Guntur: Nagarjuna Publishers.

Bhaskara Rao, Digumarti (1997). *Vidya Manovignana Sastram* (Educational Psychology). Guntur: Creative Press.

Bhaskara Rao, Digumarti (1998). *DSC Study Material.* Guntur: Nagarjuna Publishers.

Bhaskara Rao, Digumarti (1998). *Upadhyayudu Vidya.* (Teacher and Education) Guntur: Nagarjuna Publishers.

Bhaskara Rao, Digumarti (1998). *Vidya Drukpadalu* (Perspectives of Education). Guntur: Nagarjuna Publishers.

Bhaskara Rao, Digumarti (1999). *EdCET Teaching Aptitude.* Guntur: Nagarjuna Publishers.

Bhaskara Rao, Digumarti (2001). *Bharata Samajamulo Upadyayudu Vidhya* (Teacher and Education in Emerging Indian Society). Guntur: Sri Nagarjuna Publishers.

Bhaskara Rao, Digumarti (2001). *Bhoutika Sastra Bodhana Padhatulu* (Methods of Teaching Physical Science). Guntur: Sri Nagarjuna Publishers.

Bhaskara Rao, Digumarti (2001). *Jeeva Sastra Bodhana Padhatulu* (Methods of Teaching Biology). Guntur: Sri Nagarjuna Publishers.

Bhaskara Rao, Digumarti (2001). *Vidya Manovignana Sastram* (Educational Psychology). Guntur: Sri Nagarjuna Publishers.

Bhaskara Rao, Digumarti (2003). *Patasala Yajamanyam/Paripalana* (School Management and Administration). Guntur: Sri Nagarjuna Publishers.

Bhaskara Rao, Digumarti and A. Jagadish (2009). *Vignansastra Bodhana Padhatulu* (Methods of Teaching Science). Guntur: Sri Nagarjuna Publishers.

Bhaskara Rao, Digumarti and B. Prasad Babu (2009). *Pradhamika Vidya mariyu Vileena Vidya Dhrukpadhalu* (Perspectives in Primary Education and Inclusive Education). Guntur: Sri Nagarjuna Publishers.

Bhaskara Rao, Digumarti and B. Prasad Babu (2009). *Vidya Manovignana Sastram* (Educational Psychology). Guntur: Sri Nagarjuna Publishers.

Bhaskara Rao, Digumarti and G. Prasanthi (2009). *Samardya Nirmanamu* (Capacity Building). Guntur: Sri Nagarjuna Publishers.

Bhaskara Rao, Digumarti and K. Subba Rao (2009). *Elementary Vidya, Pranalika, Yajamanyam, Upadyaya Kartavyalu* (Elementary Education, Planning, Management and Teacher Functions). Guntur: Sri Nagarjuna Publishers.

Bhaskara Rao, Digumarti and M. Srihari (2009). *Vardamana Bharata Desamulo Vidya* (Education in Emerging India). Guntur: Sri Nagarjuna Publishers.

Bhaskara Rao, Digumarti, Editor (2010). *Elementary Vidya, Pranalika, Yajamanyam, Upadyaya Kartavyalu – Question Bank* (Elementary Education, Planning, Management and Teacher Functions). Guntur: Sri Nagarjuna Publishers.

Bhaskara Rao, Digumarti, Editor (2010). *Ganithasastra Bodhana Padhatulu – Question Bank* (Methods of Teaching Science).Guntur: Sri Nagarjuna Publishers.

Bhaskara Rao, Digumarti, Editor (2010). *Methods of Teaching English – Question Bank*. Guntur: Sri Nagarjuna Publishers.

Bhaskara Rao, Digumarti, Editor (2010). *Pradhamika Vidya mariyu Vileena Vidya Dhrukpadhalu – Question Bank* (Perspectives in Primary Education and Inclusive Education). Guntur: Sri Nagarjuna Publishers.

Bhaskara Rao, Digumarti, Editor (2010). *Samardya Nirmanamu – Question Bank* (Capacity Building). Guntur: Sri Nagarjuna Publishers.

Bhaskara Rao, Digumarti, Editor (2010). *Sanghikasastra Bodhana Padhatulu – Question Bank* (Methods of Teaching Social Studies).Guntur: Sri Nagarjuna Publishers.

Bhaskara Rao, Digumarti, Editor (2010). *Telugu Bodhana Padhatulu – Question Bank* (Methods of Teaching Social Studies).Guntur: Sri Nagarjuna Publishers.

Bhaskara Rao, Digumarti, Editor (2010). *Vardamana Bharata Desamulo Vidya–Question Bank* (Education in Emerging India). Guntur: Sri Nagarjuna Publishers.

Bhaskara Rao, Digumarti, Editor (2010). *Vidya Manovignana Sastram – Question Bank* (Educational Psychology). Guntur: Sri Nagarjuna Publishers.

Bhaskara Rao, Digumarti, Editor (2010). *Vignansastra Bodhana Padhatulu – Question Bank* (Methods of Teaching Science).Guntur: Sri Nagarjuna Publishers.

Bhaskara Rao, Digumarti, N. Saraja, J. Lalitha and V. Mrunalini, Translators (2008). *Vidya – Samajam (Education - Society). Hyderabad:* Dr. B. R. Ambedkar Open University.

Gopala Krishna, G., A. Rama Krishna, K. Subba Rao and Bhaskara Rao, Digumarti (2004). *Jeevasashtra Bodhana Padhatulu* (Methods of Teaching of Biological science). Guntur: Sri Nagarjuna Publishers.

Krishna Murthy, V., K.S. Sudheer Reddy and Digumarti Bhaskara Rao (2004). *Vidya Manovignana Sastra Adharalu* (Foundations of Educational Psychology). Guntur: Sri Nagarjuna Publishers.

Lalini, V., V. Dayakara Reddy, M. Srihari and Digumarti Bhaskara Rao (2004). *Vidya Adharalu* (Foundations of Education). Guntur: Sri Nagarjuna Publishers.

Sastry, G.E.P. and G. Satya Narayana, Authors, Bhaskara Rao, Digumarti, Editor (2009). *Sanghikasastra Bodhana Padhatulu* (Methods of Teaching Social Studies). Guntur: Sri Nagarjuna Publishers.

Subba Rao, K.P., P. Ayodhya and Digumarti Bhaskara Rao (2004). *Patasala Yajamanyam – Vidhya Vyavasthalu* (School Management and Systems of Education). Guntur: Sri Nagarjuna Publishers.

Sudhakar, V., B. Ravindra Babu, D.S. Kumar and Digumarti Bhaskara Rao (2004). *Vidya Sanketika Sastram -Computer Vidhya* (Educational Technology and Computer Education). Guntur: Sri Nagarjuna Publishers.

Index

D

Q